Motivating Teaching in Higher Education

A Manual for Faculty Development

Edwin G. Ralph, Ph.D.

Department of Curriculum Studies
College of Education
University of Saskatchewan
Saskatoon, Saskatchewan

NEW FORUMS PRESS INC.

Stillwater, Oklahoma, U.S.A.

www.newforums.com

Contents

Contents   v

Motivating Teaching in Higher Education

Introduction

The Purpose

I have created this manual particularly for beginning instructors at the post-secondary level, who have never had previous teacher training. I not only present the essentials of the instructional planning and implementation process, but in doing so, I provide key principles and practices that have been shown to enhance students' motivation to learn. The manual is a distillation of key information derived from the extensive body of literature on teaching effectiveness and learning motivation, and from my own thirty-five years' experience in formal education—as a researcher, a teacher (from the elementary through to the college and university levels, in both public and private institutions), a school principal, a college administrator, a career counsellor, a school-district curriculum coordinator, a president of an educational publishing firm, a presenter at numerous educational conferences, a nominee and a recipient of several teaching awards, and a father of two adult children (themselves, graduate students).

The Rationale

The last decade has seen considerable attention worldwide being paid to the importance of improving teaching in higher education. Faculty members—especially those who are newly hired—are increasingly being expected to exemplify effective teaching performance as part of their academic duties in colleges and universities. Demands for exemplary teaching are arising from undergraduate student-bodies (and their parents); from future employers in business, industry and commerce; from university/college administrators; and from taxpayers and citizens in general.

Post-secondary institutions have responded by developing a variety of initiatives to meet these challenges, such as: the establishment of campus-wide instructional development offices; the setting up of departmental or school-wide teaching centers; the conducting of seminars/workshops/courses on specific instructional topics; the organizing of (and/or attendance at) regional and national teaching/learning conferences; and the hiring of full- or part-time staff to administer these professional-development activities.

In the light of these events, I have prepared this handbook to serve as a print resource to support such initiatives. However, I have also desired to provide—in a readable format —a synthesis of the fundamental generic skills of teaching, coupled with sound motivational strategies to enhance learning, which all instructors in any field could examine and adapt to their individual teaching or training contexts.

Clearly, no specific teaching method or list of motivating ideas would be applicable to all situations. However, the principles and suggestions presented in this guidebook are based both on reported results from some of the most current teaching/learning research available, and on actual teaching practices and experiences that I and many of my colleagues have deemed effective in various fields of education.

Because instructors (and especially those who are beginning their teaching) are busy, they do not necessarily have the time nor the inclination to review the voluminous literature on teaching and motivation, let alone to attempt to extract pertinent principles and strategies for implementation into their own instructional situations. However, by means of this manual, I have performed that task for them.

I endeavoured to write in plain language and I attempted to clarify educational terms where used. Jargon was avoided. I first describe several key principles of motivational teaching, and using these as a foundation, I present several practical and useful suggestions for instructors to consider as they prepare their respective courses and/or class-sessions.

The Readers

I have created the manual for anyone interested in sharpening their instructional competencies, but particularly for neophyte instructors in any post-secondary setting, who have not had the opportunity to receive any formal teacher training. Such individuals may include: newly hired faculty members, sessional lecturers, seminar leaders, laboratory demonstrators, graduate teaching assistants, tutorial leaders, or part-time instructors.

In addition, persons whose duties may include teaching/instructing/presenting/training/coaching in several other fields of education, business, industry, commerce, or government may find the handbook useful in providing them with empirically-based guidelines for organizing and implementing motivational teaching/learning tasks.

The Format

I have designed this manual to provide instructors with guidelines for the preparation and initiation of effective teaching/learning activities. The book helps to answer such questions as: What do I do prior to the instructional session(s)? What do I do at the beginning of instruction? During? At the end? After the session(s)?

The conceptual framework I employed to organize this handbook is based on the two essential functions of the teaching process, the managerial and the instructional aspects. Each of these components is sub-divided into two parts, the planning and the implementation phases.

This manual has not been created as a research report, nor as a regular textbook—although I have based it on a synthesis of current research findings related to teaching and learning. References are indicated by the superscript numerals within the text and are listed at the end of each chapter and in the bibliography.

The contents of the manual are summarized below:

In *Chapter 1*, I answer the question: "What are the best principles/practices of effective teaching/learning and of learner motivation that are applicable to undergraduate education?"

Key definitions are given and foundational assumptions are presented.

Too, I present and describe the conceptual framework used in organizing the handbook.

In *Chapter 2*, I describe a key component undergirding all effective instruction: the establishing and maintenance of a positive, productive teaching/learning climate.

I also analyze the process of effective classroom management, in terms of the prior planning and the actual implementation (and continuing operation) of class and institutional rules and procedures. Strategies and suggestions are offered to handle interpersonal problems and conflicts that inevitably arise.

In *Chapter 3*, the heart of the manual, I describe the components of effective instruction, from both the planning and the implementation aspects. Specific motivational strategies are presented for conducting both teacher- and learner-centered activities.

In *Chapter 4*, I distill the considerable body of literature, research findings, and personal experiences regarding the evaluation of learner progress, in order to present a practical guide for measuring, assessing, and evaluating participant development.

In *Chapter 5*, I synthesize some of the critical aspects of teaching at the undergraduate level and present some concluding remarks.

Chapter 1

KEY PRINCIPLES OF MOTIVATING TEACHING AND LEARNING

What major findings may be extracted from the extensive body of research literature on effective teaching and motivation of learning that could be applied to enhance undergraduate teaching practice? In this chapter, I attempt to answer this question by: (a) defining the three terms (motivation, learning, and teaching); (b) examining how these processes are related within the instructional setting; and (c) presenting a conceptual structure, consisting of twelve major principles, which — when applied — will help guide teachers as they seek to plan and implement motivating instructional activities.

Motivation of Learning

If motivation is defined as the forces that energize human behavior,[1] then it is clear that people are motivated at all times;[2] however, a primary duty of teachers in formal educational settings is to persuade the students under their jurisdiction to learn the subject matter in the particular course they share. Yet, the challenge of this task is that students' motivation to learn is not solely influenced by external stimulation or teacher reinforcement, but that it is a product of a complex blend of individuals' needs, attitudes, emotions, competencies, background experiences, and inherited traits.[3]

Moreover, recent research on learning suggests that the degree of motivation to learn may be determined by observing the learner's effort to engage in a particular learning activity; and that this effort, in turn, is influenced by: (a) the value that a learner places on the task, and (b) the expectation the learner has on being successful at it.[4] Because these internal motivational states become deep-rooted in each learner's psyche, teachers ultimately cannot motivate students to do anything: they can only endeavour to affect some of the variables that interact to stimulate students' motivation to learn.[5]

Some researchers in learning motivation further contend that the traditionally-held distinction between extrinsic (e.g., external reinforcements for student achievement—such as grades, awards, privileges, money, or other tangible rewards) and intrinsic motivation (e.g., personal satisfaction, individual enjoyment, feelings of competency, or self-interest) is not as distinguishable as historically proposed.[6] In fact, it is believed that extrinsic reinforcement may be a source of increased self-esteem within an individual, and that this self-esteem serves as a foundation upon which one's intrinsic motivation is further developed.[7]

In like manner, other external sources of positive reinforcement (such as: learners' desire for affirmation/confirmation from significant others, their desire for recognition for achievement, their drive for affiliation and belonging, their need for power and competence, or their motive to resolve inconsistencies) all lead eventually to increased intrinsic motivation in learners.[8]

Thus, rather than being distracted by trying to diagnose all of the complexities of their students' psycho/social/emotional make-up, instructors need to develop their skills in applying the motivational principles that have been consistently shown to stimulate student learning. My synthesis of the current research literature on this subject has identified five motivational factors that teachers of all age-groups have consistently found effective.[9]

Develop Positive Relationships[10]

Teachers are responsible for setting the tone of the teaching/learning atmosphere by projecting genuine feelings of mutual respect, support, and warmth. When learners believe that they are accepted as worthwhile individuals and as contributing members of the group—and whose affiliation and belonging needs are thereby met—then they will tend to regard learning tasks with acceptance rather than avoidance. Learning, after all, includes not only the cognitive dimension, but also the affective dimension (i.e., the emotions, feelings, and spiritual aspects).

On the other hand, both the research and peoples' own personal experiences have confirmed that teachers who are typically negatively critical, intimidating or emotionally cold tend not to enhance students' desire to engage wholeheartedly in learning activities.[11]

In fact, in a recent survey of 500 graduates from 20 post-secondary institutions that assessed their degree of satisfaction with their undergraduate-education experience, the respondents expressed their greatest dissatisfaction with the institutional climate. They apparently found it non-inviting and unfriendly.[12]

A common fear of beginning instructors, however, is that in their desire to create this pleasant socio-emotional climate, they do not want to appear overly "friendly", so that their students will somehow see them as weak and/or indecisive, and consequently may take advantage of them.

Again, both the research and individuals' personal experiences affirm that effective instructors are able to balance this sometimes delicate process: it is possible to enjoy a positive, productive teaching/learning environment — and yet to confront student misconduct or classroom management problems in a direct but respectful manner.[13]

Specific details and techniques to achieve this goal are presented in later chapters.

Attract Learners' Attention[14]

Learning motivation is increased when teachers attract and maintain learners' attention and curiosity. Good instructors are skilled both at captivating students' interest at the beginning of a class session and at stimulating it throughout. However, to create and to sustain such motivational sets for each class-session is not an easy task: ingenuity and diligence are required.

Instructional personnel who are successful at this task do so in many ways. For instance, they may begin with a puzzling question about the topic; they may show an overhead transparency with a directive to the group to resolve the apparent discrepancy in the visual; they incorporate a variety of activities/methods/media/materials in one class period in order to maintain learner interest; they involve learners in active participation more than in passive reception; and they demonstrate a range of gestures/body language/movement/humor in their teaching.[15] Particular strategies illustrating these motivational activities are given throughout this manual.

Enhance Subject-Matter Relevance[16]

Motivation to learn is increased when instructors ensure that the content is meaningful to students' lives — either past, present, or future — preferably all three. Effective instructors are able to provide a convincing argument and a defensible rationale to students as to the value of the subject-matter or topic being studied. They convey an interest in and an enthusiasm about their subject, and they provide frequent opportunities for learners to apply their newly acquired knowledge and skills in authentic "real life" situations. Their instructional decisions demonstrate that: they will adjust the learning activities to meet the developmental needs of the learners; they model the desired behavior, themselves; they invite current practitioners from the field (or former students) to be classroom-guests; and they emphasize that the academic work being done is important.[17] Specific examples of these activities appear later in the manual.

Build Learner Confidence[18]

Students' motivation to learn is enhanced when they engage in activities that are optimally balanced between being challenging and being achievable. The ultimate goal of the teaching process is that the teacher will eventually make him/herself unneeded, in that the learners will ultimately internalize the material or master the skills so that the instructor (or coach or mentor or facilitator or trainer or guide or supervisor or leader) will no longer be required to assist in the learner's development.

During this process, teachers apply both their technical (knowledge or task) and supportive (human relations) skills in inverse proportions, respectively, to match the learner's developmental level in performing a specific task or in applying certain knowledge. (This developmental level consists of two dimensions: the learner's competence and his/her confidence in performing a particular learning task.)[19]

That is, if learners' competence to perform the task or to solve a problem is low, then the teacher reciprocates by meeting the students' needs for direction by giving clear, specific guidance, high task-orientation, and concise, orderly directions—in short by using "telling" behaviors. Correspondingly, if a learner's confidence, assurance, or self-efficacy in performing the task is low, then the instructor acts by meeting the learner's need for bolstered confidence by providing highly supportive and encouraging responses.

When, on the other hand, the learners' development level of mastering a particular body of knowledge or learning a skill increases (i.e., when their task-specific competence and confidence levels rise, then the teacher or facilitator reciprocates by reducing his/her application of the two leadership-style components, (i.e., the technical/task dimension, and the supportive/encouraging aspect) in order to match the learners' increasing level of ability.

Throughout this developmental learning process, the effective teacher provides an appropriate blend of directive and supportive responses to synchronize, in inverse proportions, with the particular competence and confidence levels of the learner to perform a particular skill. As the latter's developmental level improves, the teacher decreases the degree of task-direction, reinforcement, feedback and guidance given to the student in performing that task. In turn, the learner—acknowledging her/his newly acquired levels of task-specific competence and confidence—is then able to set new learning goals for other tasks at higher levels of achievement. The cycle is then repeated.[20]

Illustrations of how effective teachers help learners to develop their knowledge-and skill-bases are provided in subsequent chapters of this handbook.

Promote Learner Satisfaction[21]

Students' motivation to learn is increased when they experience a sense of achievement for accomplishing the learning tasks. If the instructor designs the teaching/learning activities by incorporating the four motivational principles just described, then learners will tend to engage in the tasks in order to complete them successfully. If the evaluation activities in a course are consistent both with the initial instructional objectives and with the type of daily learning tasks experienced by the learners, and if the evaluation feedback received is perceived to be fair and authentic, then students typically will have a desire to accomplish the learning goals.[22] The reward for this learning achievement may be of the so-called intrinsic type (e.g., the inner glow of satisfaction for succeeding at a task), or of the more traditional extrinsic kind (e.g., high grades, external awards, peer- or teacher-approval, or confirmation from others of having achieved a step in the pursuit of a series of challenges toward a long-term goal.)[23]

Key principles for instructors to apply as they reinforce learners' achievement is that the reinforcement—to be effective—must be: (a) genuine (i.e., provided for clearly describable progress—not given indiscriminately or to be perceived by learners as artificial or un-earned); (b) immediate (i.e., provided at the time of the successful task-completion); and specific (reinforcing particular points in the task performance rather than administering vague or general praise).[24]

The Teaching/Learning Process

In this manual, "learning" is viewed as a relatively permanent change in learners' behavior as a result of repeated experience.[25] Learning can occur without teaching, and vice versa. However, in formal educational settings, "the teaching act" is supposed to promote the learning process in students.[26]

Traditionally, "teaching" in post-secondary education has been seen basically as "telling", lecturing, and "expert" presenting—via one-way, instructor-directed communication. "Learning" was consequently perceived to be the passive reception of such teaching, whereby learners sat dutifully listening, copying verbatim notes from the lecture, and subsequently memorizing and regurgitating "the facts" on examinations.

In the past two decades, however, there has emerged a growing trend to reform this one-way process to one exhibiting the following characteristics: the communication act becoming more interactive and collaborative among all students and teachers; the teacher becoming more of a facilitator of student learning, and less of a dispenser of knowledge; the so-called "funnel approach" (whereby "experts" pour information into students' empty heads) being replaced by what one could refer to as the "pump approach" (in which "learning facilitators" use active-learning methods such as cooperative group-learning activities and inquiry-based tasks to "draw out" and extend learners' knowledge and skills.)[27]

Indeed, some educators are currently questioning the value of using the lecture method in any form within the learning process; while others even believe that the term "teacher", itself, is archaic and repressive, and that it should be excluded from educational vocabulary and practice—to be replaced by other terms such as "facilitator of learning".[28] However, the position taken by most educational researchers and practitioners—and the view that I advocate in this handbook—is that the processes of teaching and learning are intertwined and inter-related.[29] To try to separate them, other than for purposes of conceptual clarification and analysis, becomes a futile exercise.

Even though it may be technically true that one person cannot "teach" another person anything, but only attempt to assist the latter to learn, it is also true that peoples' own past experiences and their common sense show that there *are* times for teachers to deliver explicit, direct instruction. In such cases, lecturing—if done well—is the best teaching method to apply in these situations. (I elaborate on this assertion in later chapters of this volume.)

Moreover, the term "teaching", as defined in this handbook, represents the entire decision-making process by which a teacher plans, prepares, organizes, implements, and assesses a variety of activities and events for the purpose of promoting student learning.[30] When the decisions are enacted with clarity, precision, and most of all humanity, teachers can enhance students' motivation to learn. However, this process must be nourished, not exploited: it cannot be coerced or mechanically controlled. Above all, the fundamental integrity of the learner must not be violated.[31]

Learning Styles

By virtue of our human nature and our unique personalities, each person has a particular learning style: a specific tendency or proneness to process new information or to acquire knowledge and skills in individual ways.[32] These personal learning proclivities or preferences have been studied and categorized by several researchers into a variety of learning-style models. For instance, one model[33] classifies people, according to their dominant learning style, into four categories: (a) if they prefer concrete experience they could be called Active Pragmatists; (b) if they prefer reflective observation they could be called Cautious Reflectors; (c) if they prefer abstract conceptualization they could be called Analytical Theorists; or (d) if they prefer active experimentation they could be called Active Learners.

Another model established three learning styles: Dependent, Collaborative, and Independent Learning.[34] Still another model is based on peoples' preferences for concrete or abstract experiences, and it postulates four learning domains: Feeling Planners, Participative Implementers, Task Implementers, or Thinking Planners.[35]

In addition, studies on human brain functioning have shown that brain hemisphericity is linked to thinking styles.[36] Thus, individuals who are said to be "left-brain hemisphere oriented" tend to be more logical and linear in their thinking: they prefer rational and sequential cognitive processing, and are guided by rule-bound and structured plans. Liabilities for these individuals are that they tend to be less creative, less flexible in decision-making, less able to take a holistic view of a subject and to show less emotion in their working routines.

On the other hand, right-brain oriented individuals are generally more global in their outlook, and tend to be artistic, creative, and open in their thought processes. Liabilities for these people are that they tend not to follow through with details, and they tend to exhibit behaviors that are not compatible with set rules or formats.

The advantages for instructors of being aware of the research on learning styles are that: (a) they can better understand the differences among learners; (b) they can adjust their teaching to accommodate these differences; and (c) they can be explicit with this information for learners so that all participants will realize that "learning style" offers a legitimate explanation for classroom diversity.[37] Moreover, it will assure participants that such differences among learners is not due to the presence of some abnormality, inferior quality, flawed personality trait, or character weakness. Rather, it is simply a normal feature of being human.

Dangers of over-emphasizing the learning-style research in one's teaching, however, are that: (a) most people do not fall entirely within one category; (b) instructors realistically do not have the time nor resources to diagnose each learner's style, let alone design individualized learning activities for each student to match his/her unique learning profile; or (c) instructors catering only to learners' preferred style will do little to enhance development in weaker areas of the latters' cognitive abilities, and may rather serve to label or categorize them permanently into a stagnant state.[38]

A key implication of this knowledge for one's planning and initiation of motivation tasks is that effective teachers will select a variety of materials, methods, and media—not as an end in itself—but as a sensible means of providing *all* learners with at least some of their preferred activities, and also with some tasks that do not necessarily fall within their style range. The latter will expose students to real-world experience, in which individuals often encounter challenges and/or people, for which they do not have a particular affinity. In these situations we must stretch our capacity and learn to accept and appreciate the set of abilities and limitations of others, realizing that they may complement and/or compensate our own.[39]

Motivating Teaching

The bulk of the body of teaching-effectiveness research that emerged during the past four decades was conducted at the elementary school level. Some was done at the secondary level, and less at the post-secondary level. However, the latter has increased substantially in the last ten years—and even though more investigation needs to be done—there are enough empirical findings from post-secondary settings (both of the quantitative and qualitative types) to provide a solid basis from which educators at this level can devise motivational plans and activities for classroom teaching.[40]

What are the characteristics of effective teaching at the post-secondary level? How do effective instructors stimulate (and sustain) their students' motivation to learn? How do they balance appropriately their direct- and indirect-instruction (i.e., teacher- and student-centered learning)?

To answer these critical questions I have synthesized the current research literature on effective teaching/learning and on motivation to learn at the post-secondary level, and have coupled this with reflections and insights from my own personal and professional experiences in education during the past 35 years. From this synthesis I have created a set of twelve key factors that characterize effective teachers. This compendium is an interrelated "set" of skills and abilities that interact with and complement each other. It is not merely a recipe or list of prescriptive steps to follow. In real life instructional practice these twelve skills work together synergistically; and often, effective teachers demonstrate them consciously, but at other times they appear to perform these tasks sub-consciously, with automaticity. That is what distinguishes expert from novice practitioners.

In this handbook I have identified and analyzed these factors systematically and deliberately, whereas in the actual routines of instructional practice, effective teachers may demonstrate them spontaneously and in complex combinations. Not only that, but expert teachers have worked at developing these competencies over time through accumulated experience, reflection, and deliberate effort to improve.

Thus, by means of their diligence and commitment they have shown: (a) that teaching is both a science and an art, and a profession; (b) that effective teachers are both born *and* made; (c) that faculty (especially novice instructors) can master the generic skills of good teaching; and (d) that skilled teaching is also highly content-specific for particular subjects.[41]

The following dozen characteristics and skills form a necessary foundation upon which exemplary teaching is built; however, these basic attributes, although required, are not sufficient to produce effective teaching: the total is more than the sum of its parts. As with all learned professional competencies, to be able to apply the skills both voluntarily and involuntarily in the give-and-take of daily practice requires practitioners to have mastered and internalized the knowledge and skills to the extent that they are able to draw upon them immediately, as the particular situation may warrant. What are these foundational teaching attributes and skills? They are described in the following section.

1. Application of Knowledge Bases[42]

Expert teachers understand and apply knowledge from three essential sources: the content from their subject-matter specialty; the field of general pedagogy (basic teaching methods); and the unique area that encompasses specialized, content-specific instructional strategies.

Historically, it was believed that if instructors in post-secondary institutions knew their content, then they would naturally be good at teaching it. People's personal experience shows that this is simply not the case, however, because we have all encountered teachers who were highly knowledgeable in their subject, but who could not present it in a clear or interesting manner. Yet, the reverse situation could also be true: a teacher could be a skilled motivator, and an entertaining speaker and actor, but if his/her subject-matter knowledge was lacking, or if the teacher was not current in the field, then his/her professional credibility and integrity as an exemplary instructor would be called into question.

Furthermore, effective teachers not only understand their subject, but they also know how to apply appropriately a set generic methods/techniques of teaching that are common to all subjects and all age/achievement levels. However, they possess and apply a third body of knowledge called Pedagogical Content Knowledge (PCK).[43] With this specialized knowledge, expert teachers have developed—through their accumulated experience of practice—a specific expertise that is unique to the particular discipline, program, and/or course that they teach. Over time, as they have reflected upon and interacted with this subject-matter—and with the students and colleagues who also work with it—they have gradually devised certain tactics, perfected particular techniques, and produced pertinent "practical tips" that apply directly to specific topics, concepts, or difficult points in a course. For instance, they come to know precisely where students will typically encounter difficulties, and they will have generated effective measures to assist learners to understand and resolve these potential problems.

When teachers skillfully apply these different knowledge bases, they positively influence their students' motivation to engage in the learning activities of the course. Thus, as illustrated in Figure 1.1, to demonstrate good teaching entails much more than accumulating knowledge.

2. Accommodation of Student Diversity[44]

Effective teachers realize that no single teaching method is sufficient to help all students learn. They employ a variety of teaching/learning approaches and instructional media in order to adapt the content to meet the diversity of learning styles typically present among any group of students.[45] As mentioned earlier under "building learner confidence", skillful teachers are able to adjust their teaching style to match students' readiness level to perform specific skills: they teach to promote student understanding—not only to require rote-memory of basics (al-

. DEMONSTRATE KNOWLEDGE

Figure 1.1. How *not* to demonstrate one's knowledge of teaching.

though the latter is required in any subject as a foundation on which to build learners' later knowledge).

Thus, when instructors make provision in their procedures to move learners from the known to the unknown, from the concrete to the abstract, and from the simple to the complex, then students experience both the challenge and the reward that accompany the learning of bite-sized chunks as they progress through the subject in a course.[46] Skilled teachers create this nurturing process that leads to learner development, by reflectively adapting their instructional designs to accommodate learner diversity. As a consequence, students' motivation to continue to learn is promoted.

3. Organization and Management of Teaching[47]

Effective teachers project an image of confidence and efficiency. They convey clearly that they have planned, prepared, and organized classroom routines and procedures in such a way as to create the conditions conducive for teaching and learning to take place. They tend to exude an air of composure and assurance: they demonstrate an ability of "being in charge", yet not in an autocratic manner. They typically handle disruptions or disciplinary confrontations with an objective and "matter-of-fact" demeanor. They appear approachable and friendly, yet they maintain a business-like deportment in their teacher/student relationships. They tend to have authority without appearing as controlling or coercive; and they consistently model the values and behaviors that they wish their students to express.[48] An example illustrating poor modeling is shown in Figure 1.2.

Furthermore, on the basis of studies of responses from a variety of students at various educational levels, it is evident that students desired the following attributes in their teachers and professors: to teach well, to keep order, to explain clearly, to be interesting, to treat students fairly, and to act friendly.[49] Half of these response-categories were related to the teachers' classroom management and human-relations behaviors.

In my own teaching-practice during the past five years, I have confirmed these results with nine different groups of post-secondary students, including: first-, second- and third-year education students; graduate students in education; graduate teaching assistants taking instructional development courses; medical resident interns enrolled in a teaching-improvement seminar, and recently-graduated high-school students in summer "orientation to university" programs.

I asked individuals in each of these groups to select one teacher from anywhere in their personal background whom they felt was effective, and to write down why. Afterwards, I required them to do the same for an actual teacher whom they would rate as ineffective. In all nine groups, after listing the characteristics of these teachers on the chalkboard (or overhead), I found that the same six positive attributes (allowing for synonyms) that were listed above appeared for the effective teachers, and that opposite characteristics were used to describe the ineffective ones.

. MODEL APPROPRIATE ORAL AND WRITTEN LANGUAGE

Figure 1.2. How *not* to model appropriate oral and written language.

4. Selection of Teaching/Learning Activities[50]

Teachers who are recognized as successful consistently incorporate a variety of instructional activities and learning experiences in their instruction that invoke student interest. They stimulate student thinking, they make clear presentations, they provide for meaningful student interaction and group work, they clearly tie learning objectives to classroom activities and to evaluation processes, and they do so while exuding enthusiasm and while encouraging and using students ideas.[51]

These instructors are able to orchestrate all of these events in such a way as to establish and maintain participants' motivation to engage in the learning process.

More specific examples of these techniques are provided in later chapters of this handbook.

5. Provision for Flexibility[52]

A typical characteristic of novice teachers is that, even though they may carefully plan and present a class-session, they may become fixated in having to complete their agenda as prepared, regardless of unique conditions, and thus may miss or ignore taking advantage of a spontaneous "teachable moment" or an unforeseen opportunity to enhance student understanding.

Experienced teachers, on the other hand, are able to provide for flexibility in their teaching—allowing for pursuing an occasional tangent without destroying the overall plan for a class-session. (Too, they have developed their inner sense to know when such a diversion will be worthwhile for the class as a whole, or whether such a digression might cater to a students' attempt to side-track the proceedings and waste time.)

This allowance for flexibility, is—like the other instructional skills—developed through the wisdom of experience—whereby good teachers accommodate activities and adapt their procedures to match the group-members' unique learning backgrounds.[53] Effective instructors are not overly uncomfortable with uncertainties, and they are able to capitalize on mistakes (their own and /or their students') in a positively constructive manner. They convey that errors are steps to improvement—not something to fear. Effective teachers—by willing to take such risks—signal to learners that confidence and competence does not emerge fully perfected, but that in a psycho-social environment characterized by mutual respect and acceptance, both students and teachers can learn from one another.[54]

6. Overall Planning and Structure[55]

Although successful teachers are not rigid about following a fixed prescription for instruction, they do have an overall structure to their teaching. They move instruction along at a good pace, confirming what research has consistently indicated: that maintaining a brisk momentum influences student motivation more positively than does slowing the pace down to accommodate a few students who may be lagging.[56] The latter causes tedium, boredom, and potential classroom management problems, whereas the former helps keep the majority of students alert (and in this case, experienced teachers also insure that the slower students are not ignored, but that they receive needed assistance quickly—either from the instructor him/herself, later, or from tutorial or small-group leaders).

Other characteristics of veteran teachers' planning-patterns are that: learning objectives are made explicit; transitions and summaries are clearly stated; assignments are specifically explained; and task procedures and expectations are systematically described so that all participants know precisely what students are expected to learn and/or to be able to do by the conclusion of the teaching/learning session.[57]

Whether instructors select teacher- or learner-centered approaches, they ensure that key points and procedures are clear to all participants, as illustrated in Figure 1.3.

Experienced teachers apply this type of planning over a range of time-frames: for individual class-sessions, for weekly and/or monthly time-tables, for longer units or topics of work, and for whole semester or term schedules.[58]

It has been found that—although expert teachers may do much of their instructional planning mentally or by writing brief notations—beginning teachers seem to profit most by initially writing out more detailed plans in order to assist them to identify and conceptualize key objectives and procedures for a unit of work or for a class period.[59] By thus forcing themselves to articulate explicitly what students will learn or be able to do as a result of the particular learning experience(s), novice teachers gradually develop their ability to specify clear objectives, to ensure that course activities are geared toward meeting these objectives, and to connect evaluation tasks back to these initial objectives and classroom assignments,[60] as explained in the following section.

7. Alignment of Objectives, Tasks, and Evaluation[61]

Effective instructors not only are able to conceptualize clear learning objectives for students, but they state them orally at the beginning of a class in order to specify exactly what is to be learned. They also know and clearly state how the particular activities or tasks of the session will help accomplish these objectives. Then, in the case of evaluating student achievement

. EMPHASIZE KEY POINTS

Figure 1.3. Effective teachers emphasize key points and procedures.

(e.g., with quizzes, tests, essays, or other assignments), expert teachers ensure that these assessment activities reflect both the instructional objectives and the various learning tasks that had been assigned previously.

Some post-secondary educators believe, in fact, that instructors should indicate to students during the first class-session what will be on the final exam, how it will be graded, and what performance standards are expected.[62] Such a procedure should not be thought strange, if one realizes that each evaluation activity should coincide precisely with the particular learning objectives of the lesson or unit being studied.[63]

The reasons for ensuring that learning objectives, activities, and assessments are congruent are that: all participants involved in the learning process will be clear as to what students are to learn or to be able to do as a result of the learning activities; all will thus know how learner performance will be evaluated; students will gain confidence because they will know exactly what is expected from them; and teachers will be perceived as being organized and fair, because—for class assignments and in testing situations—students will not be trapped into revealing what they do not know, but will be permitted to demonstrate what they do know.[64] As a result, the instructor's credibility will be enhanced, and learners will tend to take increasing responsibility to become more self-evaluative about their work. Motivation to learn will thus be stimulated.

8. Relevance to Students[65]

As described in a previous section, good instructors consistently attempt to relate the subject-matter to the students' experience. For instance, they explain: how the content may help students in the future (e.g., to understand later topics, further courses, or eventual careers); how the course fits in with other knowledge-bases or disciplines; how it may connect to learners' personal lives and experiences—past, present, and/or future; or what is the rationale behind having to follow certain procedures in performing a task.

When students perceive that a certain topic is meaningful, or when they see how it may connect to the "real world" to which they are accustomed, then their motivation to engage in related learning tasks is increased. Effective instructors search for ways to emphasize the value and/or utility of the subject matter for students.

With respect to my own teaching career, I applied this principle of relevance to try to persuade certain "un-motivated" students to learn French-as-a-second language.[66] I was a teacher of Core French for several years at the junior-high and high-school levels. The conversational French courses I taught at that time were compulsory; thus, I often had classes of 30 to 35 adolescents, many of whom were forced to be there—against their (and my) will. In desperation, and for survival as a novice teacher, I was eventually able to re-arrange my course activities to make the learning of French more relevant to teenagers' interests and needs. One way I did this was to present early in the course a short and convincing message on "Why learn a second language?" I clearly and concisely stated five key reasons. I said:

Compared to monolinguals, people who know more than one language: (a) have a wider range of career and job opportunities; (b) they enjoy increased benefits when travelling—being able to converse in more than one language; (c) they possess a certain mental stimulation about their personality, in that they are more tolerant, open, and accepting of people of other cultures and groups; (d) they appear to have more relaxed personalities, and are more at ease in a variety of social situations; (e) they tend to score higher on psychological tests that assess cognitive flexibility and divergent thinking; and (f) they learn their first language better (because of the linguistic comparisons between the two languages).[66]

I found that by presenting this rationale early and persuasively and by referring back to it at pertinent times in the course, that students' negative attitudes could slowly be modified. I found that similar techniques were also productive when I worked with older students, as well, which I relate in upcoming chapters of this manual.

9. Development of Learning Climate[67]

As I stated in an earlier section, the human-relations aspect of teaching is one of the key elements in determining its ultimate effectiveness. When the participants in a class sense that they are welcome, accepted, respected and worthwhile as individuals by their instructor and peers—*despite* what their past or present record of achievement and/or behavior may have been—then their motivation to learn is bolstered.[68] All teachers convey by their visible behavior to what degree they genuinely care for students' progress and well-being.

Certain attributes and characteristics have been repeatedly identified among populations of effective teachers for creating positive, productive learning environments.[69] They are: enthusiasm, empathy, warmth, fairness, openness, and task-orientation.

When such lists of traits are generated, two possible risks arise. One danger, particularly for beginning teachers, is that they may interpret the list as being prescriptive rather than descriptive. They may misconstrue the idea that in order to become an effective instructor they must make major changes in their personality to conform to some "idealized image of the paragon of professional perfection." They may fail to realize that a key ingredient to becoming a proficient teacher is to "be yourself," to be genuine, and to build on the strengths one already possesses.[70] In time, one can take systematic steps to learn new skills and/or improve weak ones.

A second potential danger is to conclude erroneously from the list of positive traits that good instructors do not experience human-relations problems in their courses. Such is not the case, however, because all instructional personnel (exemplary ones included) have their share of occasional classroom management and discipline problems—such as learners' unacceptable language, inappropriate behavior, inattention, or unethical conduct.

The differences between effective and ineffective instructors is that the former do not ignore these events or issues, but that they confront them and deal with them, and that they concentrate on preventive strategies more than they do on remedial or "curative" ones. Specific suggestions to accomplish these goals are presented in the next chapter.

10. Clear Communication[71]

Exemplary teachers are explicit in specifying their instructional intentions, expectations, and procedures. As stated above, effective instructors clearly state to the students the objectives for the class-period, the unit of work, the term-program, and the entire course. When giving instructions and directions for classroom activities, assignments, or other learning tasks they are precise and exact: they specify clearly what is to be done, how, where, and when. Nothing is left to misinterpretation: vague and ambiguous terms are avoided, and new terms are defined and repeated for emphasis. Moreover, they make clear transitions between segments of work, so that participants understand the linkages connecting the various sections of the material. This is illustrated in Figure 1.4.

. USE CLEAR TRANSITIONS

Figure 1.4. Effective instructors make clear transitions between activities and/or sections.

Effective instructors also use their voice well: volume, tone, projection, pitch, articulation, and pronunciation are appropriate and clear. When giving explanations, they provide plenty of examples related to students' experience; and they break the particular content into appropriately sized sub-components, so that learners can readily assimilate the material without feeling overwhelmed.[72]

When giving students feedback on their work, good instructors ensure that the former know exactly how well they have performed: what their strengths are and where and how they can improve. As referred to earlier, effective teachers ensure that learners know what the evaluation standards and criteria are, against which the latters' performance is to be assessed, by clearly stating these expectations at the outset. They again ensure that these assessment standards mirror the learning objectives of the course.[73]

11. Active Involvement of Learners[74]

From the outset of the first class-session exemplary instructors ensure that learners are actively engaged in meaningful learning experiences. That is not to say that *all* classroom activities will be student-centered, or conducted in small groups, or performed in laboratory-like settings, or be centered on creative individual or group projects: indeed, effective instructors will "sample" many of these methods. Yet, a substantial part of the material in most classes is presented via formal teacher-directed instruction.[75] However, a key difference between effective and mediocre instructors is that the former will typically enliven their direct-instruction sessions by incorporating a thoughtfully planned assortment of student-centered activities at strategic points during a class period—in order to stimulate students' thinking, to encourage their input, to permit learner practice, or to require application of their newly acquired knowledge and skills.[76]

Novice instructors (or more experienced ones who have not developed their skills) are generally not as successful as exemplary teachers at accomplishing these initiatives.

Specific means of enhancing student participation as advocated here are presented in subsequent chapters.

12. Teacher Reflection[77]

A key trait undergirding effective teachers' practice is their ability to analyze and reflect on their own teaching. This enables them to orchestrate the above listed variables in such a way as to motivate students' learning within a specific environmental content. What is more impressive is that they perform this self-analysis and self-reflection on a continual, ongoing basis, in the midst of the myriad of complex processes, interactions, and consequences that occur in the daily routines of instructional life.

On the basis of these internal processes they make instructional decisions—sometimes on the spur of the moment, sometimes at the end of a session in preparation for the next class, or sometimes in revising plans for the following year. Like all professionals who have developed expertise in their particular field of interest, exemplary instructors often also apply their reflective/analytical skills to improve their own professional practice: e.g., to make adjustments in their own instructional or management behaviors, to advise students to adjust their own thinking or behavior, or to modify materials, media or equipment used in their teaching.

* * * * *

In the preceding sections I have summarized the research-based principles that sustain both effective teaching practice and motivation of learning. In the visual in Figure 1.5 that serves as a graphic conceptual-framework for this handbook, I incorporate these above principles as the foundation upon which effective instruction is designed. The remaining chapters explore the essential elements of this design.

Motivating Teaching: A Conceptual Framework

In Figure 1.5, I depict how I have conceptualized effective teaching and learning at the post-secondary level. I also use the visual to organize the structure of this handbook. In reality, of course, the teaching/learning process simply takes place; and neither the instructors nor the students are overly concerned about categorizing the activities into "managerial" or "instruc-

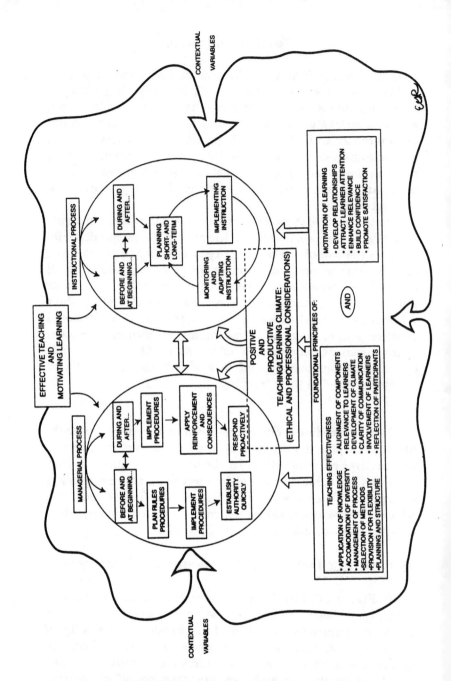

Figure 1.5. Motivating teaching and learning at the post-secondary level: A conceptual framework.

tional" components—they simply become involved in the action of the moment.

However, for analytical and reflective purposes, I isolate and examine the various components of this complex enterprise, and by doing so, deconstruct the holistic process into observable components, and thereby assist interested instructional personnel (novices, veterans, or those in between these stages) to reflect on, to practice, and to improve their own instructional competencies.

A brief orientation to Figure 1.5 follows:

I show in Figure 1.5 that for investigative purposes effective teaching may be classified into two basic categories: (a) the managerial side (i.e., what the instructor says and does—prior to and during the first class-session and the first week or so, and also later throughout the duration of the term—to create and maintain the necessary conditions under which effective teaching and learning can proceed); and (b) the instructional aspect (i.e., what the teacher does and says—prior to and during the first class-session and the first week, and also later throughout the term—to plan, prepare, present and assess motivational teaching/learning activities).

One can also see from Figure 1.5 that the key factor integrating these two sub-components and producing an effective interrelationship between them is the teaching/learning climate. I describe this climate as psycho/social/emotional tone for which the teacher has the ultimate responsibility of establishing and maintaining in the class, lab, seminar room, or wherever the learning activities take place.

Finally, I represent in the lower portion of Figure 1.5 the idea that developing a positive learning climate is contingent upon the instructor's consistent application of the foundational principles of effective teaching and motivation—as I highlighted in the earlier sections of this chapter.

References

1. See, for example, Good and Brophy (1995) and Lambert, Tice, and Featherstone (1996).

2. See Ames and Ames (1984).

3. See Jarvis (1995).

4. See Good and Brophy (1995) and Lewis (1992).

5. See Elliott, Katochwill, Littlefield, and Travers (1996) and Davis (1993).

6. See Day, Berlyne, and Hunt (1971) and Eble (1988).

7. See Amabile (1989) and Elliott, Katochwill, Littlefield, and Travers (1996).

8. See Freiberg and Driscoll (1992) and Stipek (1988).

9. See Driscoll (1994) and McCown et al. (1996).

10. See Biehler and Snowman (1993), Jarvis (1995), Wiles and Bondi (1991), and Winzer (1995).

11. See Jarvis (1995) and Rogers and Freiberg (1994).

12. See "The Landscape" (1994).

13. See Lewis (1992) and Weber (1997).

14. See, for example, Gage and Berliner (1992); Hidi, Renninger, and Krapp (1992); and Weil and Joyce (1978).

15. See, for example, Freiberg and Driscoll (1992); Lambert, Tice, and Featherstone (1996); and Virginia Polytechnic (1991).

16. See, for example, Angelo (1993), Bruffee (1995) and Weimer (1993).

17. See Eble (1988) and Thomas (1988).

18. See, for example, Gage and Berliner (1992) and Guskin (1994).

19. See Ralph (1994c, 1996a).

20. See the Bibliography for several research reports that I published on "Contextual Supervision"—a developmental learning model that incorporates these concepts. See also my forthcoming book that will serve as a complement to this present manual (Ralph, 1998b).

21. See, for example, Barell (1991), Labouvie-Vief (1992), Vojtek (1994), and Yelon (1996).

22. See Biehler and Snowman (1993), Elliott et al. (1996), Eble (1988), and Good and Brophy (1995).

23. See de Charms (1984); Amabile (1989); and Day, Berlyne, and Hunt (1971).

24. See, for example, Winzer (1995) and Biehler and Snowman (1993).

25. See Knowles (1990) and Sims and Sims (1995b).

26. See Jarvis (1995) and Wiles and Bondi (1991).

27. See, for example, Barr and Tagg (1995); "The landscape" (1994); Schnell (1996); and Wise (1996).

28. See, for example, Case, Harper, Tilley, and Wiens (1994) and Stewart (1993, 1994) for a substantial argument. See also Malcolm (1995) and Peters (1995).

29. See Jarvis (1995), Knowles (1990), Thomas (1988), and Wiles and Bondi (1991).

30. See Hoyle and John (1995).

31. See Jarvis (1995), Rogers and Freiberg (1994), and Thomas (1996).

32. See Sims and Sims (1995b).

33. See Gunter, Estes, and Schwab (1995), and Sims and Sims (1995a, 1995b).

34. See Sims and Sims (1995a, 1995b).

35. See Sims and Sims (1995a, 1995b).

36. See Sims and Sims (1995b).

37. See Gunter, Estes, and Schwab (1995), and Sims and Sims (1995a, 1995b).

38. See Good and Brophy (1995).

39. See, for instance, Bruffee (1994), Good and Brophy (1995), and Rockwood (1996).

40. See Angelo (1993), Elliott et al. (1996), "Nothing succeeds" (1994), and Wiles and Bondi (1991).

41. See, for example, Biehler and Snowman (1993), Chiarelott, Davidman, and Ryan (1994), Dillon, (1986), and Palmer (1993).

42. See Dillon and Sternberg (1986), Good (1990), and Lim (1996).

43. See Shulman (1987).

44. See Edgerton (1996) and Katz and Henry (1993).

45. See Jarvis (1995) and Moore (1984).

46. See, for example, Brookfield (1991), and Lambert, Tice, and Featherstone (1996).

47. See Bonwell (1996), Hoyle and John (1995), and Wiles and Bondi (1991).

48. See, for example, Good and Brophy (1995).

49. See Weimer (1993) and Winzer (1995).

50. For busy instructors who desire access to practical ideas presented in a concise form, the following sources are excellent: *The National Teaching & Learning Forum* and *The Teaching Professor*.

51. See, for example, Berkowitz (1995a), Brookfield (1991), Lim (1996), and Peters (1996).

52. See, for example, Angelo et al. (1995), Brookfield (1991), Gunter, Estes, and Schwab (1995), Lambert, Tice and Featherstone (1996), and McNeely (1995).

53. See, for example, Good and Brophy (1995), Marken (1997), Wiles and Bondi (1991).

54. See Brookfield (1991).

55. See Gustafson (1996), and McCown et al. (1996).

56. See Good and Brophy (1995), Weimer (1996d), and Winzer (1995).

57. See Good and Brophy (1995), Lim (1996), and Lambert et al. (1996).

58. See Barell (1991), Freiberg and Driscoll (1992), and Elliott et al. (1996).

59. See, for example, Gage and Berliner (1992), Thomas (1988), and Winzer (1995).

60. See Elliott et al. (1996) and Slavin (1994).

61. See Good and Brophy (1995), Popham (1998), and Weimer (1993).

62. See Thomas (1988) and Yelon (1996).

63. See, for example, Ralph (1994f).

64. See Biehler and Snowman (1993), Eble (1988), and Thomas (1988).

65. See, for example, Berkowitz (1995a), Brookfield (1991), Rogers and Freiberg (1994), and Sternberg (1994).

66. See Ralph (1982, 1989, 1994d).

67. See the first section of this chapter, "Motivation of Learning."

68. See, for example, Rogers and Freiberg (1994).

69. See Bonwell (1996), Daloz (1986), McNeely (1995), and Moore (1984).

70. See, for example, Borich (1994), Brookfield (1996), and Lambert et al. (1996).

71. See Kuh (1997), Lim (1996), and Weimer (1993).

72. See, for example, Eble (1988), Heinich, Molenda, and Russell (1993), Yelon (1996), and University of Saskatchewan (1997-1998).

73. See, for example, Brookfield (1991), Lewis (1992), and McCown et al. (1996).

74. See, for example, Edgerton (1996), McCown et al. (1996), and Weimer (1998).

75. See Jarvis (1995) and Lim (1996).

76. See Elliott et al. (1996), Freiberg and Driscoll (1992), and Lewis (1992).

77. See, for example, Brookfield (1995), Chiarelott et al. (1994), Davis (1993), Shulman (1993), and Wise (1996).

Chapter 2

CONDITIONS CONDUCIVE TO LEARNING: CLIMATE AND MANAGEMENT

In Chapter 2, I apply the foundational principles of teaching effectiveness and motivation of learning outlined in Chapter 1 (and as depicted in Figure 1.5), in order to present specific strategies and suggestions for instructors to consider implementing or adapting as they engage in two primary tasks. One task is to create a positive teaching/learning climate, and the other is to establish and maintain an appropriate classroom management plan.

Part 1: Creating a Positive Teaching/Learning Climate

I have endeavoured to illustrate in the lower portion of Figure 1.5 that the key integrating factor that links the managerial and instructional functions of effective teaching is the presence of a pleasant socio-emotional environment pervading the learning situation. The onus rests upon the instructor to attempt to establish and maintain this positive working relationship for class participants.[1] While it is true that other factors may influence its effectiveness, the ultimate responsibility for setting the tone in the group remains with teachers— by virtue of their legal, professional, and ethical position: they have been hired to conduct the course.

If the instructor consistently applies the foundational principles of effective teaching and motivation described in Chapter 1 (and as shown in Figure 1.5) during the class routines, then an inviting and productive atmosphere will prevail. However, a critical question—especially for novice instructional personnel—is how, in fact, does one accomplish this? I present five practical norms of action garnered from the research literature and from my own educational experience. These behaviors are rooted in the foundational principles, and they have been shown to promote a productive and appealing learning atmosphere. Although there are elements in each of these actions that are interconnected, I separate them here, in order to emphasize their importance in the motivation of learning.

1. Portray a Humane Attitude

Because the teaching-learning enterprise involves both the intelligence and the emotions, for a teacher to neglect the latter would hamper the effectiveness of the process.[2] When instructors demonstrate sensitivity to the "non-academic" interests and needs of students, they begin to create an accepting climate that is conducive to learning.

Furthermore, they tend to demonstrate their genuine interest in students by what they say and do, both in and out of class. They exhibit a professional yet approachable manner in their relationships by consistently showing empathy and understanding—especially when students raise questions or concerns; and they deal with them privately or publicly, as required.

Other examples of this caring attitude are: instructors consistently show respect for students (even for the occasional obnoxious one); they endeavour to incorporate students' ideas or suggestions into the learning situation; instructors consistently show that they are available by often arriving for class early or leaving a little later, so that they may dialogue with students and/or respond to their inquiries about the course; they post—and keep—office hours for student advising; and they use a discrete amount of self-disclosure—through, for instance, the occasional sharing of personal anecdotes, or the prompt apology for an error made in a lecture, or in mis-calculating points on a student's test.[3]

Responses such as these—when implemented consistently and genuinely—promote the creation of an inviting work environment for all participants.

2. Be Honest[4]

When teachers gain a reputation for being truthful and trustworthy, students become less cynical about how they may be treated, and also less suspicious about possible hidden agendas in the teaching/learning situation. Presenting the subject-matter accurately, examining alternative viewpoints system-atically, avoiding dogmatism, withholding judgment pending investigation of all available evidence, and maintaining honesty in conducting research and reporting results are all examples of professors' behavior that promote the development of trust within the student/teacher relationship.

Research[5] among adult students has revealed five indica-tors of "instructor authenticity" (i.e., the perception among students that their teachers are honest and open with them): (a) Maintaining congruence between words and actions; (b) revealing some of their own personality, occasionally; (c) accept-ing students' suggestions and being willing to incorporate them into the program; (d) disclosing the full agenda of a course and all of its expectations early; and (e) being willing to acknowledge their own mistakes.

The importance of truthfulness as a norm to govern teach-ers' actions and as a means of building an affirming learning atmosphere is apparent.

3. Be Fair[6]

Although this admonition appears to be a cliche, it is critical in establishing the instructor's credibility and in nurturing an environment of trust among group-members. Key factors influ-encing fairness are consistency and impartiality. When evalu-ating and grading students' work, the same standards must apply to all, and to all sections of course that one may teach. Moreover, to prevent major inconsistencies, the instructors teaching several sections of one course should collaborate in setting common course goals and assessment-standards. If re-quirements or results are too divergent between and among sections then students would have reason for complaints.

In formal teaching situations instructors need to be seen as showing no favoritism. For instance, effective teachers typi-cally: distribute oral questions equitably around the classroom; provide individual attention equally; request "monopolizers" to permit others to contribute; avoid stereotyping or discriminat-ing on the basis of age, gender, background, race, or disability—and stop students who do so; use objective rather than subjec-tive criteria when calculating students' final grades (i.e., refrain from allowing "personality factors" to influence, either positively or negatively, a component of a student's grade, such as "class contribution, attendance and attitude"—unless related criteria for assessing this item have been previously and publicly communicated); and frequently ask themselves, "Would I want an instructor to treat either me or my nineteen-year-old this way?"

Fairness in Handling Diversity[7]

Virtually all instructional personnel believe in the principle of equal opportunity for every student, but effective teachers take consistent and deliberate action to apply it in daily practice. By doing so, they model for all class participants how to interact with students of diversity, and to work at removing barriers of exclusion and alienation.

Good instructors are, first, aware of unacceptable practices that mitigate against the acceptance of diversity, and second they counteract these negative patterns with specific and overt responses, as illustrated below.

Gender issues. The following gender inequities in post-secondary education have been documented: female students are called on less than male students; in group discussion women are interrupted more often than are men; both men and women make less eye contact with women, in group work; both are less attentive when female students speak; in classrooms the latter are asked fewer open-ended questions than males; women are given less time to answer questions than are men; women's self-esteem is lower when they finish post-secondary education than when they begin (especially for minority women); as women's self-esteem is diminished their academic aspirations also tend to decline; and students (both sexes) expect female faculty to be more understanding than their male counterparts.

To help reverse these discriminatory images, effective instructors not only present these facts to their classes, but during the teaching/learning situation they ensure, on a consistent basis, that they: call on female students as often as males, listen attentively to all students' contributions, ask a variety of questions of all students, allow adequate wait-time for all participants to answer, and convey a spirit of concern and understanding for all students.

Exemplary instructors also model non-discriminatory language[8] (e.g., using "people" for "mankind", "nurse" for "male nurse", "chairperson" for "chairman", "gay male' for "homosexual", "Inuit" for "Eskimos", "First Nations" or "Aboriginals" for "natives", or "Jane Smith" for "Mrs. Peter Smith." Using such language is not just a matter of being "politically correct", but of advocating *and* practicing fairness and equality.

Multicultural issues.[9] In keeping with the motivational principle of creating an inviting environment for teaching/learning interaction, expert instructors seek to empower individuals who belong to diverse groups of people for the purpose of granting them equal opportunity to pursue learning goals without attached advantages or disadvantages. Because teachers are the creators of the classroom group-climate, they not only model responsible behavior, but they establish group norms that rule out unacceptable remarks that would offend any individual or group with respect to racial, ethnic, cultural, linguistic, or religious background.

Effective instructors treat minority students as if they belong—taking them as seriously as any other student, while simultaneously respecting their ethnic or cultural differences. They recognize similarities and differences between and among diverse groups, and they stress the former. In the classroom, they will not tolerate overt racism, ethnic slurs, or disparaging comments against anyone—minority or not.

Because multiculturalism is a key part of every country's make-up, today, it should be emphasized in universities and colleges—and ultimately addressed directly or indirectly in all courses. Teachers who do so are serious about reducing stereotyping and about celebrating what all individuals share—not just what makes them distinct.

Students with disabilities.[10] If the fundamental norms of fairness, respect, and human understanding are prevalent in a learning situation in which any students with disabilities participate, then there is little opportunity for inappropriate or discriminatory reactions to develop against them. However, unintentional misinterpretations or negative feelings may occasionally arise, but effective instructors are sensitive to such events and they act quickly to prevent them from escalating.

For instance, they use language like, "A student with a disability" (or "Samuel, who has a hearing impairment..."), *not* "A disabled student" or "Samuel is a disabled person". They state, "A person with (or "who has") epilepsy", *not* "An epileptic." They say, "A student with [stating the disease]...," *not* "A student suffering from (or "afflicted with")...," nor "A man confined to a wheelchair" but "...uses a wheelchair."

Vocalizing such sensitive and sensible descriptions places the individual ahead of the impairment because the whole person is *not* disabled; emotionally negative descriptors are not used that label a person as hopelessly handicapped. (In fact, the word "impair" is preferred to the word "handicap," because of the latter's negative overtones.)

People with disabilities do not want to be treated stereotypically, and yet from both the legal and the moral standpoint, instructors are obliged to accommodate the special needs of these individuals—*not* to provide them with unfair advantages over regular students, *not* to dilute the course objectives nor alter the basic curriculum content, *not* to hold them less accountable for learning tasks, or *not* to reduce standards or relax requirements.

Rather, based on a desire to help equalize the opportunities in assisting these individuals to overcome personal obstacles, responsible instructors—in collaboration with the student and the campus's office of student services—incorporate modifications in the delivery and/or format of the course. For example, alternative arrangements may be made for student examinations (such as responding in an oral, tape-recorded format, re-locating the exam to a different room, providing extra time, or using a scribe [or note taker]); and during regular class-lessons provision may be made for the use of an interpreter, tutor, reader, or auxiliary material and equipment.

Students with disabilities do not want to receive prejudicial treatment, but they do want to participate in learning on an equal playing-field. In fact, one university[11] described three "disabling myths" that students wished were eliminated from people's thinking:

1. *The Myth of the Helpless Invalid*, which manifests itself in excessive deference and solicitousness.

2. *The Myth of the Heroic Cripple,* which places the person with a disability on a pedestal, making it difficult for him or her to assimilate and to function.

3. *The "Spread" Phenomenon,* which generates from a single disability and assumes there are also intellectual, social, and other physical defects. An example is speaking more loudly to a person who is blind.

4. Show Respect[12]

This norm of action is presented neither as a platitude nor a slogan, but rather it represents a major integrating factor pervading all of the normative behaviors that promote solid social-emotional cohesion in classrooms. Students repeatedly report[13] that when they sense that instructors acknowledge them as worthwhile individuals with unique ideas and talents to contribute to the learning situation, then their interest and motivation regarding the subject increases. Students do not want to be regarded as children, but they want their teachers to treat them with respect, and to respond to their inquiries and questions seriously.

They, as do their instructors, wish to be granted consideration, civility, and courtesy in their working relationships. Ineffective teachers do not consistently reflect these qualities. Some instructors are not self-disciplined and they allow themselves to display anger, hostility, and resentment toward certain students who may not conform to their standards; or they may project an air of arrogance, selfishness, arbitrariness, or indifference in the teaching/learning situation. Such behavior, if maintained, is unprofessional and unacceptable.

Although every teacher will experience occasional "bad days," those who are committed to creating a positive communicating process will refrain from such negative reactions. They deal with teacher-student conflicts in private: they do not let the problems that inevitably arise with one or two of their students interfere with or detract from the positive relationships that have been developed with the great majority of the remainder of the group, who are productively engaged in the learning activities. (More of this issue will be discussed in the upcoming section on the managerial and organizational aspects of teaching.)

Build Trust[14]

Teachers who are skilled at their craft show respect for learners by creating a relationship of mutual trust, which is the psycho-social bond that holds groups together. In one study when a group of teacher-award winners[15] were asked to account for their success in the field, they all identified the human-relation aspect of their craft as critical: to get acquainted with their students, and to serve their needs first; to involve the learners *and* be involved, themselves, in learning; and to be respectful, encouraging, and concerned about students' development.

Such teachers foster a climate of trust among class-members; however—even though students experience more freedom of expression and choice in such contexts—the instructors also do not neglect to provide structure, but they do so in a humane manner. Thus, they draw from their wisdom of experience to provide learner choice without license, direction without rigidity, and opportunity for learner expression without being offensive.

The building of trust and respect in a group is not the product of implementing any single technique, but of an accumulation of events over time. It must be earned. This process engenders risks, in that instructors begin to share some of their authority, while simultaneously maintaining their credibility (i.e., still being perceived as knowledgeable, competent, expert, but also as helpful and patient). This risk also entails being open (but not overly so) about and critiquing one's own weaknesses.

Effective teachers, although being genuine and open, do not undermine their professional expertise and experience in learners' eyes by being overly self-effacing or artificially humble. Students readily perceive whether or not an instructor is nurturing the trust relationship by granting them voice, by being a genuine listener, by entering their world, and by balancing support with challenge. Exemplary instructors are considerate and generous, yet they maintain a deliberate professional distance in their relationship with students: they may attend students' social or athletic events, for instance, but they refrain from appearing solely as buddies, or as "one among equals."

5. Keep Promises[16]

An essential component of producing an agreeable working climate in a learning group is for leaders to demonstrate their integrity and credibility by keeping their word. Dedicated instructors maintain consistency between what they declare and what they do, in such areas as: the course syllabus (Do they follow it?); the evaluation procedures (Are they consistent?) the office-hour schedule (Are they present?); or the commitment to "...answer it tomorrow..." (Do they follow through?)

With respect to these issues the golden rule is applicable: How do instructors react if their supervisors or administrators break their promises? Undoubtedly, they feel frustrated, disappointed, betrayed, or cynical — and their respect for these leaders often declines. Likewise, with adult learners and their instructors who are not faithful to their word.

Keeping one's promises not only enhances one's credibility but it bolsters the trust relationship. Research[17] among adult learners has shown that students will tolerate a wide variety of teaching styles and approaches, provided that a climate of trust has been formed in the relationship. Students will place confidence in instructors' experience and competence if: the latters' words are congruent with their behaviors, they admit their fallibility, they are approachable in non-formal settings, they show respect by seriously considering student input, and they refrain from showing favoritism.

* * * * *

The five behavioral norms just presented have been identified, both in the research and in practical classroom experience, as promoting the growth of a harmonious working atmosphere in educational settings. A central theme interwoven through all of these norms for action is that the teaching/learning process is essentially a *human* undertaking, and that the socio-emotional domain is as equally important as the cognitive and academic components.

What I have endeavoured to demonstrate in this section is that the intellectual part of learning is promoted when learners' psycho-social needs are met. This relationship between feelings and thinking shows that:

...both the teachers' role performance and the teaching methods they employ should never undermine, but always seek to enhance, the dignity and humanity of the learner: to do less than this is a misuse of the teachers' position, immoral and falls below the high ideals of education.[18]

Ethical and Professional Considerations

Closely aligned with the development of a positive work environment in classrooms is the whole realm of professional ethics. Not only does the legal, contractual arrangement between employer and employee obligate instructors to abide by established professional expectations in their work, but—at a deeper level—there are fundamental moral and ethical standards, which effective teachers use to guide their practice.[19]

Based on a review of pertinent literature, I present a condensed grouping of essential ethical qualities that current educators believe should guide the professional conduct of teaching personnel at the post-secondary level.

It is important to note at the outset how closely these ethical standards are interrelated with many of the foundational principles of good teaching and the qualities promoting a positive working climate—as shown in Figure 1.5. Indeed, abiding by these ethical criteria serves to nurture and support the application of all of the principles of effective teaching in the instructors' daily routines of practice: both in the managerial and the instructional domains.

Most post-secondary institutions have extablished formal policies in sub-sections of their collective agreements that delineate expectations for the professional conduct of their faculty-members. These documents often identify ethical principles of professional responsibility in three areas: commitment to students, to colleagues, and to the institution. These statements serve as guidelines for professors' behavior in their teaching role.

Examples of these principles are provided below.[20]

Commitment to Students

Exemplary faculty members assist all students to reach their potential in learning. They do so by applying their knowledge and skills in several areas: (a) the content of the subject-matter, (and how the particular course they teach fits into the range of courses offered in their discipline); (b) the generic skills of teaching; (c) the more specific pedagogical content knowledge (i.e., the specialized instructional and learning approaches unique to their field); (d) the appropriate explorations of relevant topics, and alternative viewpoints about them; (e) the respectful, equitable, and impartial treatment of all students; (f) the maintaining of confidentiality of students' academic or personal matters; and (g) the avoidance of any type of exploitation of students due to the instructor's professional status or authority.

Commitment to Colleagues

Effective faculty-members respect and cooperate with their peers in pursuing the common goal of promoting student learning. They fulfill their ethical obligation to resolve any professional or personal disagreement with a colleague in private. If an instructor believes that a colleague has acted unethically in a matter, he/she first discusses it with that person before reporting the situation to supervisors.

Commitment to the Institution

Good instructors adhere to the policies of the employing institution with regard to teaching, research and public service. They avoid conflicts of interest (e.g., engaging in other work that may interfere with their professional duties), and they ensure that the institution's procedures and regulations are followed regarding both the students' and their own academic affairs— such as with academic honesty, fair assessment of student work, administration of examinations, and reporting of grades.

On the one hand, these ethical standards could appear as a cold and remote list of idealistic prescriptions that "everyone knows about," but that are either carelessly followed or largely ignored.[21] This negligence becomes even more serious when students sense a discrepancy between "the policy" and "the practice." In fact, recent research investigating student satisfaction with teaching practice in undergraduate education has reported their views that: their classes were too impersonal; their professors were uncaring and uninterested in them as individuals; that mutual respect among the professor and students was lacking; and that the interpersonal atmosphere in the institution was non-inviting.[22]

On the other hand, there is ample evidence to show that effective instructors are able to accomplish two tasks related to their professional responsibility for creating a humane working atmosphere. One task is to reverse the negativity if it did infiltrate the class environment.[23] This is achieved, in part, by encouraging students to share personal opinions and experiences within the teaching/learning situation. This type of active-learning exchange permits all participants to see one another's "human side," and consequently generates feelings of mutual respect and of contributing to the group's well-being.

A second task accomplished by exemplary teachers in producing a pleasant learning climate is their capacity to prevent, from the start, undesirable attitudes and conduct from developing.[24] From the first class session, and consistently throughout the term, these instructors; (a) personally model the desirable qualities by exemplifying in both action and word, "This is how we act and work here." (e.g., the instructor is always well prepared, prompt, accurate, respectful, honest, and self-evaluative); (b) clearly explain "why we...use reasoned judgment...; ...value critical thinking...; ...avoid cheating...; or ...refrain from intimidation..." and so forth; or (c) occasionally exhort students about these ethical standards, by means of a brief pep-talk, a serious reminder, an appeal for empathy, or a request for cooperation.

However, some educators assert that anything even resembling the above three actions smacks of indoctrination, compulsion, forced "character repair," and even sectarianism;[25] and that such inducement to conformity should have no place in a modern classroom. Yet, I believe that these three instructional strategies not only promote desirable moral and ethical principles that should be advocated and practiced universally (i.e., "a moral imperative"),[26] and further that by reflectively applying and/or adapting these actions (according to the context of the teaching situation), instructors will achieve two goals. These actions will (a) directly help to produce a positive group atmosphere, and (b) indirectly help to satisfy the growing societal demand for college graduates who exhibit principled ethical conduct.[27]

A Caution

A potential risk arising from my strong advocacy for instructors to emphasize building up the human-relations element in classroom life is that—like any other educational practice—it could be over-used, misused, or abused. Indeed, if the promotion of group cohesion and the satisfaction of participants' psychosocial needs becomes the end rather than a means to enhanced learning, then the process may indeed fall short.

This creation of an agreeable classroom environment by ethical teaching does not represent a "laissez-faire" or overly-permissive ethos, where everyone "feels good" and does only what they want. On the contrary, effective instructors who pattern their practice on these ethical principles are also task-oriented:[28] they maintain high expectations for student achievement by demanding diligent work, academic mastery, and personal integrity—both from the class participants and from themselves. "By teaching ethically, faculty members model and advocate appropriate behavior to students in a voice far more effective than any proclamation."[29]

Such a professional stance has been shown to help motivate both the learners *and* the teacher to develop favorable attitudes toward the field of study.

How do effective teachers, who hold these values, actually plan and conduct the managerial and organizational function of the teaching process?

Specific answers to this question are presented in Part 2 of this chapter.

Part 2: *The Managerial Process: Organizational Routines and Strategies*

As shown on the left-hand side of Figure 1.5, the classroom management component of the teaching process constitutes a substantial portion of the teaching/learning initiative. This managerial process is defined as what the instructor says and does—outside of the strictly instructional portion—to create the conditions conducive for teaching/learning to take place.[30] For reflective and analytical purposes, I have categorized this classroom management and procedural component into two segments (as illustrated in Figure 1.5): (a) What successful instructors do to motivate learners prior to and at the beginning of a course; and (b) What they do during and after the session(s) to maintain this motivation, with respect to the routine procedures, policies, and organization of the teaching/learning situation.

It is noteworthy that although classroom management and procedural routines may seem trivial, research has revealed that this area of teaching is critically important.[31] Findings show that: students expect their instructors to exercise management and control; new teachers are more concerned about content than about management—until after they begin teaching (when they realize significance of it); exemplary teachers practice sound management techniques, and ineffective teachers do not; and effective management produces positive results (e.g., minimizes disruption, enhances task engagement, maintains learning momentum, and maximizes learning). In settings deficient in sound management practices, these results do not materialize.

Management: Before and at the Beginning of a Session

Of course, in actual practice both the management and instructional components of the teaching/learning process occur simultaneously, but in order to assist interested instructors to examine and to develop their own professional competencies, I have separated these two domains and analyzed them in terms both of current educational research and of my personal experiences in a variety of educational settings.

My expectation is that instructors will: (a) consider what the research indicates as best managerial and instructional practice, (b) compare their own present practice with these findings, (c) reflect on any similarities and differences between them, and (d) decide if (and how) they might adapt their own teaching performance in these dual categories and/or how they might improve it.

Before a Session

Research[32] has consistently revealed that skilled instructors at all levels and in all subjects, plan, prepare, and organize their teaching before the actual event transpires. They must do so—especially if they are guided by the foundational principles for effective teaching, motivated learning, and ethical practice —as presented in earlier sections of this manual.

These teachers not only sense a moral obligation to enhance students' learning, but they genuinely desire to develop and/or improve their own professional skills.[33] However, many instructors often do not receive the necessary support, feedback, and opportunity to engage in reflective practice in order to do so. As a consequence of this and other institutional conditions that may run contrary to instructional development,[34] many faculty personnel may not improve their managerial and instructional competencies to the extent that is possible if they had the necessary support.

Planning for Procedures and Routines[35]

Prior to the first class-meeting successful teachers will have thoughtfully prepared for the administrative arrangements, facilities, policies, rules and routines that will enhance the smooth operation of the class proceedings.

Physical setting.[36] They will have examined the meeting location and facilities to check for: ease of access, adequate seating/heating/ventilation/lighting, availability of instructional-media equipment/hardware, access to "break-out" areas for group-work, and overall comfort level of the setting. If any of these items are deficient or require modification, good teachers will have attended to the task, or will have made arrangements for it to be done.

Administrative routines.[37] Although many of these procedural matters may seem of minor importance, effective teachers realize that, if neglected, these seemingly insignificant details could lead to frustrations, delays, student inattention, and escalation of confusion and dissatisfaction. Routines such as distributing handouts (having them pre-counted in stacks, sorted by row), making clear transitions from large-group to small-group work, and consistently abiding by accepted social conventions for contributing to discussions or answering questions are all thought out ahead of time and then explained to group-members by the instructor.

This efficient handling of pre-established procedures and management tasks results in minimal intrusions into class learning time.

Rules and procedures.[38] When planning rules (i.e., the stated expectations for student conduct) and procedures (i.e., actions designed to implement the rules), good instructors anticipate the typical behaviors and responses of learners with whom they are working. They also consider the institutional policies and regulations that pertain to student deportment on campus, as they formulate, beforehand, a basic set of ground rules that will apply to their particular learning setting.

Often, beginning instructors may dismiss such forethought as being "uptight or paranoid" or as being too authoritarian. In fact, it may appear to be contradictory to the position advocated earlier in this handbook for the creation of a humane and positive atmosphere. Yet, both the formal research[39] and the professional experience of many faulty-members attest to the fact that teachers who do establish (and, sometimes who do so with student input)[40] a set of fundamental classroom guidelines (and, the fewer the better[41]) to serve as standards for student deportment are more effective than those instructors who do not. Thus, a rule might be "We are courteous, here." A corresponding procedure applicable to small-group work would be: "When addressing anyone, we may attack their idea, but we do not deprecate the person."

If instructors are in a position where they meet and teach a new class, or if they inherit the proverbial "bad group," or if they are assigned to a group in which they are only a year or two older than the students, then one of the best ways to present themselves in these cases is to portray a business-like, task-oriented, confident manner, and to move activities along at a brisk pace.[42] (One researcher[43] has proposed that in such situations the teacher should take the role of "benevolent dictator"—being firm but kind, until he/she has established credibility and authority, and then gradually move the group toward more democratic interaction later in the term).

Positive speech. Another element in planning a core set of classroom rules and procedures is that expert instructors tend to accentuate the positive rather than the negative aspect of learner conduct,[44] thus conforming with the goal of applying ethical principles to help create an inviting socio-emotional learning climate. For instance, in a science-lab setting, rather than berating a group for not following procedures, a laboratory coordinator could deliberately select a group—or at least some individuals of a group—and comment positively on how they performed the task. Of course, this would be done in a tactful manner that does not ridicule or demean the offending group, or that does not appear artificial.

Moreover, in the rule-planning stage, proficient instructors will prepare a sound rationale for the rules and procedures[45] (e.g., "Because we hold that every member, here, is important we all practice respectful listening. Offensive remarks are therefore unacceptable.")

Hence, when presenting the operational policies to the group, strong instructors will verbalize them in specific rather than vague terms. Thus, a command like "Answer right" is best replaced by the above explanation.

Classroom rules. Effective instructors will have also reflected on how to deal with such management issues[46] as: student absenteeism, arriving late/leaving early, eating/drinking in class, talking during or disrupting proceedings, submitting late assignments, or working on other course assignments in class.

Some teachers choose to provide detailed rules, procedures, and consequences for these misdemeanors in the course syllabus, so that it is public information, and that all participants are thus aware of the expectations and the consequences for non-compliance. Other instructors deal with such questions orally in the group—either at the beginning of the course, or later, whenever a violation arises. For example, for attendance policy, they might have a rule: "For three or more unexcused absences the penalty is that you are not permitted to write the final exam." The key point is not merely to state a rule, but to enforce it consistently. If it is not, then it is best not to have the rule in the first place.

Part of the pre-planning process for these rules and procedures includes thinking about the implementation phase. For instance, some faculty-members would reject such rules as the one just mentioned, as being unacceptably restrictive for adult students, and would possibly say: "They are old enough to know what must be done. I am *not* going to spend valuable time taking attendance, reading notes from physicians (and determining whether such notes are fake or not), and policing students' behavior as if they are elementary-school children!"

Although there inevitably will be increased teacher responsibility for monitoring any rule, skilled professionals thoughtfully weigh the pros and cons of the alternatives of administering these procedures, before deciding on any action —and they do so prior to the beginning of the course. Their ultimate goal is preventive[47] rather than remedial procedural management.

Neophyte instructors who plan such procedures would benefit from collaborating with experienced colleagues and/or their department-heads to discover what faculty and/or departmental policies and/or practices have been previously used in this area. One cannot go against the management structures that have been previously established in one's department.

Alignment with institutional policies. Proficient teachers, when they pre-establish their own class rules, will have considered the institution's policies and regulations concerning student conduct with respect to the area of academic honesty.[48]

Questions of cheating (i.e., the giving or receiving of any unauthorized assistance or unfair advantage in any form of academic or unfair advantage in any form of academic work), plagiarism (i.e., the copying of the language, structure, or idea of someone else and claiming or attempting to imply that they are one's own work), falsification (i.e., any type of forgery, tampering, adding, deleting, changing of any academic documentation, or unauthorized accessing of another's computer files) or academic sabotage (i.e., any purposeful vandalism, tampering, theft, destruction of any academic equipment or materials) are usually addressed in the institution's code of honor, academic calendar, or other public documents. The onus is on students to comply with these standards; however, some may not have even realized that such codes exist—let alone to have previously read them or considered them.

In fact, current research[49] indicates that cheating by students in higher education has increased, both in exam situations (e.g., copying, helping others cheat, or using crib notes), and in written work (e.g., ignoring footnoting, submitting work done by another, collaborating on work—without authorization).

Expert instructors experience their share of these incidents, but on the basis of their desire to build a cooperative learning atmosphere, they will have pre-established a brief set of policies that reflect their ethical standard: to treat all students as if they desire to do right. However, if certain students choose not to do so, effective instructors will have also anticipated how they might handle the few cases that inevitably arise regarding these matters.

The Beginning of a Course

Implementing Procedures and Policies

It is important to have planned specific rules and procedures, but to implement what was written down and/or reflected upon is even more critical. How do exemplary instructors introduce and implement these policies during the first few class meetings?

Experienced instructors have found through practice that pro-active, preventive management is better than re-active, remedial or "curative" procedures.[50] It is easier to present one's expectations the first day, and subsequently to deal with any infringements, than to wait and let them escalate into major problems. Therefore, these teachers typically address the key rules in a matter-of-fact and objective manner (either in the syllabus or in introductory remarks) explained during the first class meeting.

The first session.[51] Despite how conscientiously one has reflected upon, planned, and stated management procedures, the work is futile unless one is serious about enforcing the rules.

It would be wiser not to have established a rule, than to state it and not to carry through with it. Because first impressions are critical, good teachers do not over-emphasize the rules and procedures, but they state them succinctly and directly as they move through the course outline with the group-members.

In general, successful instructors complete three tasks the first day: (a) they introduce themselves and the students, (b) they describe the course—its objectives, key topics, evaluation process, and basic expectations (the key rules and procedures are typically stated at this point), and (c) they provide an actual portion of the course content and/or process (many experienced educators advise instructors *not* to dismiss the class early the first day,[52] because of possibly leaving an impression with students that "the prof is too easy"—an idea which later may prove problematic. For instance, it may be difficult to reverse that impression when attempting to engage the learners in sustained academic work, or when having to confront a student for a misdemeanor.)

With respect to task "(a)" above, after referring to the course name and number and briefly introducing themselves (highlighting their background, qualifications and teaching interests), effective teachers typically introduce an "ice-breaker" (an exercise where students become acquainted). Examples are: (a) to have each individual introduce her/himself; (b) to have pairs interview each other for three minutes, then stand and introduce their partner to the group; (c) to conduct a similar type of "interview", except the interviewer must *not* talk (but only write) for the three minutes then change roles for the next three minutes; (d) to distribute numbered cards such that each numeral appears twice among the group. Students are to find the other person with their number, and then discover three educational- or family-related facts about their partner. They later stand as a pair and present these facts to the group; or (e) instead of formally reviewing the syllabus with the group, the teacher might assign students to silently read it (or a certain section thereof), and individually to write one key topic or idea from the outline that interests them, and also one key concern or question they may have about the course. Then, as a whole group, each pair shares their findings, while the instructor records these results, in two columns on the chalkboard or overhead. The instructor subsequently helps summarize and synthesize the students' perceptions, and also responds to their inquiries. (This activity would thus include all three of the first-day tasks mentioned above.)

In most cases, the class regulations and procedures would emerge from this interchange, but if not, the teacher would incorporate them into his/her remarks during the discussion.

The first few days.[53] Exemplary instructors are able to balance their confident, business-like style with a positive non-threatening manner.[54] These qualities are not mutually exclusive; and these teachers reflect the fundamental ethical norms described in earlier sections of the manual (i.e., a humane attitude, respect, honesty and fairness), while at the same time implementing the management procedures in a consistent and reasonable manner: they are serious about the tasks—yet supportive and encouraging; they are professional and "in charge" —yet pleasant and approachable. In doing so, they learn and use student names,[55] which in itself, is a powerful management tool.

During this critical implementation period, effective teachers present structure and motivating learning activities (see Chapter 3), and they continue to monitor student conduct— providing timely and diplomatic feedback concerning student compliance with the management rules and expectations. These faculty-members administer both positive reinforcement (e.g., "I appreciate how each of your group-members demonstrated self-discipline when debating that issue: You were able to analyze the weak areas of the argument and suggest improvements, without demeaning the presenters"); and negative consequences (e.g.,—to a student in private after a class—"I want you to know that two of your group's members informed me, today, that they feel you are not doing your share of the work. They mentioned that they spoke with you about this, but that nothing seems to have changed. Thus, they asked me to talk with you about this. What are your views on this situation?...").

During the first few class sessions, good instructors are constantly aware of student and group action and inaction: they are efficient at scanning the class—observing, monitoring, providing necessary assistance, questioning, probing, praising, and correcting, as the situation warrants. If required, they may review or re-teach a managerial expectation or a rule with the entire group, or with small groups or individuals as required.

A fundamental principle underlying all of these managerial activities and interventions is the instructor's desire to create a positive group feeling and a high task-orientation.

Solidifying Authority[56]

Skilled instructors know the importance of establishing one's authority early—not by means of dictatorial or autocratic control—but by clearly demonstrating their teacher leadership. By virtue of the basic structure of the instructional enterprise (where students pay to come and learn, and teachers are paid for fulfilling their responsibility to design activities to ensure that this learning occurs), teachers are granted this authority; however, they need to use it without exploiting it.

Successful teachers exercise this authority by being perceived as competent, confident, and knowledgeable (on the content and instructional side), and as being perceived as pleasant, fair, and honest (on the human-relations side)— points that have been emphasized in previous sections of this manual. Specific actions that they take to maintain their leadership position with respect to classroom management are described below.

Assertiveness.[57] Because novice instructors desire to be respected and accepted by students, their initial friendliness may be interpreted by some learners to represent uncertainty and weakness. Effective instructors tend to project a confident and assertive manner, and they recognize the distinctions between being assertive, aggressive, and non-assertive.[58]

For instance, an aggressive instructional approach would be characterized by intimidation, sarcasm, rudeness, fear, and coercion, in which the aggressor projects "I win, you don't win." Instructors who are aggressive may gain in the short-term, but lose in the long-term because they engender resentment, bitterness, and hostility among learners.

Teachers who are non-assertive project an image of "You win, I do not win," in which they allow others' views and decisions to control them. Unassertive instructors are self-denigrating, apologetic, and fearful of conflict.

Assertive instructors emphasize a balanced consideration of all sides in a conflict, where "I win and you win." They seek a mutually supported solution to relationship problems, in which teachers directly present their position but also understand the others' stance.

Three examples of these responses to a typical managerial problem are presented below.[59]

A student wishes to submit a major assignment that is five days late.

An *aggressive* response by an instructor would be: "Excuse me! If you had been listening the first day of class—or were you skipping?—when I clearly stated from the syllabus—did you even read it?—that in no way would I accept late assignments. You get zero."

A *non-assertive* response would be: "Well, let's see...uhm...you know that the syllabus mentions something about late assignments...I really shouldn't accept it...but, well, I might be able to this time...but you know we should abide by the rules...(heh, heh, heh)...but...well...I guess...okay..."

An *assertive* response would be: "No, I will not accept it for credit, because—as you know from our discussion of the syllabus the first day—late assignments get zero. If you wish, though, I will give you some feedback on your paper that may help you for the next assignment."

Presence.[60] Other ways that exemplary teachers use to project confidence and authority is the "I mean it" tone of voice, and the use of speech that is articulate and precise and that avoids nervous laughter or fillers like "ah" and "uhm" that may project images of instructor insecurity or indecision. Furthermore, they make frequent eye-contact with all members of the group, which adds to their image of assertiveness.

They teach with conviction and enthusiasm, and always secure the attention of learners before beginning, or before continuing to speak. Without appearing to be arrogant or rude, they insist on everyone attending to the presentation or event occurring at the moment. They may say, for instance, "Is everyone with me?" (using a pause and deliberate eye-contact, for example, with a pair of learners who may have started visiting during the class).

With respect to demonstrating enthusiasm, some teachers argue that unless one is born with "enthusiasm" it is futile to try to manufacture it. Although it is true that instructors should "be natural and be themselves" in the teaching context, it is also true that — regardless of their own personality traits — they can learn new and/or refine present skills that will help to create interest and motivation, both within themselves and among students.[61] For instance, effective teachers do the following:

1. They use *mobility* by breaking "the invisible six-foot leash" that typically holds presenters at the front of a classroom, and by casually moving about the room, and occasionally positioning themselves in the middle, at the sides, or at the back of the room while teaching. Such movement produces tangible results. It gains student attention, keeps them alert (by adding a certain amount of discomfort: "What is she doing meandering around over here?"), and tends to create a degree of group cohesion—in that the instructor's proximity will not solely be limited to the people who sit at the front.

2. They use their *voice* by varying their pacing, pitch, volume, tone, modulation and projection as the situation warrants, and sometimes when it may not—to add occasional humor or novelty. These variations tend to promote interest, create expectancy, or emphasize key points.

3. They use *pausing* appropriately. Pauses can add dramatic effect, stress the importance of a statement, provide time for students to think, attract attention, make transitions, or promote expectancy.

4. They use *gesturing* to focus learners' attention on main concepts in a lecture, or to point to certain items on the chalkboard or on a visual or a specimen. Such gestures are often accompanied by key phrases, such as: "Watch this." (as the teacher uses progressive disclosure on a projected overhead transparency showing the step-by-step solution to a problem); or "Listen to the taped voices while I point to each person on the slide shown on the screen who sings the various parts of these popular songs."

* * * * *

In this section I have summarized how exemplary instructors initiate effective managerial procedures by both planning and implementing a variety of techniques during the first few sessions of a course. I have emphasized that they attempt to create both a high task-orientation among learners and an inviting work climate. The next section of the chapter seeks to answer the question, "How do they *sustain* the managerial process, once it has been established, for the remainder of the term?"

Management: Maintenance of Procedures

As described in the preceding section and as displayed graphically in Figure 1.5, proficient teachers stabilize their authority by establishing their credibility and authenticity directly from the first session and during the first few classes. However, it is one thing to establish one's initial professional reputation, but to conduct oneself so that one's authority is maintained is quite another. One way that effective instructors accomplish this goal after the initial "break-in period," appears to involve a contradictory strategy, because it involves sharing their authority[62]—to gain and retain it, one begins to give it away!

During and After Sessions

Expert teachers accomplish this sharing process—not by relinquishing their leadership or forsaking their responsibilities to permit a laissez-faire spirit to pervade the group—but by systematically facilitating conditions so that collaboration and creativity are promoted. For instance, they respect learners' input and feelings about the course; they incorporate some of these ideas into the learning activities; they attempt to tailor some of the content to match participants' expressed interests; and they provide for increased learner choice, within a range of alternatives, in meeting the instructional objectives of the program.

During and after each session, as these teachers reflect on the day's activities and results, they continuously monitor the effect of their decisions — sometimes making adjustments immediately to deal with spontaneous events, and sometimes deciding to make either partial or substantial revisions for the next class or for future terms, as illustrated below.

Reviewing Managerial Routines[63]

Occasionally instructors discover as they progress through the course that their initially established rules and procedures may not be functioning as planned. Proficient teachers are sensitive to such feedback and begin to consider how these policies might be altered. They demonstrate flexibility—avoiding the appearance of being rigid on the one hand, and of appearing indecisive or showing partiality on the other.

For instance, in the example presented earlier about the rule of giving zero for late assignments, the teacher may not at the time feel as strongly about the rule, or may see it as not being completely fair or reasonable, or he/she may not be monitoring it as closely and consistently as some students believe it should be (thus causing these students to accuse the professor of showing favoritism to someone who might have been one-half hour late with an assignment).

In such cases, teachers have at least three options. They can modify the rule, say, to provide for a de-escalated loss of points for each day that the work is overdue. They can review and re-explain the rule—not in a threatening manner—but in an objective and personable way, just as if they were re-teaching a subject-matter concept for students who were not clear about it. (Perhaps, students were genuinely confused about the implementation of a specific procedure.) The third option is that teachers could remove the rule altogether.

Whatever the decision, good teachers—at this juncture in the course—would be encouraging student input and discussion, and it may be timely at that point to consider learners' suggestions for restructuring the rule. Again, effective teachers use their assertiveness to consider all input in a balanced fashion in order to attempt to arrive at a solution with which all participants can live.

This may not be easy, because it is time-consuming and often intensive; and it may be virtually impossible to accomplish, depending on the contextual variables. Nevertheless, experienced instructors—at the very least—give the appearance of being fair,[64] and even though they have the professional responsibility for the final decision, they do consult with students. One way to do this is to have each student anonymously write in one sentence on a card their solution to the issue. The teacher would collect and collate the data, and on that basis, could make the decision and explain the process to students in the next class period.

Using Reinforcements and Consequences[65]

A key element in how exemplary instructors enact their plans of maintaining their management routines during the implementation phase is their skillful application of positive incentives, for student compliance, and the administering of negative consequences for non-compliance, with respect to the ground rules and procedures of the program or course in question.

Reinforcement.[66] Although reinforcement practice is rejected by some as being cold, mechanical, and "behavioristic," the fact is that adult learners are motivated by a variety of reinforcers,[67] such as: peer approval, independent work, privileges and responsibilities, expectations of success, feelings of autonomy, pursuit of interests, personal goals, avoidance of failure, fear of punishment, aversion for displeasure, or achievement anxiety.

To deny the influence of these influences would be to ignore powerful incentives applicable to the motivation of learning—as indicated in Chapter 1 of this manual.

Key positive rewards that expert instructors apply during teaching/learning activities are: praise, smiles, nods, gestures, grades, privileges, and independent time. There are, of course, negative responses: using sarcasm, frowns, negative facial expressions and body language; giving low grades and, punishments; and assigning laborious, tedious or meaningless tasks. Wise teachers tend to incorporate the former and to avoid the latter.

Praise.[68] Research[69] on the extent of the use of teacher praise in both K-12 and post-secondary education reveals an alarming lack of it in classrooms.

Yet, if it is administered appropriately, praise can positively influence learning for learners of all ages. Moreover, both extremes are dangerous: indiscriminate praise soon becomes meaningless (where every learner and every comment and task is reinforced, without regard to the effort expended or the quality of the response); and giving no praise ignores major reinforcement opportunities, and may lead to sterile learning environments.

Praise is more effective in motivating introverts than extroverts, while extroverts are more motivated by blame than by praise, as compared to introverts. Furthermore, students from families of lower socioeconomic status are more motivated by praise than are students from high S.E.S. homes.

For praise to be effective in rewarding students' desirable behaviors, it should progress beyond simple feedback, and should reward individual learners' clearly describable progress, high achievement, or serious effort. Furthermore, genuine praise is even more meaningful if it is administered personally by an instructor with high status. (Thus, competent teachers use their professional reputation and credibility to support their reinforcing behaviors, and vice versa.)

If praise is given indiscriminately or without being earned through honest effort, learners will tend to see it as being artificial. Too, effective praise needs to be selective: it is most powerful when presented immediately after the desired action (or as soon thereafter as is feasible), and with sincerity rather than superficially.

Praise is also effective when it is administered for specific accomplishments, rather than given in blanket terms. For example, when positively reinforcing a student's oral presentation a competent instructor might say:

> Your introduction with the puzzle on the overhead was catchy, and you referred back to it twice—once in the middle, and then, again, in your conclusion. This motivational technique not only highlighted the main concepts for us, but you also reviewed it, when you got us excited about guessing the answer (and explaining our thinking) at the end. We were stimulated.

This is much better for both the students' and audience's learning than is a vague general comment like, "You did well."

Praise also needs to be provided in sufficient amounts. Effusive praise is typically judged by adults to be ingenuine; and intermittent reinforcement is more effective than constant reinforcement.

When learners first began to practice a new learning task—regardless of their age—they require positive feedback for what they do correctly. Then, as they progress by succeeding at step-by-step successive approximations toward the final goal, expert instructors reinforce each improvement. However, they occasionally hold back reinforcement so that it does not become automatically expected. In these cases, learners experience needed periods of cognitive dissonance, in which they are forced to struggle with a problem, and in which they must substantiate for themselves whether their proposed solution is correct and their response is defensible.

A mistake often made by neophyte instructors with their reinforcement reactions is that they tend to over-use certain oral responses. Various hackneyed expressions become neutralized in that they lose their desired effect because of triteness. Classic neutral responses are: "Okay" (or "Kay"), "Good," "Right," or "Yeah." Effective teachers supplement these with a variety of reinforcing expressions and actions,[70] such as: "Good thinking," "I see," "Please elaborate," "Tell us more," "Yes," "Precisely"/"Exactly"/"Absolutely," "That's an interesting answer," "Correct," "How do you prove that?" "Thank you," "That is an insight!" "I never thought of that," "That shows some ingenuity," "A creative response," "Great," "Do we all agree?" "That is logical," or the nodding of the head accompanied by a smile, or giving the "superb" sign (a raised hand with the thumb and forefinger touching, indicating "perfect").

Consequences.[71] Successful instructors also enforce negative consequences for rule infractions in implementing their overall classroom procedures and standards. Although most instructors do not relish administering aversive judgments, they occassionally must do so to maintain their professional credibility and the authenticity. However, those that do so have also developed their skill to be able to discern between infractions that require intervention and those that are minor in nature.

If consequences are warranted, expert teachers are able to maintain their overall positive manner without appearing overbearing or provocative to students—and yet they are able to administer the necessary penalty objectively, and judiciously—and usually in private with the student(s) involved. They seek to minimize any humiliation and embarrassment of the offenders, as demonstrated by their use of "I-messages" that express the teacher's actions and perspectives (e.g., "I observed that you were using unauthorized crib notes during the quiz. I understand that you may have been under pressure, but I will give you zero for this quiz. I am disappointed. I am also willing to permit you to do a "partial make-up" paper to regain some of the lost ground. It would be worth one-half the value of the quiz, that is 5 out of 10; so that if you were interested, you could possibly get a few points for credit for some work, rather than the zero. Do you wish to accept this proposal?"

Applying a consequence of this sort preserves the integrity of the instructor through an appeal to ethical conduct on the part of both the teacher and the learner.

Handling Management Problems[72]

Because effective instructors emphasize preventive and proactive classroom management, and because they integrate this process with their motivational instructional design (see Chapter 3), student disciplinary problems—although present—tend to be fewer in number than those that arise with less competent and/or inexperienced teachers. As mentioned in previous sections, a major influence on successful teachers' management skills appears to be their strong commitment to the ethical teaching principles of humanness, honesty, fairness, and respect. The teachers' application of these principles in the daily routines of class-life gradually generate the desired learning climate characterized by both task productivity and a positive attitude.

Because such an atmosphere is present, when instructors must deal with non-routine student misconduct or serious discipline matters, a fundamental tone of stability and fairness seems to undergrid the entire process—even though some unpleasant feelings, words and decisions may arise.

Academic Dishonesty.[73] Experienced faculty-members recognize that they must have firm evidence of student's academic cheating, plagiarism, or falsification before any accusations are made. Where this evidence does exist, there is a relatively straight-forward process of following the institution's published procedures for dealing with these matters. The instructor initiates the process with the student, in private, and then a chain of events unfold, leading eventually to formal disciplinary action being administered by the institution.

Although these cases are sometimes unpleasant and lengthy, the ethical standards upon which academic and professional conduct are based cut both ways: to build students' (and instructors') confidence and competence, but also to correct and reprimand anyone who violates the code of honor.

When an experienced teacher suspects that a student has plagiarized in an assignment, but cannot prove it, he/she may write a comment on the paper in question, such as: "Be sure to quote all references, here," or "Should this line be in quotation marks and referenced?", or "Have you acknowledged all of your sources?"

When students must be confronted for academic dishonesty, experienced instructors do so assertively—not aggressively nor un-assertively—in a one-to-one meeting. They remain calm, at all costs, and they present the facts in a straight-forward manner—not asking if the student cheated, nor accusing him/her of it. They tend to take an non-adversarial approach, and simply state what was observed and what evidence exists.

If a student becomes hostile and aggressive, expert instructors attempt to accommodate this reaction without losing their own composure or integrity. They do not retaliate with humiliating or demeaning remarks. Because they are professionals, they realize that their obligation is to work *with* people—not to let ego-confrontation escalate. They tend to be able to defuse the emotional level of the situation, and deal with the actual incident in a systematic manner.

One comforting point in this whole issue of academic dishonesty is that findings from current research coincide with one of the main messages of this handbook, which is:

> Students consistently indicate that when they feel part of a campus community, when they believe faculty are committed to their courses, and when they are aware of the policies of their institution concerning academic integrity, they are less likely to cheat. The social pressures not to cheat in such an environment, are substantial.[74]

Successful instructors and their institutions, who create a strong sense of group- and campus-community, use various strategies to achieve this, such as: establishing a campus-wide honor code (in which students who observe others cheating are obligated to report it); providing for significant student involvement in settling cases involving academic dishonesty; having students sign an honor pledge upon applying to the school; initiating some type of "honor assembly," whose members make presentations across campus on various topics about academic honesty; examining how all instructors can seek to prevent/reduce cheating in their courses; and promoting student/instructor discussion of these issue in classes.[75]

Questioning the Instructor's Authority.[76] In rare cases—even when an instructor has established a reputation for being open, patient, considerate, and respectful—a student, or a group of them, may refuse to accept the instructor's authority, especially if the teacher is new, or is only slightly older than the students. This situation may also arise, however, when a teacher brings on the problem him/herself by trying too hard to be assertive, by demonstrating aggressive tendencies to establish their authority, or by demonstrating false confidence. In these cases the instructor lacks true command of self and the situation, and is actually insecure.

Another cause may be the teacher's failure to plan either the managerial or the instructional components (or both) appropriately. In this situation students may reject the instructor's authority by ignoring and/or ridiculing him/her. Or, if the teacher—in an attempt to rescue the faltering management process—responds with an increased number of threatening statements or reprimands, then students may further retaliate with more uncooperative reactions.

Sometimes, too, inexperienced instructors will induce students to question their credibility by attempting to bluff their way through a situation that is beyond their capacity. In such cases, sensible responses to a difficult question might be: "I do not know, but I will find out for next class." (The teacher must keep the promise, though); or "I do not know. Who thinks they might know?" or "I don't know, but it's a good question. I would like you to find the answer for next class."

Similarly, if instructors make mistakes in presenting erroneous material or procedures in the subject-matter, the best response is a brief apology given with the corrected information.

To ignore the error or wait until someone brings it up ultimately detracts from the instructor's credibility.

Effective teachers, who may encounter any of these above problems (experience does not prevent them, but it provides a repertoire of possible ways to deal with them), tend to respond in characteristic ways; they are candid, and they face the situation openly. If they realize that they are at fault, they admit it, make necessary changes, and move on.

Occasionally, they request students for input and feedback on what they feel is both positive and negative about the point in question. They may have an open discussion about a mutual problem in the class. Making this decision does not show insecurity, but rather it can signal to students that the instructor is human, and that he/she is willing to welcome their suggestions in resolving the problem.

In all of this, experienced teachers realize that they have "position power"—by virtue of their academic status and the institutional hierarchy; but they tend not to rely on it. Rather, they depend on their "personal power": the authority that emerges from their professional credibility (i.e., the confidence that others have in a person by virtue of his/her experience, expertise, self-assurance, commitment, and vision) and authenticity (i.e., one's openness and honesty with others).[77]

Because teaching is essentially a human profession, it is a complex often unpredictable enterprise. Many instructors (who may be forced to teach because of the particular position they hold in the institution) may eventually leave because they do not like teaching, for various reasons: it is not rewarded adequately, it involves hassles and pressures, it can be chaotic, alone it does not lead to promotion, it can be boring, it can be difficult to do correctly, and it takes time and energy to improve one's teaching skills. (Incidentally, these same arguments can be made against any other activity, such as parenting or truck-driving.)

However, many of those who decide to make a career of instructing excel at it.[78] They get their "rewards" not only from salary and merit increases, status, or promotion, but from fulfilling their desire to help learners develop their knowledge, skills, and attitudes for the future. They do not abhor chaos, but they see it as a challenge from which to learn. They are able to sense when the teaching/learning process begins to get tedious for learners or for themselves, and they are able to adjust their plans accordingly. They seek ways to motivate students and to enliven their interest. They enjoy creating and implementing stimulating activities. Moreover, they find time and expend energy to enhance their own instructional skills.

Finally, they know that they are not trained counsellors or ministers, and that they are not responsible for changing students' personalities or character flaws. They know that things may not always go well in the "people-business," but they do not hold grudges when things do not go well. In fact, many of them have cultivated the habit of being able to laugh—both *with* students, and at *themselves*. This ability appears to add an emotional lubrication to reduce the frictions that invariably arise in the complex world of teaching in higher education.

* * * * *

In this chapter I have examined how exemplary teachers typically apply some of the foundational principles of effective teaching and of motivation of learning (described in Chapter 1), in order to create a positive classroom environment. I have also described how they rely on this climate, as they implement their plans for designing productive managerial procedures and routines.

Effective teachers' credibility and authenticity are enhanced when they deal with people humanely, honestly, fairly, and respectfully. These norms guide the way they both plan and incorporate their classroom procedures, and the way they deal with infractions of these rules. Their authority is established and maintained by their strong commitment to helping students learn: their positive attitude is instrumental in increasing learning motivation.

References

1. See, for example, Brookfield (1991), Love and Love (1996), Rhem (1997), and Weimer (1996c).
2. See, for example, Biehler and Snowman (1993) and Borich (1994).
3. See Eble (1988) and Slavin (1994).
4. See Brookfield (1991, 1996).

5. See, for example, Beachem (1996), Daloz, Keen, Keen, and Parks (1996), and Weimer (1996c, 1996d).

6. See "Old-fashioned" (1996), Weimer (1996c), and Wentz and Yarling (1994).

7. See Lambert et al. (1996), Orlich, Harder, Callahan, Kauchak, and Gibson (1994), Scherer (1997-1998), and Virginia Polytechnic (1991).

8. See, for example, American Psychological Association (1994, Chapter 2) Cheney (1994), and University of Saskatchewan (n.d.).

9. See Cheney (1994), Lambert et al. (1996), Wentz and Yarling (1994), and Weimer (1996c).

10. See, for example, Ahluwalia and McCreary (n.d.), and American Psychological Association (1994).

11. See Virginia Polytechnic, (1991, page 49).

12. See, for example, Barell (1991) "But I made" (1996), Cornett (1983), and Jarvis (1995).

13. See Chiarelott et al. (1994), Dunkin and Barnes (1986), Rogers and Freiberg (1994), and Shils (1983).

14. See, for example, Brookfield (1991), Daloz (1986), Gunter, Estes, and Schwab (1995), and Sergiovanni (1992).

15. See Beidler (1986). See also Brookfield (1991, 1996) and Weimer (1996d).

16. See Brookfield (1991), "Old-fashioned" (1996), and Weimer (1996c).

17. See Brookfield (1996).

18. See Jarvis (1995, p. 104).

19. See Shils (1983) and Weimer (1996c).

20. See Davis (1993), especially Chapter 9.

21. See, for example, Brookfield (1991) and Love and Love (1996).

22. See Gardiner (1997) and "The landscape" (1994).

23. See Beachem (1996).

24. See Barell (1991) and Chiarelott et al. (1994).

25. See Kohn (1997, p. 436).

26. See Doyle (1997, p. 440). See also "Old-fashioned" (1996).

27. See Gardiner (1997).

28. See, for example, Borich (1994), Daloz (1986), Good and Brophy (1995), Shils (1983), and Wiles and Bondi (1991).

29. See Linc Fisch's quote in Weimer (1996c).

30. See, for example, Dembo (1994), Ralph (1994a), and Weimer (1993).

31. See, for example, Borich (1994), Weimer (1993), and Wiles and Bondi (1991).

32. See, for example, Berkowitz (1995b), Biehler and Snowman (1993), Orlich et al. (1994), and Winzer (1995).

33. See, for example, Ralph (1996b) and Weimer (1990a, 1990b, 1990c).

34. See Barr and Tagg (1995), Eble (1988), and Haycock (1996).

35. See Biehler and Snowman (1993), Borich (1994), Dembo (1994), Lewis (1992), and Yelon (1996).

36. See Gage and Berliner (1992), Gunter et al. (1995), and McCown et al. (1996).

37. See Biehler and Snowman (1993) and Borich (1994).

38. See Dembo (1994), Lambert et al. (1996), Orlich et al. (1994), and Vale (1995).

39. See, for example, Borich (1994), Dembo (1994), Weimer (1993), and Wiles and Bondi (1991).

40. See Biehler and Snowman (1993), Hopkins and Moore (1993), and Rogers and Freiberg (1994).

41. See, for example, Chiarelott (1994) and Elliott et al. (1996).

42. See Borich (1994), Brooks (1987), and Wiles and Bondi (1991).

43. See McCandless (1967). Also see Biehler and Snowman (1993) and Ralph (1989).

44. See Gage and Berliner (1992) and Orlich et al. (1994).

45. See Elliott et al. (1996) and Lambert et al. (1996).

46. See Weimer (1993).

47. See, for example, Gunter et al. (1995) and Yelon (1996).

48. See, for example, Virginia Polytechnic (1991).

49. See Eble (1988), McCabe and Trevino (1996), and "Thirty years" (1996).

50. See, for example, Eby (1992), Elliott et al. (1996), and Ralph (1994d).

51. See, for example, Lewis (1992) and Weaver and Cotrell (1987).

52. See Lewis (1992), Lambert et al. (1996), and Virginia Polytechnic (1991).

53. See Biehler and Snowman (1993) and McCown et al. (1996).

54. See Biehler and Snowman (1993).

55. See, for example, Lambert et al. (1996) and Yelon (1996).

56. See Aronson (1987), Borich (1994), and Brooks (1987).

57. See Borich (1994) and Gunter et al. (1995).

58. See Svinicki (1992).

59. See Svinicki (1992).

60. See, for example, Aronson (1987), Brooks (1987), Rogers and Freiberg (1994), and Weaver and Cotrell (1987).

61. See, for example, Gage and Berliner (1992), Good and Brophy (1995), and University of Saskatchewan (1997-1998).

62. See Dembo (1994), Eble (1988), and Poole (1994).

63. See, for example, Elliott et al. (1996) and Ralph (1993a, 1994b).

64. See, for example, Notterman and Drewry (1993).

65. See Borich (1994) and Orlich et al. (1994).

66. See Elliott et al. (1996) and Yelon (1996).

67. See Stipek (1988) and Yelon (1996).

68. See, for example, Dembo (1994), Gage and Berliner (1992), and Langrehr (1988).

69. See Dunkin and Barnes (1986).

70. See Freiberg and Driscoll (1992) and University of Saskatchewan (1997-1998).

71. See, for example, Rogers and Freiberg (1994) and Yelon (1996).

72. See Eble (1988).

73. See, for example, Eble (1988), Lewis (1992), University of Saskatchewan (n.d.), and Virginia Polytechnic (1991).

74. See McCabe and Trevino (1996, p. 33).

75. See McCabe and Trevino (1996).

76. See, for example, Dunkin and Barnes (1986), Eble (1988), Elliott et al. (1996), and Virginia Polytechnic (1991).

77. See Brookfield (1991, 1996) and Eble (1988).

78. See Brookfield (1991) and Lambert et al. (1996).

Chapter 3

MOTIVATING INSTRUCTIONAL PROCESSES

The other major component of the teaching process—in addition to the managerial element—is instruction. It embodies not only the content of the subject-matter of the course being taught, but also both the generic and specific pedagogical knowledge and skills employed by instructors to assist students to learn this content.

In Chapter 3—as was the case in the previous chapter—I utilize the basic principles of effective teaching and motivation of learning (described earlier in Chapter 1) as a foundation upon which to ground my synthesis of three generic instructional approaches. This synthesis represents a summary of best practices applicable to undergraduate education, which I condensed from current research literature on teaching effectiveness and learning motivation. In it I also refer to activities that were found to be motivating from my own and my colleagues' teaching practice in a variety of educational settings.

To the often-posed question, "What is more important to effective teaching: classroom management or the instructional process?" I respond that this is a non-question. It is like asking, "What is more important to breathing, inhaling or exhaling?"[1] Both the managerial and instructional components are integrated and essential: one collapses without the other, and both processes are necessary for effective teaching and learning to occur in the formalized educational structure as it exists at present. These two aspects are mutually inclusive.[2]

The organizational format I follow in Chapter 3—as pictured in Figure 1.5—is to present the planning and implementation stages of the process.

In both of these sub-sections, I present the information in pragmatic terms, suitable for practicing instructors, who desire to apply and/or adapt basic generic skills of planning and presenting in order to motivate learners (and themselves) in their daily routines of teaching. Moreover, the evaluation of student learning—which in essence is also the evaluation of effective teaching—is an integral component of the instructional process. Because of its importance I will examine it separately in Chapter 5. However, this logistical separation of evaluation in the manual is by no means to infer its isolation from the actual instructional process.

Part 1: Planning for Instruction

For the purpose of this manual, I do not make as sharp a distinction between "teaching" and "instruction" as some educators make.[3] I define "instruction" (closely resembling my definition of teaching in Chapter 1) as: "the deliberate arrangement of experiences to help a learner achieve a desirable change in performance."[4]

The Planning Process[5]

Although trite, the adage "To fail to plan is to plan to fail" is a truism. All successful teachers plan—both for their management of classroom logistics and student conduct and for their instructional procedures. Often, for experienced instructors the planning process is almost automatic—and they may have little or no written agenda.

Novice teachers, on the other hand, lack the accumulated wisdom of teaching practice from which to draw; and they thus find it useful—for both organizational and survival purposes—to write detailed instructional plans and procedures for each class session, and to attempt to follow and/or adapt these plans during the actual teaching event.

Reasons for Planning[6]

There are several sensible reasons why successful instructors engage in planning:

1. It helps them give direction to instruction.
2. It provides them with increased self-assurance because they know where they are going.
3. It enables them to prepare materials/methods/media ahead of time.

4. It gives them an opportunity to reflect on events before and after they occur in order to modify the process for the future.

5. It provides them with some "breathing space," rather than barely keeping one-step ahead of the students.

6. For teachers who "despise structure, but fly by the seat of their pants" planning helps prevent the destruction or ripping of "these pants."

7. It assists them to "keep on track" and prevents unproductive tangents—or, alternatively, it permits occasional tangents, but it helps in returning to the path, later. (Ineffective planners may not know when they get off track—let alone, know where the main road is.)

8. It helps them align assessment of student learning with original learning objectives.

9. Long-range planning (by the term, month, week, or unit of work) makes planning for individual class-periods much easier, because once the large plan is complete, the single sessions can be designed in much less time, than if the work is being planned only one day at a time.

10. It helps enhance instructors' overall credibility in the eyes of students. Compared to disorganized or poorly-planned instructors, they are perceived as being more competent, confident, and prepared.

11. This in turn, enhances students' perception of the faculty-members' authenticity: they are seen as matching their rhetoric with reality.

12. It helps satisfy departmental, faculty, and institutional standards: some units require samples of instructors' teaching record.

13. Planning documents could also be used by instructors, themselves, as part of a "teaching portfolio," if they were seeking promotion or another position.

14. It helps them to "see the forest plus the trees." By doing both long- and short-range planning, instructors understand the course's major and minor concepts; the topics to emphasize and/or to de-emphasize; the scope, sequence and depth of the content to pursue; and the relationships and patterns between/among the key ideas. (Of course, it is the instructor's goal to help learners' master all of this, as well.)

Realities of Planning[7]

How do effective teachers plan? Research[8] on the subject shows that although they reflect upon their teaching practice and make adjustments before, during, and after the process, seldom—except when they are at the beginning stages of learning to teach—do they follow a prescribed set of systematic and logical steps that many teacher-training educators and institutions recommend. Most practitioners plan in practical terms, beginning with pragmatic questions: "What does the curriculum, or course of study, or textbook say I am supposed to cover?" "How many days or class periods will I have to fill?" "How can I best match the two?" and "What types of activities can I incorporate to enhance motivation in the course?"

These are normal worthwhile questions that all instructors need to answer; however, they have limitations. For instance, they all deal with "I": they center on attention for self, thereby reflecting a lower level of professionalism than that typically exhibited by expert teachers. Research[9] on concerns about teaching expressed by teachers throughout their professional careers revealed that they tend to reflect three different stages or levels of attention: When they begin a new task or job they are pre-occupied with "self": "Will I be a good teacher?" "Will they like me?" "Will I come across properly?" (This state may explain the situation described in Chapter 2 where certain neophyte instructors encounter classroom control problems and student resistance because of their drive to be seen as competent.)

A second stage is reached after beginning teachers become more confident in their role, and the level of their attention is diverted somewhat from ego-protection and enhancement to that of the "task". Here, with increased experience and decreased nervousness and self-consciousness, instructors' thoughts turn mainly to performing the instructional skills: "How can I present this information clearly?" "Will my motivational set work?" "How is my questioning?" or "Do I still stand tied to my invisible six-foot leash?"

A third level is reached, as the instructor gains yet more competence and assurance, and that is a concern for the learners and their learning. Here, the spotlight switches from the teacher, as performer, to the student, as learner: "How will they use the material outside of the classroom setting?" Effective instructors typically operate at this level: they are aware of how learners process information, they understand the concept of "learning style," and they continually seek to apply the foundational principles of effective teaching and motivation to enhance learning (see Chapter 1).

A problem with relying upon this three-stage model to categorize practitioners is that it may not always reflect reality with accuracy. For instance, some experienced teachers may not reach the third stage; or many instructors demonstrate all three stages—depending on the context and situation; or teachers may simultaneously be at different levels for specific tasks or skills—depending on their comfort level.

Nevertheless, the 3-level structure does offer limited value in providing an approximate gauge of instructors' confidence levels.

A Key Planning Principle[10]

Before presenting some general planning guidelines, I emphasize one fundamental premise that is essential for all effective instructional planning. This proposition is critical—particularly in the light of the current socio/economic/political situation in the Western World, in which sustained pressures are being exerted upon all levels of education for improved accountability in producing better teaching and learning. This key principle, depicted in Figure 3.1, is that there must be congruency among the learning objectives, the activities, and the evaluation of learning. That is, the objectives (what students are to learn and/or be able to do at the end of instruction) must be embodied in both the teaching/learning activities (i.e., what is done by instructors and learners to achieve the objective) and the evaluation procedures (i.e., the processes/products used to determine if the objectives have, in fact, been accomplished).

Thus, it is feasible for instructors—in the first session of the course—to present the general format of the final examination, within the overview of the course syllabus, because the test(s), as well as *all* of the learning activities throughout the course, are to reflect the instructional objectives. Evaluation and testing, then, simply ascertain the extent that individuals have internalized what they have been learning *and* doing in the various course activities throughout the term—as initially stated in the objectives for each class-session, for each longer unit of work, and for the course as a whole.

This principle of aligning and integrating the assessment of student learning with the objectives and the course's teaching/learning activities is simple in concept, yet profound in its potential to provide instructional personnel with a vital framework with which to guide the planning and implementation phases of instruction.

* * * * *

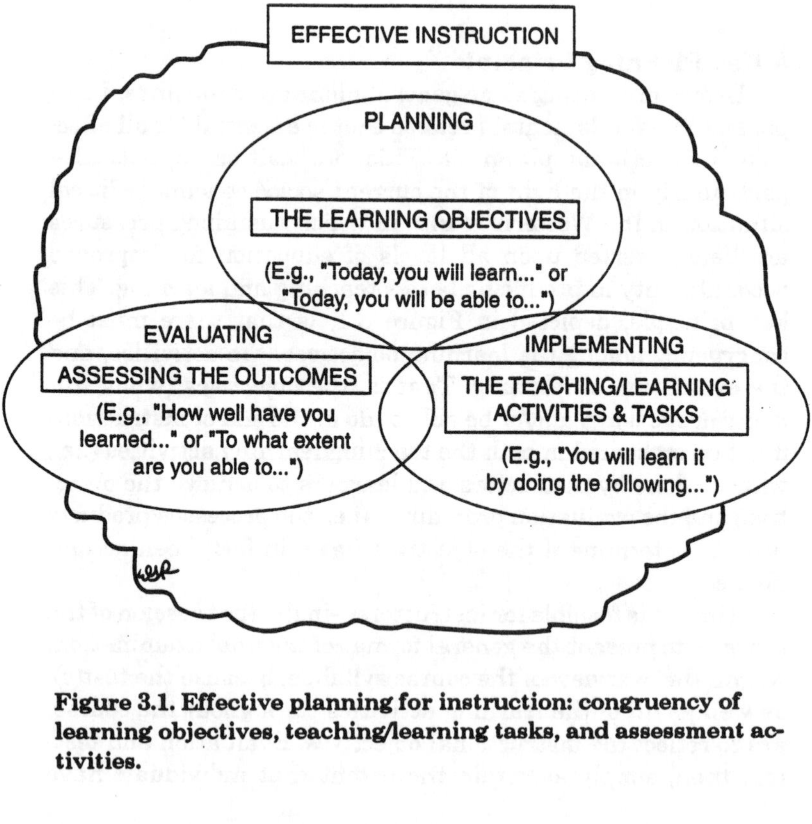

Figure 3.1. Effective planning for instruction: congruency of learning objectives, teaching/learning tasks, and assessment activities.

A Caveat

In the following section I outline some generic planning skills and techniques that exemplary teachers from all levels and in virtually all subjects and contexts have used and/or adapted in one way or another as guidelines to their own teaching.[11]

Again, I stress that it would be *unwise* for anyone to regard these skills and approaches as mandatory, prescriptive formulae to apply unconditionally to every teaching context. It is unwise for three reasons. One is that teachers *could not* do so, because each teaching situation is so unique that no one could possibly conform to the details of a rigid planning script for a few minutes—let alone do it with regularity.

A second reason is that instructors *would not* do so anyway, because human nature is such that no professional would condone—let along tolerate being chained to an externally imposed set of mechanical rules to be unreflectively adhered to in all cases.

The third reason is that instructors *should not* do so, because the essence of professional development is that—although practitioners do not ignore research-based principles, they examine them and select/adapt/modify (or reject) them for incorporation into their personally constructed repertoire of effective teaching ideas.

Some Planning Guidelines

If instructors accept the essential planning premise that objectives, activities, and evaluation are to be consistently congruent, how do they plan and prepare for meaningful learning experiences for their classes? Successful teachers typically engage in planning for both the long (i.e., the course, the term, the month, and perhaps the week) and the short-term (i.e., the individual class-session or daily lesson).

Although expert instructors seldom write out detailed lesson-plans, they probably once did so, early in their careers. On the basis of my supervisory experience, I recommend in this handbook that neophyte instructors write out detailed instructional plans (using the suggestions presented below) for the first few units and class periods. My rationale for this advice is that by doing so: (a) beginning teachers will force themselves to conceptualize more clearly the particular unit and/or class-period of work to be covered; (b) they will understand how the three essential components (i.e., objectives, activities, and assessment) fit together; (c) they will not forget certain key items (that they may have if they were not recorded); and (d) they will experience some sense of relief that they have clearer direction for their instruction, than if they simply acted on such assertions as: "Let's cover the next chapter in the text," or "Do the reading and answer the questions on the handout."

Unit planning.[12] A "unit" of work is a specific subject, topic, theme, or area of content in a course that usually takes several class-periods to complete. As mentioned in a previous section, good teachers spend time preparing unit plans because it gives them a holistic vision of the topic and allows them to extract more easily their daily lesson plans from this larger unit plan. (In fact, I found through a decade of supervising teacher-interns during their 4-month extended-practicum program, that many of them begin by spending up to two hours planning and preparing for a single class-period. However, after planning a larger unit of work—which, itself, often takes several hours to do well—they are able to extract from it a daily plan in only 10 to 15 minutes.)

A formal unit plan[13] typically consists of 5 components: an introduction (1/2 to 1 page), a brainstorming page, a concept-map (1/2 to 1 page), an orientation-outline (1 or 2 pages) that presents in a few rows and columns the essential instructional components, and a bibliography.

1. The *introduction* summarizes the course's context: the subject, the student background, and perhaps how the unit fits into the course and discipline. The introduction gives the needed orientation to help instructors plan for meeting learners' instructional and learning needs, interests, stages of development, and motivations.

2. The *brainstorming* section records the teacher's initial ideas about presenting the topic, and is typically arranged in two columns: "*What* should I include?" (i.e., the content), and "*How* might I teach it?" (i.e., the pedagogy: "What methods, approaches, strategies, media, materials could I use?").

The instructor's brainstorming process occurs prior to any extensive research on the course curriculum or textbook. The brainstorming process also provides for teacher creativity. (Teachers may even record topics and strategies that are not possible to implement in the unit; however, such events are not problematic, because the purpose of brainstorming is to explore a variety of possibilities.)

3. The *concept map* is a diagram that shows, usually with geometric shapes and connecting lines, the typical four or five major concepts or topics to be learned in the unit, along with several connected sub-topics or minor concepts. This visual helps to organize, on a single page, the overall structure of the unit. Instructors then estimate how many class periods will be needed to teach the unit, and place consecutive numerals (to represent Day 1, Day 2, etc.) according to time and coverage beside each part of the map (see Appendix A).

4. The *organizational chart* takes the consecutively numbered concepts and topics from the concept map and arranges them in a tabular or column format that represents a logical time-table. In this chart, the consecutively numbered days are placed down the left-hand side and a series of column headings are placed across the top that shows the key instructional components that will form part of each class period.

These top headings would be: Topic (or major concept), Instructional Objectives, Procedures/Activities, Materials/Resources, and Evaluation Strategies. Then, for each day, instructors would summarize in point form the key information required under each heading. (Because a plan is a skeleton outline of the intended instructional activities, it does not include the content material, per se, but only the essential steps and brief notations.)

Effective planners ensure that what is written within the various categories for each day in the column format is grounded in the foundational principles of effective teaching and motivation (as described in Chapter 1, such as: using a variety of methods and approaches, aligning evaluation with activities and objectives, providing for relevance, involving learners actively, and keeping their attention).

5. The *bibliography* lists all resources used in presenting the unit, such as: curriculum guides, textbooks, audio-visual media, instructional kits, other teachers' materials, invited guests, and so forth.

Veteran instructors will rarely write out all five parts of a unit plan, because much of that information is embedded in their accumulated wisdom of practice that their past teaching experience has provided them. Neophyte teachers, however, profit from the planning experience because having to conceptualize and to articulate precisely *what* and *how* they will arrange and implement the instructional activities will also force them to grapple with: *why* they chose the activities, *how well* the activities worked, and finally what might be *changed* or retained for the future.

On the other hand, merely following the chapters of a textbook, or presenting a series of topics on the course outline—although probably covering the content—may do little to address the following key questions: (a) Are students motivated to learn? (b) Are instructors varying their learning activities to enhance this motivation? (c) Are they deliberately stating their objectives to the group? (d) Are the teaching/learning tasks congruent with these objectives? (e) Are the tests, quizzes, and other evaluation activities congruent with the objectives and the classroom activities? and (f) Are instructors willing and able to improve in any of their teaching areas that may be weak?

I emphasize that following the textbook or the course outline is not unsound, in itself, because it would be unacceptable to expect instructors to somehow "to reinvent the wheel" or to discover and re-write an entire curriculum for a particular course or program (although this sometimes may occur). Rather, my point here is that by being compelled to think through how to formulate systematically their intended rationale and procedures for motivating learners to understand and apply the subject-matter will ultimately help instructors conceptualize more clearly their entire teaching practice.

Planning individual sessions.[14] I recommend that neophyte teachers engage in writing out their plans for individual class-periods—at least for the first few sessions, until they begin to internalize the process of effective instructional planning, and until they can clearly conceptualize how these components need to be integrated to enhance student learning.

Having just mentioned that individual session plans can be extracted easily from the column format of a well-prepared unit plan, I offer the following guidelines for a single-period plan. The format contains nine headings (compared to the five in the unit-plan columns), because, by nature, the individual class-session plan must be more detailed in order to provide specific structure to instructors for a typical 50-minute class period.

A class-period plan[16] is an overall outline of the main procedures and activities to be presented during the instructional session. A good session-plan is generally one to two pages in length: ones longer than that contain more than a basic outline. (If instructors find they need additional notes and other materials, these extra documents do not actually belong in the plan, but they can be an addendum for the instructor's use.)

Planning and presenting. Below, I describe a typical session- or lesson-plan, and also offer comments on how effective instructors actually deliver or present the session: that is, how they actually transfer the lesson "from the paper" and enact it in live classroom practice.

1. The *Title* presents the topic of the day, the course, and the date, time and location (1 or 2 lines).

2. The *Objectives* (two or three) state precisely what students will *learn* or be *able to do* by the end of the session. (When teaching, effective instructors explicitly state these objectives *to* the students: "Today, you will learn to..." (or "You will be able to...") apply the criteria we learned yesterday for judging...".

On the other hand, for an inquiry- or discovery- or open-ended type of period where instructors do not want to specify beforehand what students will learn, they will still state explicit objectives, such as: "Today, you *will be able* to solve this problem after having followed the..." or "You will *learn* to apply this series of procedures to discover how to resolve the dilemma...". The writing out of the precise objectives on the period plan may take 3 or 4 lines. Again, the key words are what students will *learn* or *be able to do*; and when the instructor makes a habit of stating these objectives during the sessions, both the instructor and the learners know exactly what the intentions are for each period. Stating clear objectives for each session gives direction and assurance to participants regarding their work. See Figure 3.2, for example.

3. A *Motivational Set* is a short activity or item that the instructor presents at the beginning of a period to gain learners' attention, to pique their curiosity, or to provide impetus for the duration of the session. It occupies 1 or 2 lines on a period plan. It may consist of a brief demonstration accompanied by a question posed to the class, a simple question alone, a dilemma or puzzling statement, or a visual showing discrepant information accompanied by a statement like, "I wonder why this appears to be...". Sometimes the motivational set precedes the stating of the objectives; but, in any case, to be effective, the teacher should refer back to the motivational set sometime later during the class period. In Figure 3.3, the instructor is asking

Figure 3.2. Effective instructors state learning objectives explicityly.

how two distinct elements can be combined to form an entirely new compound.

Specific examples of motivational sets are:[16] (a) in a Mathematics or Logic course, students could be asked to explain "How to divide by 1/2" (it is *not* "to divide by 2"); (b) in a Philosophy course the professor could project via an overhead projector the one-word question "Why?", then pause for two or three minutes for learner reactions; (c) in a Psychology course the instructor could project a Peanuts cartoon on the overhead and ask, "Why is Charlie Brown so often down on himself?"; (d) in a Physics course, a laboratory demonstrator could bring in a new bottle of catsup, and at the front of the class by a table with a pail on it, tap its cap firmly with a rubber mallet, and have the bottom of the bottle (and its contents) fall out into the pail. She could

Figure 3.3. Effective instructors present a motivational set to create student interest.

then ask, "Why did this happen?" (e) in any course studying the concept that things are often not as they appear, the instructor could pick up a small candle that she had just lit, blow it out, and eat it. She then could field and/or ask pertinent questions (The "candle" was carved out of a potato or an apple, and the wick was made of slivered almond); or (f) in an Animal Sciences course, a professor could replace his "old" motivational set (in which he used to project a colored slide of a chicken and used to state, "Here is a sick chicken. I will explain the ailment...") with a "new", motivational set. In it he could show the same picture but would alter the oral component by asking, "What disease does this chicken have?" Student motivation would tend to increase because of the question.

Each of these motivational sets would be followed by a clear statement of objectives for the session. For example, after "(f)", above, the instructor would state, "We are going to learn the causes, treatment, and prevention of two major poultry diseases..."

4. Under the *Method(s)* heading of a lesson plan is written (in 1 or 2 lines) the instructional methods, approaches, or strategies that the instructor has selected to lead to the achievement of the day's objectives.

Effective teachers use a variety of methods in a single period, and during a week/month/term—not for the sake of incorporating variety, per se, but because of grounding the experiences in the sound principles of learning motivation, such as: gaining/holding learner attention, arousing curiosity, making the tasks relevant, avoiding tedium/boredom, accommodating divergent learning styles and interests, relating to real-life experience, and enhancing active learning.

On the single-session plan, only the written names of the selected approaches are necessary, some of which are: lecture, small-group tasks, role plays/simulations, demonstration, debates, panel discussions, laboratory investigations, small-group discussions, whole-group discussions, or independent study.

5. The longest section of the class-period plan is the *Procedures/Activities* component. However, it need not be longer than a half-page, because it lists in chronological order what

will happen during the period. It is helpful to divide the section into two columns, labeled "Instructor" and "Students". Here, the teacher can plot out in brief who does what, when. For instance, to remind themselves to perform the motivational set and state the objectives, the instructor would write down those instructions (see Appendix B).

As they plan the activities, teachers ensure that each activity reflects the instructional objectives: Are learners engaged in learning/practicing/applying what the plan states they should be?

Occasionally, beginning instructors confuse the "method" component with the "activities" portion of a plan; however, the former lists instructional approaches or strategies to be implemented, whereas the latter lists, in order, the instructional steps to be followed in the session.

Also, in the activities section, novice instructors have found it helpful (and sometimes mandatory) to indicate how long they estimate that each step will take (see Appendix B). Many beginning teachers typically experience difficulties in gauging their time accurately—and often have more material planned than alotted time permits. However, forcing themselves to estimate the time-frame—and then verifying if the length of the segments were accurate—will assist new instructors to improve their pacing/momentum/and timing. In this way, they are able to prevent slow-downs.

By writing out the proposed activities, new instructors also verify that the tasks selected reflect the principles of motivation and sound teaching. However, as illustrated in Figure 3.4, novice teachers often take longer to accomplish their goals than initially planned.

6. The *Key Questions* that neophyte instructors intend to ask during the period should be written down—either under this heading, or earlier, under "Instructor" in the Activities component of the plan. As will be emphasized in a subsequent chapter of this manual, oral questions that are posed clearly and concisely by the instructor can serve as powerful motivators of student learning. There are typically two to five key questions in a session.

Under this heading, instructors will not write every question they might ask in a class period, but only the ones that refer to important concepts or points in the content. The key questions must directly connect to the learning objectives. In this way, teachers again ensure that their instructional intentions are aligned with the actual learning experiences provided. The key questions may be posed at any time during the session, but most often they are either a part of the initial motivational set, or they are posed at main junctures and transition-points in the presentation to summarize key concepts or skills that learners have just studied or practiced.

Research[17] on teacher's use of oral questioning indicates that it is one of the most challenging instructional tasks to master. I address this skill in a later section. Suffice it to say that when learners are questioned orally (and are expected to respond), their level of motivation increases, as compared to when they are simply "told" information.

. MAINTAIN TIME-SEQUENCE AND TIME-FRAME

Figure 3.4. Effective instructors maintain an appropriate pacing/momentum/time-frame.

7. A *Summary* is generally provided not only at the end of a class session, but at strategic points throughout the period in order to help learners synthesize what has been accomplished in each segment of learning. There are two types of summaries: teacher- and learner-initiated summaries. The latter is preferred, because students will have to be more actively engaged in cognitively processing the material and in publicly stating/defending their current understanding of the topic. Thus, student motivation is stimulated.

Summaries do not only occur in formal lecture situations, but they are provided—and are especially important—after small-group work and discussions, in order to help distill both what has been, and what may still need to be, decided by the group concerning the subject at hand.

Research shows that students learn more effectively when instructors ensure that summaries are presented during and at the end of a session, than if only a review of the previous class work is provided at the start of the following period.[18] Of course, effective teachers have found it beneficial to use both of these strategies in one's teaching practice.

On the period-plan, new teachers write brief statements as to where and what the summary will be. Again, teachers verify that these summary statements are congruent with the learning objectives (*and* with the key questions, *and* with the learning activities used in the class-session).

8. The *Assessment* or evaluation segment of the session-plan is a specific task, event, or activity that instructors incorporate to determine if the learning objectives have been achieved: Have group-members *learned* or are they *able to do* what was intended?

The evaluation may be formal (e.g., an examination, quiz, essay, individual or group project; or a performance/demonstration/simulation of some type that requires learners to apply their newly derived knowledge and skills in a real-world situation—such as having a beginning college instructor to teach a class of first-year students). With formal assessments, students would have been previously informed of the task and how it was to be evaluated (e.g., the standards, expectations, and criteria by which it was to be graded had earlier been explicitly stated and clarified).

Evaluation could also be informal, in that the instructor may not award specific credit for classroom work but would be vigilant in observing students' work habits, attitudes, classroom demeanor, and sense of group cooperation. Informal assessment could also be conducted on various academic tasks: quizzes, short-papers, speeches or presentations, assignments, readings, or reports. Teachers could provide feedback to students about their performance on these tasks in order to assist them in developing their own self-assessment skills.

The evaluation component of a class period could also be classified as either *formative* (i.e., ongoing, continual, or periodic—and often informal—throughout the term to show learners how they are developing or being "formed") or *summative* (i.e., assessment that is typically more formal, which evaluates students' progress at the end of a unit or term: a "sum" of their achievement).

On the written plan, however, instructors write only two or three lines indicating succinctly what students will do to demonstrate that they have, in fact, *learned*, or are *able to do*, what the session's objectives have specified. It may be as simple as "They will answer the seven questions on page 101 in the text." However, instructors should indicate with a word or two, whether this assignment is "practice," or informal; and whether it "counts" (e.g., Will it be submitted for grading and credit? or Will it be "corrected" in the next period?)

Whatever assessment method is employed, exemplary teachers are aware that evaluation is not separated from but integrated with the learning experiences; and that by being creative in devising different assessment tasks, instructors can add to the motivation already inherent in the process.[19]

9. *Materials* needed during the class-period are *all* listed on two or three lines on the plan. Teachers show forethought by having all equipment, hand-outs, and other required resources ready for the session. As they plan and prepare these resources, effective teachers select them on the basis of their motivational impact on students.

Occasionally, unforeseen events may occur to cause distractions for teachers and students alike. Not being fully prepared (e.g., not becoming familiar with the audio-visual equipment beforehand, and not knowing what to do when the projector bulb expires, or not bringing the extension cord) is not only frustrating and embarrassing, but if it happens habitually, then the instructor's credibility may decline in the eyes of the group-members.

Other planning formats.[20] Instructors may use other methods by which to plan their coursework, as well. For instance, some may plan *weekly* or *bi-weekly* agendas—depending on the number of times they meet their classes within the institutional time-table. Others may plan via *tri-weekly*, *monthly*, or whole *term* formats. In such agendas, experienced teachers tend to jot down only broad outlines of main topics, with brief but specific notations for using particular activities, media, materials or personnel, where applicable.

Veteran professionals do not write much in their plans, but beginning teachers appear to benefit, initially, from conceptualizing their proposed actions on paper, in fairly detailed steps.

* * * * *

I have presented the above information for planning individual class-periods and longer units in the spirit of assisting novice instructors in preparing for teaching. It is not meant to be a restriction, but a framework; not an algorithm, but a guideline. It is not only provided for those who may be instructing for the first time, but also for those more seasoned practitioners who may wish to reflect on the effectiveness of some of their own planning and teaching skills.

Part 2: Implementing Generic Instructional Skills

A mark of distinction of exemplary instructors is not just how logical, detailed or motivating their teaching - plans appear on paper, but, ultimately, it is how they implement the proposed activities in the live-action of the teaching/learning environment. The purpose of Part 2 is to provide instructional personnel with practical applications of three generic teaching skills that are based on the key motivational principles stressed up to this point in the handbook.

In order to expedite this task, I analyze the three generic skills separately; however, such a categorization is artificial, in the sense that—in the real world teaching—these skills and other motivational techniques rarely operate in such discrete compartments. In reality, they often over-lap and are "mixed and matched and blended" according to the unique contexts of each situation.[21]

Moreover, competent instructors virtually apply these skills all of the time—regardless of the specific teaching method or learning activity they may be incorporating in a particular class-session. My colleagues and I have emphasized the following three sets of instructional behaviors in our work in the improvement of teaching:[22] (a) structuring (i.e., clarity and organization of the activities); (b) questioning (i.e., the posing of oral questions to guide learning); and (c) responding (i.e., what the instructor says and/or does after learners say and/or something).

Three Generic Instructional Skills

Structuring

Because formal education is largely conducted in classes led by teachers, who structure and deliver coursework to groups rather than to individuals, successful instructors have had to be well-organized in this process.[23]

A characteristic of exemplary instructors of any subject, with any age or level of learners, is that they demonstrate clear organization in their teaching—whether they are presenting a formal lecture, or whether they are filling a facilitative role in assisting small-groups in conducting investigations and presentations. Not only do they model excellent communication skills, but these instructors structure the teaching/learning experiences in such a way that all participants know exactly what is expected of them. Yet, even though these teachers are organized and systematic in their planning and implementing of various activities, they have also learned to be flexible, open, and inviting in their dealing with students.

Research[24] indicates that students in post-secondary education evaluated instructors who demonstrate structuring behaviors in their teaching higher than they did professors who do not. Students prefer instructors who express themselves clearly and who also structure sessions to encourage discussion.

Ten specific sub-skills have been identified by several researchers[25] as key structuring behaviors practiced by effective teachers. It is interesting to note that all of these skills relate directly or indirectly to the foundational and motivation of learning described in Chapter 1 of this handbook. These ten structuring skills are described below.

Clarity.[26] Effective instructors are characterized by their ability to give precise and lucid directions and explanations. They present material intelligibly and are explicit in their communication with learners.

They consistently model correct oral and written language, and they avoid vagueness, ambiguity, redundancy, verbal mazes, false starts, halts in speech, tangles of words, unessential content, annoying verbal mannerisms, and "fillers" (such as, "ah," "uhm," "okay," "kay," "right," "good," "yuh know," or "yuh know what I mean") or poorly enunciated words (such as: "yeah," "gonna," "wanna," and the dropping of "ing" endings— "teachin' " for "teaching").

Effective instructors also present their subject-matter clearly: by using a sequenced series of understandable steps to minimize student frustration, by incorporating appropriate illustrations and/or analogies to clarify newly defined terms, and by connecting new material to students' prior knowledge. They also present summaries not only at the end of a class-session, but at key junctures throughout a session. Occasionally they will also ask students to summarize the content learned, as illustrated in Figure 3.5.

Research[27] in higher education settings has indicated that students not only express satisfaction with classes whose professors exemplify instructional clarity, but that these students demonstrate better understanding, higher achievement, and more accurate work habits in these same classes. Apparently, instructor clarity helps to reduce classroom tedium, anxiety and uneasiness among students.

Pacing.[28] A second structuring skill observable among competent instructors is pacing: they are able to conduct or facilitate the various teaching/learning activities at a brisk tempo, rather than permitting the proceedings either to get draggy (which often leads to students' off-task behavior and potential classroom management problems) or to advance too rapidly (which may lead to students getting behind in their work, which, in turn, engenders potential frustration and resentment).

As described in the earlier section on classroom management, these exemplary teachers also establish classroom procedures and routines early, so that they do not waste time repeating organizational and logistical directions, and so that all students quickly become accustomed to the basic ground rules and expectations in the course.

This is not to say that effective instructors never alter the class momentum: in fact, they change the focus of the routines regularly by incorporating a variety of teaching/learning activities. This enhances student motivation to learn.

. SUMMARIZE (DURING AND AT END)

Figure 3.5. Effective instructors incorporate both teacher- and student-centered summaries.

Task orientation.[29] Related to the quickened pacing and timing of activities is how exemplary teachers structure class-room proceedings to emphasize time-on-task. They convey the message that the academic or course work is important, that "we are all here to accomplish some goals," and that all are expected to focus their time and energy to that end. Although good instructors portray this serious approach they are also skilled in providing the necessary socio/psychological support and group environment that also rewards individuals' achieve-ments—as well as challenging their efforts.

Student involvement.[30] A fourth instructional skill is struc-turing class routines to require students to become actively involved in learning activities. Experienced instructors apply the basic principles of effective teaching and motivation to ensure that, in every class period, students are engaged in relevant and meaningful activities that apply to some facet of their own life experience—past, present, and future—and de-sirably all three.

By using familiar examples, asking questions, introducing physical activities, varying audio-visual stimuli, having stu-dents set achievable goals, reinforcing their accomplishment of the goals, and having learners practice their newly acquired skills, effective teachers are able to move students from being passive recipients to being active participants in their learning.

This goal is accomplished when instructors involve students immediately in applying their newly acquired knowledge in "real-world" practice, as illustrated in Figure 3.6 (for a class in second-language acquisition).

Gaining and maintaining student attention.[31] A fifth structuring behavior demonstrated by expert instructional per-sonnel is how they get and keep learners' attention on the task at hand. They utilize a variety of techniques and tactics to do this. One that has already been described earlier in this manual is their incorporation of a motivational set at the beginning of a formal class session. This short activity may take the form of: a brief demonstration showing a puzzling or discrepant event; a simple question that has no ready answer; a brief anecdote illustrating a concept being learned; a quotation from a famous literary, political or entertainment personality; an audio-visual clip raising a particular issue; or a short problem posed on the overhead screen.

Typically, effective instructors pair the motivational set with their explicit statement of the class-session's objectives for the period. Thus, this combination might proceed as follows: a physics instructor[32] walks silently to the front of the classroom where there are a small glass aquarium (two-thirds filled with water) and two non-opened cans of soft drink beside it on the table. The drinks are of the same brand: but one is "diet" and the other is "regular".

The instructor waits until students are all attending, then—without comment, but with slow, deliberate, and exaggerated movements (along with appropriate gestures, and with distinct pointing to the labels on the tins), she first puts the can of diet drink into the water. It should float. She removes it,

. ENSURE STUDENT PRACTICE

Figure 3.6. Exemplary instructors provide for learner practice and application of new skills.

again pointing to its label, and then does the same for the can of regular soft drink. It should sink.

She then switches on the overhead that projects the following questions and instructions:

1. You have 10 minutes to answer these questions.
2. Individually, write a brief description of what happened.
3. Explain the results.
4. Verify if these results hold when one uses different brands of diet and regular soft drinks. (There are several samples in the box beside the aquarium.)
5. With a partner compare your answers to the above items.
6. Be prepared to share your findings in the large group.

After the 10-minute motivational set, the instructor has 3 or 4 pairs report their answers to the class then states the objectives for the period, like this: "Using the observations you have just made today, we will learn how density of liquids functions."

In addition to employing motivational sets, effective instructors also maintain student interest by incorporating occasional humor, such as: puns, plays on words, riddles, brief jokes, cartoons, theatrics, voice modulation, novelty events, biographical incidents, or written humor (e.g., Watch your punctuation:[33] "Woman, without her man, is a savage." or "Woman! Without her, man is a savage.").

Although humor can be motivating, there are certain dangers in attempting to incorporate it into one's teaching:[34] (a) it cannot be forced; it cannot be inappropriate, too obvious, or too subtle; (b) it should emerge naturally and spontaneously from a situation; (c) cognition is required to understand some forms of humor, but understanding it does not necessarily mean that it will be greeted with levity. Certain types of humor appeal to specific individuals; (d) it is contextual: it may not be funny unless "you had been there;" and (e) it must be used judiciously and tastefully.

Do the following humorous events meet the above criteria?[35]

1. A Psychology instructor who saw a student asleep in her class woke the student and said to him: "I don't mind your going to sleep, but it hurts when you don't say good night."

2. An English professor lamenting the poor speaking and writing skills of first-year students commented: "They need to take a basic course in English so they'll know another language besides their own."

3. A Philosophy instructor received a student's exam paper with this answer printed in the center of the page: "GOD KNOWS EVERYTHING. I KNOW NOTHING." The professor wrote this notation at the bottom of the sheet: "RIGHT. GOD GETS 100%. YOU GET ZERO."

4. A Biology laboratory-assistant, in response to his supervisor who was requesting some information on one of the lab students—who was also the class-president—said: "Yes, I have worked quite closely with her...I mean...we have had a good relationship...I mean...in a biological way...I mean..."

5. An Education professor, wanting to eliminate some midwinter blahs, staged a ploy on Valentine's Day. Prior to the class-period he wrote a poem on a valentine, put it in an envelope, and set it on the chalkboard ledge in the classroom before anyone entered. Later, he commenced the period, as normal; then at an appropriate juncture, he purposefully glanced around at the envelope on the board ledge, stopped, stared a moment (until everyone followed his gaze), and then said, delightfully, "A valentine!" Picking it up, he read the envelope: "To Professor Jones, from Your Curriculum Studies Class." He warmly thanked the class, and opened the envelope, from which he extracted the fancy valentine, and held it up for the class to see. While silently reading the back of it, he could hear giggles and whispers, such as: "Who sent it?" "Who is it from?"

Slowly, a frown replaced his smile. He then asked firmly, "Who sent this?" After pausing, he said, "I shall read it to you..."

Violets are blue.
Roses are red.
Honey is soft.
And so is your head.

He glared around the room. Some students were quietly chuckling, some looked shocked, and others glanced embarrassingly at one another or looked down at their desks. Still maintaining a serious appearance, the professor said, "I thought something like this might happen, and I anticipated such an event. Thus, I brought *you* people a valentine."

From his brief-case he pulled an almost identical envelope, labeled, "To my Curriculum Studies class, From Professor Jones." After opening it and showing the class their valentine, he read them this verse (still with a straight face):

You are at mid-term,
and things are really humming;
But if you think you'll pass this course,
You've got another thing coming!

At that point, he opened the classroom door and wheeled in a cart with containers of juice and Valentine's cookies, and spent the last few minutes of that class period informally visiting with the students. (He still thinks that a few of the group are not certain to this day as to what actually occurred during that particular incident.)

Logical presentation.[36] Whether they are lecturing as "the sage on the stage" or facilitating student group-work as "the guide on the side," proficient instructors ensure that the learning activities are organized, sequenced, and presented in "bite-sized chunks" so that learners are able to understand, practice, and assimilate the material.

In doing so, they frequently employ the following techniques: (a) providing "advance organizers" at the beginning of a session to inform students of the planned "path for the day"; (b) displaying concept maps that explain in diagrammatic form the major ideas and generalizations of a topic and how they relate to each other (see Figure 1.5 in Chapter 1, for an example); (c) helping students set achievable short-term goals that result in providing them with a sense of mastery and that eliminates feelings of being overwhelmed with assigned tasks or of seeing only drudgery; (d) utilizing "cognitive scaffolding" or specific explanations that help bridge the gap between students' prior learning and new information and concepts they encounter; (e) helping learners construct new knowledge by moving from: theoretical to practical applications, simple to complex concepts, concrete to abstract thought, familiar to unfamiliar information, and known to unknown experiences.

Skilled instructors also use and/or adapt a variety of instructional materials, methods, and media to structure the teaching/learning environment for the purpose of guiding the learning of all students. Using a variety of approaches not only adds interest and novelty to the learning process, but it helps the instructor provide for the range of divergent learning styles and preferences among class-members. Not surprisingly, research[37] has in fact shown that the incorporation of instructional variety in teaching is correlated with higher levels of student attention, involvement, and achievement.

Demonstrating enthusiasm.[38] Exemplary instructors convey that they are both interested and interesting, with respect to the subject-matter that they teach. Even on the occasional days that they may not feel particularly enthused about teaching, they are able to switch on their personal vigor for the class session. This is not in contradiction with the ethical principles of being genuine and authentic with students, but it does highlight the fact that instructional personnel are professionals, and that they may occasionally have to ignore their personal feelings, and "play the role" and project the appropriate image. I believe that teachers are actors, and that their professional ability is to maintain their interest to help students learn the content.

Although some educators reject this notion, and claim that teachers are not "entertainers," nor should they attempt to be something or someone they are not, my stance is that if teachers desire to be effective they can learn specific skills to increase their instructional enthusiasm. Here, I do not mean undergoing some sort of personality change or psychotherapy to alter one's basic temperament, but rather to engage in the following four behaviors that are known to project animation and vigor into the teaching process.

1. Using one's voice appropriately to attract and hold students' attention by varying the pitch, volume, projection, tone, and articulation is effective in creating enthusiasm. Doing these things can emphasize key points, arouse interest, create suspense, signal transitions, and add humor to the proceedings.

2. Incorporating pertinent pauses into a presentation can also create interest, arrest inattention, increase expectancy, indicate a transition, or provide reflective time. Pausing, rather than confronting, can occasionally be utilized to stop inappropriate student behavior in a class setting from disrupting other students.

3. Instructor movement in the classroom can also help increase student attention and enthusiasm. Research[39] on teacher movement indicates that it is directly proportionate to student-teacher and student-student interaction in discussions, and that it is inversely proportionate to student inattention and off-task behaviors.

Plus, instructors who have intentionally broken their invisible six-foot leash and who occasionally change their location to teach from the sides, middle or back of the classroom find that: they are able to monitor student work more accurately; they can maintain student attention; and that they can promote more of a whole-group climate in the class because they are "closer" to all parts of the room.

4. Directing students' focus is also used by effective teachers to help motivate learning. Calling students' attention to specific objects, visuals, or concepts is done verbally, non-verbally, or using both. Examples are: statements like, "This is a key point"; or "You need to remember this"; or gestures such as pointing, extending the hand, or looking and nodding in a certain direction; or combinations of these, such as the instructor pointing to the lines on a graph on an overhead and saying, "Look! These two trends are distinctly different!...Why?"

Expert teachers do *not* rely on the following cop-out regarding the attribute of enthusiasm: "Well, the Lord never made me with an enthusiastic personality, so I'll just do what I've always done in the class." Rather, they consciously apply or adapt the above four skills in their teaching—regardless of their personality characteristics.

Figure 3.7 illustrates some of the means that good instructors employ to generate enthusiasm in their teaching.

Making smooth transitions.[40] A ninth behavior that effective instructors apply in their structuring is signaling clear transitions from one segment of a session to another. They indicate these by stating such phrases as: "That completes the first section of the topic, now we will advance to viewing the video-clip;" "Let's summarize what we have learned in the last problem;" or simply, "Next, number three..."

Although veteran instructors enact these transitions almost effortlessly, beginning teachers often have difficulty in clearly and consistently articulating them because (a) they tend to think that learners see and understand the material in the same way they do, or (b) they forget to cue students deliberately for the transition.

Provide for student understanding and practice.[41] A tenth structuring skill that expert instructors consistently apply is to ensure that students comprehend and master the newly

. **CREATE ENTHUSIASM**

Figure 3.7. Effective instructors use a variety of approaches to maintain enthusiasm.

acquired knowledge and skills that they have encountered. Periodically, these teachers check for student understanding by posing questions or by observing students practicing and applying the material. However, practice alone, although essential for learning new skills, is insufficient. Feedback and reinforcement are also required to solidify learning.

In other words, they realize that teaching is not merely "telling", nor is learning merely "listening", but rather they arrange the learning and evaluation processes in order for students to engage actively in performing the learned skills or tasks in a manner that as closely as possible resembles real-world experience.

As learners practice the sub-skills of the new subject-matter content, the instructors assess their progress and provide appropriate feedback. This reinforcement is often given in brief portions, and the goal is to enhance students' retention and transfer of the fresh knowledge to new applications. Effective instructors may administer both oral and written praise, but they avoid the two extremes of either providing indiscriminate praise (given to *all* students for *anything* they do) or no praise at all.

Expert practitioners are aware of the following research results[42] that help guide their appropriate distribution of reinforcement: (a) praise must be earned for clearly describable progress, (b) it should be given in specific rather than in global terms, (c) it must be perceived as genuine not superficial, (d) it is more potent when administered by a person with status and credibility, (e) it tends to motivate individuals who are introverted more than those who are extroverted (the latter tend to be more motivated by blame or negative feedback than are introverts), and (f) little or no praise is typically ever given by instructors in post-secondary education settings.

Effective instructors incorporate praise judiciously, also recognizing that it can be over-used or under-used.

Oral Questioning[43]

A second generic instructional skill employed by instructors is oral questioning. It has been one of the most widespread techniques of teaching, next to lecturing; however, it tends to be one of the most difficult teaching behaviors to implement on a consistently effective basis. These skills—like other teaching behaviors—are not internalized automatically; teachers must learn and practice them in order to master them and make them a part of their professional repertoire.

Reasons for posing oral questions in the teaching/learning process are: to ascertain the level of students' understanding, to evaluate their progress, to encourage learner reflection, to help plan future classes/courses, to facilitate classroom management, and to involve students interactively in the learning process.

One could deliver a presentation via the formal lecture approach, and students would be passive recipients of the material; however, if one presented the same information, while incorporating an effective set of oral questions, then students would immediately become more alert, aware, and active in the entire process—because of the possibility of being asked to respond to a question.

At the same time, good instructors recognize potential dangers in the use of oral questioning, such as: (a) adult students sometimes feel uncomfortable with a question/answer format, but tend to prefer group discussions; (b) it may create an unbalanced power hierarchy, in that the instructor is perceived as "the expert in control," while the learner is seen as "the subservient, defensive subordinate"; (c) feelings of anxiety, threat, or hostility may arise; or (d) asking too many questions may actually deter group discussion.

Skilled instructors, however, arrange their oral questioning format based on the principles of ethical and motivational teaching—as described in earlier sections—in order to build a climate of trust and collaboration.[44]

A taxonomy. Many competent teachers ground their questioning activities in an organizational framework that categorizes questions into a hierarchy according to the cognitive abilities used by students to process the question and to respond to it. One such widely used structure is "Bloom's Taxonomy,"[45] that classifies questions and cognition into six levels:

1. Knowledge. Knowledge-level questions are the basic factual recall kind that typically answer What? Who? When? and Where?

2. Comprehension. Comprehension level questions ascertain if learners understand a particular concept or fact. Possible verbs that may be used to assess comprehension are: translate, interpret, explain, draw inferences, predict, or relate.

3. Application. Application level questions (or requests) ask learners to transfer newly acquired knowledge to new contexts. Students utilize their learning to attempt to resolve issues or figure out solutions to problems.

4. Analysis. Analysis level questions seek to determine students' ability to separate material into its constituent parts in order to study the relationships among components and how they are inter-connected. Verbs that seem to activate this cognitive ability are: examine, break down, investigate, identify, or justify.

5. Synthesis. Synthesis questions request learners to do the opposite of analysis by requiring them to create or produce a new entity by combining assorted components. Possible synthesis activities are: create an art piece, produce a creative piece of writing, invent/fabricate/develop a new object or process, or develop a new proposal or plan.

6. Evaluation. The evaluation level seeks to have learners assess and judge the value of concepts, ideas, or objects according to specific standards or criteria. They do not merely state an opinion or preference, but they are to justify their selection.

In simplifying these six types of cognitive functioning, successful questioners ensure that they pose questions from a variety of levels by classifying them into two basic categories: remembering (i.e., level 1: Knowledge) and thinking (i.e., levels 2 to 6, often using such stems as "How does one...?" or "Why...?"; or as requests, like: "Tell us how you arrived..." or "Explain the steps you followed to..." or "Justify how you could..."

Basic questioning competencies.[46] A conceptual framework that I have found particularly useful over the past decade to develop my oral-questioning strategies in my own teaching (and also to help pre-service and in-service instructional personnel from a variety of institutional settings to enhance their questioning skills), consists of a set of five key questioning behaviors. This "package of skills" consolidates what I believe to be the best of current, pertinent research and practice into a valuable and manageable questioning guide.

1. Determining students' level of knowledge.[47] Competent instructors pose questions to ascertain the level of students' understanding of specific topics. They ask these questions at three basic stages: at the beginning of instruction, at key intervals during teaching/learning activities to monitor how students are grasping the new material, and at the end of a session to evaluate the extent of learning and thereby the effect of the instructional activities.

2. Posing succinct, lucid questions.[48] Teachers who are proficient in oral questioning tend not to ask questions that are vague or cumbersome. They avoid error patterns. ("Patterns," here, refers to the fact that if approximately 30% or more of an instructor's oral questions fall within one or more of these negative categories, then other instructional problems will ensue.) These error patterns are:

- indefinite questions (e.g., "How about motivation?" This is ambiguous and incomplete. It could be rephrased as, "How do oral questions motivate students?")

- multiple questions (e.g., "What are the six questioning errors? That is, define them. What are some examples?" To correct a multiple question, instructors should ask each one separately.)

- interrupted questions (e.g., "How can teachers—if it were possible and feasible—how could they really improve—it would take time and dedication to do so —how could they improve their questioning skills?...Of course they must want to, as I said...". This run-on question could be corrected by having the asker to remove all of the intervening fillers, and simply ask a concise question.)

- "yes/no" type questions. Instructors who pose too many questions requiring either a "Yes" or "No" response run several risks, some of which are: it encourages student guessing; it may lead to "chorus-type answers" (where no particular responder is identified or held responsible for the answer, because of several students calling out); and it tends to waste time and to increase teacher talk because the response almost always require a follow-up question (e.g., "Why?" or "Why not?"). Most "yes/no" type questions being with "Can you...?", "Is (Are) there...?", "Do you...?" or "Can you...?"; but they can be re-worded, such as "Why do you think that...?"

- cue type questions. Cue questions provide clues to the answer within the question, such as: "If the litmus test wasn't pink, what was it?" To correct this error, one would ask "What color was the litmus test result?"

- rhetorical questions. Rhetorical questions are often posed when no answer is expected or desired, or if the questioner intends to provide the answer him/herself. Simply waiting for someone else to answer is how such questions could be modified.

Again, it must be noted that the overall *pattern* of these negative questions is what causes problems—not whether a teacher poses one or two of them during a particular class session.

3. Posing high and low order questions.[49] Exemplary instructors ask questions from all levels of Bloom's taxonomy, as described earlier in this section. Research[50] indicates that most post-secondary instructors tend to ask many more low order questions (i.e., knowledge level, recall, and convergent [those having a single correct answer] types) than the high-order type. However, teachers who are skilled questioners consciously blend both orders—according to the particular situation (e.g., the level of the course, the background of the learners, the point of time in the term, and the prior questioning experience of the instructor and students).

Teachers well-versed in the skill are aware that the posing of higher level and divergent [those having a variety of appropriate answers] questions has several positive results:[51] (a) it encourages reflective thinking, (b) it promotes creative and critical thinking, (c) it leads to significant gains in student understanding and higher student achievement, (d) it yields a higher number of student responses and statements (than does posing only low-order questions), and (e) it correlates with students' positive evaluations of the teaching they received.

4. Using directed questions.[52] In both my own instructional practice and in my supervision of novice teachers, I have found that directed questioning accompanied by adequate wait-time to be a critical instructional skill. The effectiveness of this skill appears to directly influence the effectiveness of the other four questioning behaviors.

A directed question is a question posed by the instructor to the entire group, followed by a pause of three to five seconds wait-time, after which the teacher designates a specific student to answer. Although this action seems simple enough, only experienced individuals who have mastered the skill are able to execute it consistently.

Inexperienced instructors invariably encounter the following difficulties in their questioning approach: (a) their wait-time averages only one-half to one second; (b) they do not "teach these procedures" to the group—and *re-teach* them as necessary so that *everyone* knows how the directed-questioning format operates; (c) they fail to control the typical two or three verbal "monopolizers" in almost every group, who will persist in answering out for every question, unless reminded politely and/or firmly (with such censures as: "Thank you for your comment. May we hear from someone else?" or "Remember, I am giving everyone an opportunity to think of an answer; then, I will choose someone to respond." or "Please do not answer out. We want to give everyone a chance to reflect on a response, before we select someone...Be ready..."); (d) they revert either to "targeting" students (i.e., naming a student first, prior to the question—which immediately excuses all other students from engaging in thinking about an answer) or to asking non-directed questions (not indicating a specific person to answer, and thus permitting anyone to respond—again, in all probability, it will be the few "talkers"); and (e) they are afraid of silence and thus tend to fill it up with extra words or activity rather than letting participants think about the response.

Effective questioners also leave a second wait-time pause of three to five seconds after a designated student responds to the initial question, in order to provide time for the responder to elaborate on or clarify the answer, or for other students to add a comment. All of these directed-questioning techniques must be practiced and assimilated by teachers who desire to develop their questioning skills. People are not born with such competencies: they must learn them like any other skills in life.

Some of the benefits of using directed questions with adequate wait-time (compared to questioning that does not follow these procedures) are: (a) learners give longer responses, (b) they respond more often, (c) they pose more questions, themselves, (d) they are more actively involved in the class proceedings, (e) they show an increase in their reasoning abilities, (f) they are more likely to venture a response, (g) they respond with more appropriate answers (rather than, "I'm not sure..."), (h) they display more confidence in both the content and the process of their answering, and (i) they respond from a higher level of cognition.

It is important to stress, however, that not all questions require 3 to 5 seconds wait-time (e.g., low-order questions). Furthermore, occasionally an instructor may want either to target someone with a question (i.e., placing a student's name first) if, for instance, that person is off-task; or to use an undirected question (i.e., to let anyone respond) in order to generate group-interest at the beginning of a class discussion.

A fourth important point I wish to re-emphasize in oral questioning is that the degree of effectiveness is determined by *the overall pattern* of questions—not isolated cases or occasional errors.

A fifth note of significance is that directed questioning—like all instructional tools—needs to be adapted and applied appropriately to one's context.

5. Apportioning questions equally.[53] Expert questioners are careful to select both volunteers and non-volunteers to answer, and not to permit the former to dominate. The effectiveness of using directed questions, with appropriate wait-time, permits instructors to distribute questions equitably to the group, because they—not the few verbal students—are in charge of the

questioning process. Thus, they will ensure that everyone will have an opportunity to contribute to the discussion.

Quieter students may never participate unless instructors facilitate their involvement, and they do so by watching for cues from such students indicating that they wish to respond. In keeping with the basic tenets of their ethical and professional values, effective instructors are sensitive to student's feelings — constantly balancing the need to challenge their existing cognitive performance with their need for feedback, reinforcement and acceptance.

Responding[54]

Closely integrated with effective oral questioning are instructors' responding skills (i.e., what a teacher says and/or does after students say or do something, such as after a student answers a question). People often remember a teacher's characteristic responding behaviors long after they have forgotten the subject-matter of the particular course, because teacher responding is so closely connected to the human-relations aspect and psycho-social climate that pervades the teaching/learning activity. How an instructor typically reacts to learners' input and responses will largely determine the ultimate effectiveness of the entire learning process, as was emphasized in Chapter 1 of this handbook.

Research[55] has consistently shown the importance of feedback in promoting learning, because individuals' improved functioning in any skill will not occur unless they receive some type of information about the results of their progress.

Although learners at the post-secondary level are accustomed to receiving written evaluatory comments on returned papers and grades on examinations, little oral reinforcement and praise is provided by instructors in regular classroom settings. In fact, in advanced courses, instructors tend to accept and use students' ideas more than they do in beginning courses, and even more so in the humanities than in the physical sciences and mathematics areas.[56]

These findings suggest that the nature of each program or course does influence the extent that good instructors are able to engage in oral discussion and question/answer sessions with students. Yet, my message in this book is that *all* instructors can implement at least some facet of oral interchange in their courses, and that by managing it effectively—according to some of the guidelines provided here—they will enhance learners' motivation to learn.

What effective responding behaviors do exemplary teachers exhibit in such oral exchanges with students? A group of my colleagues and I in the institution where I work have developed a set of eight basic responding skills[57] — which are based both on a review of the current research literature in the field and upon several years of accumulated teaching and supervisory experience. These skills are described below:

1. **Respect students.**[58] Consistent with the ethical and professional considerations presented in Chapters 1 and 2 of this manual, competent instructors ground their responding actions in the key premise that every individual is unique, worthwhile, and to be respected. By conveying this humanitarian attitude of acceptance and by creating a learning environment where group-members have their affiliation and belonging needs genuinely satisfied, effective instructors are also able to establish a reciprocal arrangement where they, themselves, gain the respect of the group-members.

As described in earlier sections of this book, effective instructors demonstrate this respect by such simple but crucial tasks as: arriving early and remaining behind after class to answer students' questions or to chat informally with them; portraying a professional yet approachable demeanor in addressing learner concerns; maintaining one's credibility and authenticity by treating all students equitably and by keeping one's promises; and avoiding any sarcastic, belittling or rude behavior (even to those few group-members whose negative conduct may require the instructor's intervention).

Research[59] on post-secondary students' evaluations of their professors showed that their ratings all decreased on five criteria if the instructors employed negative or threatening desists and reprimands, than if the teachers used supportive or constructive criticism or desists. (The five criteria were: instructor's competence, authority, fairness, likability, and openness to communicate with students.)

2. **Reinforce students.**[60] A second responding skill employed by skilled instructors is the positive reinforcement of

student progress. Proficient instructors provide varied forms of praise and encouragement to reward individuals for demonstrating achievement; however, these incentives must be seen as being worthwhile by the recipients to be of value.

When giving oral feedback, these instructors supplement the overused reinforcers of "right," "yeah," "good," "uh huh," and "kay" with other appropriate techniques, such as eye contact, smiles, nods, facial expressions, gestures, and fitting oral expressions (such as, "Great," "I see," "Yes," "That sounds logical," "Well expressed," "Thank you for that point," or "Sounds fine"). To be most effective, the reinforcement must be genuine, specific, and as immediate as possible.

Within short instructional segments where there may be rapid question-answer exchanges between the instructor and students—such as correcting a previous assignment or reviewing a section of work in which teachers ask convergent, low-order questions and students respond with brief answers—effective instructors generally respond with short words or phrases.

In more involved discussions[61] teachers may often ask students for clarification, elaboration, or reaction to previous comments. In the latter cases, instructors desire to encourage creative and critical thinking on the part of students. Here, they may pose additional provocative or hypothetical questions to stimulate this process, such as: "Does today's television programming lead to violence among young viewers?" (in Sociology), or "How do fish communicate?" (in Biology), or "How would one go about finding out?"

Other reinforcers may include: (a) referring to a student's idea later in a discussion; (b) asking a participant to repeat a response because of its appropriateness; (c) in the case of having to administer a "mild punishment" (for such infractions as constant interrupting), experienced instructors might frown at the student, or hold up a hand to cue, "Stop," or shake their head signaling, "Not now"; (d) occasionally reflecting on a student's comment (e.g., "So you believe that..."); or (d) using deliberate silence to stimulate further reflection among students, or to solicit a reaction or an additional comment from someone else.

3. **Probing for additional input.**[62] Effective teachers reinforce appropriately the correct portion of a participant's response, but also solicit more information from responders to

help correct any erroneous or inaccurate thinking. This task requires tact and skill, but exemplary instructors perform it smoothly by asking a second question, such as: (a) "Your logic seems correct on the first part, but tell us how you arrived at the second;" or (b) "Explain how you arrived at that conclusion;" or (c) "You lost me on the last part. Help clear up my confusion...;" or (d) "Yes, I follow you to the point where 'x' occurred; but then what happened?" or (e) "What might happen if...?"

In all of these probing activities successful instructors are mindful of preserving students' dignity and of using a gentle but firm approach in challenging their thinking or persuading them to substantiate their claims, to provide good evidence for their assertions, or to offer defensible arguments for their position. However, instructors do so by avoiding negative criticism or threatening disapproval.

Good teachers do not probe students' responses merely to increase the latters' cognitive dissonance—although dealing with this dissonance is how learners develop new levels of thinking—but research[63] on this instructional practice has confirmed several findings. They are that: (a) probing is associated with higher measures of student achievement; (b) it leads to increased quality and quantity of student involvement; (c) it reduces the frequency of non-responding by students; (b) it leads to higher level responses from almost *all* students in a class; and (e) it helps responders (and onlooking non-responders) to attempt to provide more clarity and detail in subsequent answers.

However, unless this entire probing activity is done in a positive and accepting spirit, its success is limited.

4. **Rejecting answers positively.**[64] Related to the diplomacy demonstrated by skilled instructors in praising correct portions and probing incorrect parts of students' responses, this fourth skill requires teachers to maintain a sensitive balance between stimulating students' cognitive development and hindering the group's cohesion or damaging individuals' self-esteem. This process requires that teachers know their students' needs and personalities, so that they may provide the appropriate type of feedback to students.

Some educators[65] believe that when a student's response is wrong, the instructor should clearly reject the answer with a

"No! That is incorrect!". To do less, they feel, suggests that the teacher is afraid to be direct, and as a consequence the student may be uncertain as to the correctness of his/her response.

Other educators,[66] however, advocate refraining from being so blunt, but rather to couch the rejection of the answer in milder terms, such as: "You're on the right track..." or "Not quite" or "Try again."

The most sensible solution to this dilemma is for the instructor to be prepared to use both approaches according to the personality of the responder. For instance, individuals who have a positive self-image or who are extroverted and confident can profit from a precise "No. That is wrong." response. However, such students also deserve to know why their response is incorrect; and exemplary teachers follow up this statement with an explanation, or a simpler, re-phrased question, or a request to another student to "Help us out, here." By doing so they will not discourage the responder (or other students observing the exchange) from attempting to answer again.

Good instructors do not intimidate participants, yet they are skilled at modelling how to identify errors clearly and concisely and to help students correct them.

If students question the validity of the professor's ideas, the latter can model for students how *not* to react negatively nor retaliate. Rather, effective teachers, themselves, (a) take the criticism seriously—but not personally, and (b) work at resolving the problem—not concentrating on protecting their own ego and self-esteem.[67]

5. **Avoiding "parroting" student answers.**[68] Expert teachers do not fall into the trap of echoing student responses. They have consciously trained themselves to use other forms of reinforcement without repeating, verbatim, what students say. Many teachers, however, parrot the responses, unthinkingly, immediately after students state them. If this happens consistently, students tend not to attend to their peers' responses because they realize that the teacher will be the "instant play back" of what was answered. Hence, a sort of unconscious dependency on the instructor is reinforced, while the opportunity for encouraging student-student interaction is nullified because of the instructors' dominance in giving constant commentary.

Effective instructors use a variety of reinforcing responses,[69] such as: (a) praising (e.g., "Well structured."); (b) providing a declarative statement (e.g., "The driver was inebriated."); (c) reflecting (e.g., "So you believe that she was innocent..."); (d) describing their own reaction (e.g., "Your analysis puzzles me, for one reason, and that is..."); (e) requesting clarification (e.g., "How does your solution fit with the fact that...?"); or (f) permitting a period of silence, to encourage further thinking and or comments.

6. Being aware of students' reactions.[70] Experienced teachers are not only skilled at reacting to learners' oral and written responses, but they show sensitivity to the students' non-verbal behaviors, as well. Just as instructors realize the power of their own body-language in either strengthening or weakening the effect of their own responding behavior upon students, so they also become increasingly aware of students' facial expressions, grimaces, frowns, gestures, body posture, and other non-verbal cues. These cues often signal how learners are reacting.

Expert instructors pick-up on these cues and are able to adjust the teaching/learning situation—often instantly—to clarify a point, to change instructional tactics, to reduce tedium, to avert frustration, or to de-fuse a potential conflict. This responding skill is closely linked to effective classroom management, and as was indicated in Chapter 2, successful teachers use it to help maintain their proactive and preventive management style. With this preventive emphasis, they are able to anticipate and avert possible problems from escalating by demonstrating "withitness"[71] (i.e., the ability to be aware of all happenings in a classroom setting, and to detect and resolve potential instructional or managerial difficulties early).

7. Exhibiting interest in students' input.[72] This responding behavior is also consistent with the foundational philosophy undergirding effective teaching: the treating of all group-members with respect. Skilled instructors demonstrate active attention to students' relevant responses and suggestions in various ways, some of which are: (a) reinforcing correct answers, (b) probing to help learners improve incomplete or partially correct responses, (c) inviting elaborations or clarifications, (d) requesting other students to react to an answer, (e) paraphrasing a student's comment, (f) using "inviting" facial expressions and body-language to show attention and interest in learners' contributions, (g) exploring for reasons why a student has expressed a certain point, (h) demonstrating empathy (e.g., "I felt that way, too, when I first read it...")

However, the instructors' interest must be perceived as being genuine and not as representing artificial reinforcement: they cannot be seen as being "over sweet."[73]

8. **Prompting student participation and interaction.** During group-discussions, expert instructors not only select learners to respond to questions or react to comments, but they are proficient at involving them in student-to-student inter-changes—where the teacher acts as a facilitator, while students interact with each other concerning the subject in question.

In these cases, the students become the focus of attention, and the teacher's role changes to one of resource-person or occasional guide. Instructors also encourage students to pose questions as a response to another student's answer or comment. In this way, students begin to enhance their own listening skills and logical reasoning abilities by devising questions for and probing their peers for clarification and elaboration of their ideas.

To sustain this type of student-student interaction in a discussion format in an undergraduate setting for longer than a few minutes is rare and takes patience and skill, because most undergraduate students have not had adequate experience and/or preparation to engage in such activities.[75]

* * * * *

In this section I have described three key generic instructional skills that effective teachers apply contextually in the majority of their teaching/learning activities. Each of these skills—structuring, questioning, and responding—consists of several sub-skills that instructors adapt and apply according to the specific teaching methodology (or combination of methodologies) that they are implementing for a particular session or series of periods.

In the next chapter, I describe several practical and motivational techniques that skilled instructors use to implement two basic teaching approaches: instructor-centered and student-centered methods.

I ground these strategies not only within the foundational principles of teaching-effectiveness and learning motivation, as described in Chapter 1 of this handbook, but also within the relevant generic instructional skills just summarized in this chapter.

References

1. See, for example, Ralph (1994d).

2. See Shulman and Colbert (1988).

3. See, for example, Gunter et al. (1995).

4. See Heinich et al. (1993, p. 445).

5. See, for example, Elliott et al. (1996), Orlich et al. (1994), and Weimer (1993).

6. See Gunter et al. (1995), Wiles and Bondi (1991), and Yelon (1996).

7. See, for example, Danielson (1996), Good and Brophy (1995), and Tierney (1996).

8. See Gage and Berliner (1992) and McCown et al. (1996).

9. See, for example, Fuller and Bown (1975) and Smith and Sanche (1992).

10. See, for example, Kennedy (1995), Notterman and Drewy (1993), Popham (1998), Schon (1995), and Slavin (1994).

11. See Angelo (1991a, 1991b), Brookfield (1995), and McNeely (1995).

12. See Barell (1991), Lorber (1996), and Waldron and Moore (1991).

13. See a sample unit plan in Appendix A. Also see University of Saskatchewan (1997-1998).

14. See University of Saskatchewan (1997-1998). Also see Lambert et al. (1996), McCown et al. (1996), Winzer (1995), and Yelon (1996).

15. See a sample lesson plan in Appendix B.

16. See, for example, Berkowitz (1995b), Gage and Berliner (1992), Kruse (1988), and Raffini (1993).

17. See, for example, Dunkin and Barnes (1986), Jarvis (1995), Ralph (1998a, 1998c), and Weimer (1993).

18. See, for example, Gage and Berliner (1992), and University of Saskatchewan (1997-1998).

19. See Gage and Berliner (1992), Dembo (1994), Ralph (1994f), and Yelon (1996).

20. See, for example, Barell (1991), Elliott et al. (1996), and Freiberg and Driscoll (1992).

21. See, for example, Brookfield (1995), Dunkin and Barnes (1986), Jarvis (1995), and Notterman and Drewry (1993).

22. See, for example, Ralph (1993a, 1994b) and University of Saskatchewan (1997-1998).

23. See Good and Brophy (1995).

24. See Dunkin and Barnes (1986).

25. See, for example, Armstrong and Savage (1994), Evans (1994), Gingell (1997), Reigeluth (1996).

26. See, for example, Albright and Graf (1992), McCown et al. (1996), Tierney (1996), and Winzer (1995).

27. See Dembo (1994), Dunkin and Barnes (1986), Lambert et. al (1996), and Slavin (1994).

28. See, for example, Draves (1988); Freiberg and Driscoll (1992); Gagne, Briggs, and Wager (1992); and Katz and Henry (1993).

29. See Elliott et al. (1996), and Wiles and Bondi (1991).

30. See Draves (1988), Good and Brophy (1995), and Weimer (1998).

31. See, for example, Albright and Graf (1992), Gage and Berliner (1992), McCown et al. (1996), and Tierney (1996).

32. This example is adapted from Raffini (1993, pp. 258-259).

33. This example is taken from Clipperton and Leong (1985, p. 1).

34. See, for example, Chiarelott et al. (1994), Eble (1988), and Gage and Berliner (1992).

35. These jokes are adapted from some found in Clipperton and Leong (1985).

36. See, for example, Albright and Graf (1992), Gagné et al (1992), and Wiles and Bondi (1991).

37. See, for example, Gage and Berliner (1992).

38. See Good and Brophy (1995), Raffini (1993), and Winzer (1995).

39. See Bender, Dunn, Kendall, Larson, and Wilkes (1994); Freiberg and Driscoll (1992); and Tierney (1996).

40. See Freiberg and Driscoll (1992) and Tierney (1996).

41. See Chance (1986), Dembo (1994), Gagné et al (1992), and Slavin (1994).

42. See Dunkin and Barnes (1986) and Torrance and Myers (1973).

43. See Freiberg and Driscoll (1992), Gage and Berliner (1992), Ralph (1998a, 1998c), and Vale (1995).

44. See Barell (1991), Lambert et al. (1996), and Peters (1995).

45. See Bloom, Englehart, Furst, Hill, and Krathwohl (1956).

46. See, for example, Latham (1997), Sternberg (1997), and Waldron and Moore (1991). See also Kraft (1990), University of Saskatchewan (1997-1998), and Weimer (1990a, 1990b, 1990c).

47. See Freiberg and Driscoll (1992), and Winzer (1995).

48. See, for example, Browne and Keeley (1990), Good and Brophy (1995), and Weimer (1990a, 1990b, 1990c).

49. See Gage and Berliner (1992) and Winzer (1995).

50. See Dunkin and Barnes (1986), Torrance and Myers (1973), and Wiles and Bondi (1991).

51. See Dunkin and Barnes (1986), Gage and Berliner (1992), Garmston (1994), and Winzer (1995).

52. See Barell (1991), Freiberg and Driscoll (1992), Lambert et al. (1996), and Ralph (1998a, 1998c).

53. See Gage and Berliner (1992), Good and Brophy (1995), and Slavin (1994).

54. See, for example, Chance (1986), McCown et al. (1996), Tierney (1996), and Wiles and Bondi (1991).

55. See Dunkin and Barnes (1986), and Gage and Berliner (1992), and Torrance and Myers (1973).

56. See Dunkin and Barnes (1986).

57. See University of Saskatchewan (1997-1998, pp. 124-129).

58. See Beachem (1996), Biehler and Snowman (1993), Borich (1994), and Weimer (1996d).

59. See Dunkin and Barnes (1986).

60. See Barell (1991), Gage and Berliner (1992), Paul (1987), and Tierney (1996).

61. See McCown et al. (1996) and Torrance and Myers (1973).

62. See Dunkin and Barnes (1986), Gage and Berliner (1992), Orlich et al. (1994), and Slavin (1994).

63. See Gage and Berliner (1992), Waldron and Moore (1991), and Winzer (1995).

64. See Elliott et al. (1996), Gage and Berliner (1992), Orlich et al. (1994), and Winzer (1995).

65. See Freiberg and Driscoll (1992), and University of Saskatchewan (1997-1998).

66. See, for example, Dunkin and Barnes (1986), Gage and Berliner (1992), and Winzer (1995).

67. See Gage and Berliner (1992).

68. See Orlich et al. (1994), and University of Saskatchewan (1997-1998).

69. See Barell (1991), Dillon (1983), and Torrance and Myers (1973).

70. See Good and Brophy (1995), Tierney (1996), and University of Saskatchewan (1997-1998).

71. See Elliott et al. (1996), Kounin (1970), and Orlich et al. (1994).

72. See Barell (1991), Dunkin and Barnes (1986), Good and Brophy (1995), and Wiles and Bondi (1991).

73. See Elliott et al. (1996) and Gage and Berliner (1992).

74. See Dunkin and Barnes (1986), Good and Brophy (1995), Tierney (1996), and Wiles and Bondi (1991).

75. See Dunkin and Barnes (1986), Orlich et al. (1994), and Winzer (1995).

Chapter 4

MOTIVATING METHODS OF TEACHING/LEARNING

In this chapter I examine several specific methodologies that effective instructors employ in assisting learners to internalize the subject-matter of the courses being taught.

The framework I employ consists of two basic divisions: instructor-centered and student-centered approaches, referring to who is most actively involved in the process at the time. Under instructor-centered methods, I present motivational strategies to implement lecturing, demonstrating, and discussion.

Then, under student-centered processes, I describe stimulating approaches to incorporate small-group work, cooperative learning, discovery/inquiry learning, panels/debates, and dramatics (i.e., role-play and simulations).

Before examining these methods and strategies, I wish to re-emphasize two points. One is that any categorization scheme that one chooses to use to analyze teaching has deficiencies, because of the complex nature of the enterprise. Many of the sub-categories could fit equally under either section depending on a multiplicity of factors, such as the age/level of development of the learners (and the instructors), or the subject and level of the course being taught. For example, the discussion approach could be classified under the teacher-centered category if it was led by the instructor in such cases where students were new to the process; or it could fit under the student-centered approach if the discussion was conducted by small-groups themselves.

The second point is that things may not be as they appear. For instance, just because learners seem passive during a teacher-centered presentation does not necessarily translate into a poor learning situation. Similarly, with respect to student-centered activities, instructors may appear to be doing little, and yet in such cases, more teacher preparation and monitoring of group progress is often required than for a lecture or instructor demonstration.[1]

Part 1: Teacher-Centered Approaches

A teacher-centered method is a sequence of learning activities that the instructor has designed to follow a logical path.[2]

I describe three popular instructor-based methods (i.e., lecture, demonstration, and discussion) using the following outline: definition, purpose, strengths, limitations, and implementation. However, I supplement the standard delivery-format of each one with a variety of techniques, tactics and suggestions that have been found to motivate students' engagement in learning.

Lively Lectures

Numerous studies[3] have shown that lecturing is not only the most common method in teaching at the post-secondary level, but also that it is as effective as any other instructional approach in helping learners acquire new information.

Definition.[4] A lecture is a carefully prepared oral presentation by a qualified person. It is a familiar method for transmitting information or, combined with a demonstration, to show how a skill is to be performed.

Purpose.[5] Its purpose is to convey information efficiently and effectively, particularly if the material is not readily available elsewhere, or if it is widely dispersed among several sources. Lectures—if well presented—serve to motivate or inspire learners; to introduce a subject; to explain or describe objects, procedures or ideas; to summarize; to stimulate reflection; to promote creative and critical thinking; to clarify or update information; to organize material in a special way; or to provide alternative points of view.

Strengths.[6] The lecture method has several advantages that effective instructors exploit. Some of the lecture's strengths are:

a. it can be made more current than print materials,
b. the lecturer can immediately add to, delete from, and adjust the material as required, whereas print and other media cannot be as easily modified,
c. it can be used to synthesize or preview an entire topic in a live setting,

d. it can be enlivened by incorporation of enthusiasm, dramatics, humor, warmth, intensity, and other methods and materials,

e. it permits audience interaction, questioning/answering, discussion, and social reinforcement,

f.it is adaptable and flexible,

g. it is logistically and administratively efficient and economical,

h. it is controlled by the lecturer in terms of content, pacing, organization and time management, and

i. the presenter can re-explain or re-teach any ambiguous segment immediately.

Limitations.[7] Many educators believe that the lecture method is inferior, and yet, as with any instructional tool, it may be misused, abused, not used—or used appropriately. When lecturing has been maligned or rejected as a method, a closer examination of the negative cases show rather than instead of dismissing the approach as being deficient, the more rational explanation is that the persons implementing it have been in error. Their expertise in making the lecture as motivational and enlivening as possible must be called into question—not the method itself.[8]

Thus, rather than attributing weaknesses as residing integrally within the method itself, it would be more sensible to perceive the limitations as the lecturer's inappropriate or unskilled application of the approach. Some of these ineffective uses of the lecture are:

a. instructors may try to use lecturing to change learner's values, attitudes, and feelings; but lecturing is not as effective as the discussion method for modifying participants' attitudes,

b. teachers may make lectures too lengthy, boring, unorganized, irrelevant, or redundant,

c. instructors may attempt to over-use lecturing to promote learners' thinking skills, rather than employing problem-solving, inquiry, interactive, or discovery activities,

d. instructors may not be trained to use other methods to enhance lecturing,

e. instructors may not have nor accept the evidence of the effectiveness of other approaches,

f. they may only be familiar with the lecture method because of tradition or insecurity,

g. they may agree with some students who prefer lecturing to other participative methods so that both teacher and students will not have to disclose gaps in their level of knowledge,

h. teachers may believe that "covering the course" is their goal,

i. instructors may be preoccupied with this coverage and ignore interaction, questioning/responding, discussion, and reflection,

j. they may insist that "teaching is telling" and "listening is learning"

k. pure lecturing is tolerable only for students who are intrinsically motivated and who are skilled note-takers and synthesizers; the remainder become increasingly passive, detached, and unmotivated, and

l. instructors who overuse lecturing often provide little opportunity for student-student interaction, they emphasize low-order thinking, they cannot easily ascertain the progress of student learning, and they fail to meet class-members' various learning needs—believing that they all learn in the same way.

Thus, two key points emerge from these facts. The first is not "*Should* the lecture be used, but *when* should it be used"; and the second point is "*How* can lecturing be implemented to optimize students' motivation to learn?"

Implementing Lively Lectures

I highlight key motivational strategies and activities based on the foundational principles described earlier in this handbook, which successful instructors employ to enliven their lectures.

1. **Structuring activities.**[9] As indicated in Chapter 3, effective instructors maintain structure in their implementation of learning activities: they state objectives explicitly to students early in the class-session; they use a motivational set to arouse learner interest; their explanations and directions are

precise; they make clear transitions from one segment to another; the activities proceed with brisk pacing and momentum to keep participants alert; they summarize (or get students to do so) during and at the end of a period; they ensure that learners practice applying the newly learned concepts and skills—and provide students with feedback and reinforcement of their progress in this practice; and, what is especially important, they do all of this with both smoothness and flexibility—allowing resilience for spontaneous events and contextual adjustments.

Clear explanations typically consist of the eight components shown in Figure 4.1.

Other means of structuring presentations that excellent teachers employ are: associating new material with learners' previous experiences and learning; using advance organizers

. GIVE CLEAR EXPLANATIONS

REVIEW   **4. PURPOSE**   **6. EXAMPLES & NON-EX.**
ADVANCE ORGANIZER   **7. SUMMARY**
SMALL STEPS   **5. DEFINITION(S)**   **8. PAUSE(S)**

Figure 4.1. Exemplary teachers provide clear explanations.

(an outline set of major topics or concepts to be learned); sequencing the material in logical, understandable hierarchies; using conceptual maps, charts, diagrams, or other visuals to help students organize the information; helping students in making meaningful connections to earlier work; using as many sense modalities as possible to help learners internalize the material (i.e., sight, sound, touch, taste, movement, and speech); helping students "overlearn" (which does *not* mean rote memorization but assisting them to focus more clearly on the main ideas of a topic and how they are related); consistently using verbal and visual clarity in their organization and presentation of material, such as explicitly stating objectives, directions, and verbal cues of importance (e.g., "This point is the most crucial in the entire series. Note it well!")

However, skilled instructors do more than structure their presentations; they incorporate other motivational devices and techniques to stimulate learning. Some of these activities are described below.

2. Creating motivation. To increase learners' *intrinsic motivation*,[10] good instructors consciously build and maintain a positive group climate where students: feel emotionally safe, have a sense of affiliation, develop their self-esteem, and are given an opportunity to make some decisions about their learning (e.g., they may choose learning activities from among several options).

Students tend to be more motivated to learn if they: (a) understand the value of the course being taught; (b) believe that it will help them meet personal goals; (c) believe that they are able to learn it, and (d) have expectations to succeed at it. Effective teacher's thus spend time helping students attain these four expectations.

3. Varying stimuli. Expert instructors structure the presentation into 10 to 20 minute segments in order to add *stimulus variation*.[11] For instance, they inject relevant humor and laughter into a lecture—either as a deliberate act, via a cartoon on an overhead, or as a spontaneous event emerging from the class work (i.e., puns, plays on words, or laughing at one's own one error).

They also employ gestures, voice inflections, questions, pauses, analogies, anecdotes, audio-visual media, and brief periods of small-group work.

4. Teaching interactively. Experienced teachers enhance their lectures by using *interactive teaching*[12] to motivate students. Interactive teaching gets learners actively involved in learning activities other than writing notes, watching the teacher, and listening to the lecture. The lecture segments are interspersed with oral question/answering episodes, pair problem-solving, short discussions, resource-based learning segments (in which pairs or small-groups use resources provided to answer a question or resolve a problem), or brief independent-study activities.

When effective instructors implement interactive teaching they do so in a smooth, organized fashion so that all the activities fit and flow easily; and they carefully design each segment of the class period so that it is brief, interesting, and challenging (but that can be accomplished with reasonable student effort).

A specific example of a successful modification made to a traditional lecture-style approach was provided by a Physics professor in an Eastern American university.[13] He was not satisfied with how his first-year Physics course was progressing. Although noted as a fine instructor, he felt students' achievement, attitude, and attendance were mediocre; but he desired to re-vitalize his classes. After searching for some ways to do this in a large class of several hundred students, he decided to "start small" and adjust only one component at first, and then to evaluate its effect. He did not want to change radically his entire instructional process, but rather to incorporate incremental improvements.

Thus, he simply inserted an interactive element into his regular lecture. For instance, during one of his presentations on the topic of mass, density, buoyancy and volume, he stopped his lecture after 15 minutes (when he completed one sub-topic) and to the class stated the following procedures:

Now, I want you to look at the test-answer sheet that the TAs passed to you as you entered this morning. I am going to put a visual on the overhead. On it you will see a multiple-choice question about the picture (a sailing ship at sea), and four response choices. You will have to perform no calculations, but, individually, simply select the best response pertaining to the principle of buoyancy that we have just studied. You will have one minute.

Then, I will give you two more minutes to convince the person sitting beside you why your answer is correct. (I will tell you when time is up.)

Thirdly, if after your paired conversation you wish to change your original answer, "X" it out and blacken in your corrected response on the sheet.

This is not an examination. Your responses only belong to you, but I want to collect the sheets at the end of the period for analysis purposes in order to help me improve my teaching of the course.

Now, here is the overhead picture. You have one minute. Begin.

At the end of this interactive activity the professor resumed the second part of his regular lecture.

This professor, who had taught the course in the conventional manner for several years, reported three major improvements after adding this interactive element to his lectures. At the end of the term his analysis of students' achievement scores, their attitudes towards Physics and science in general, and their class attendance showed that *all* three increased—compared to the measures of those criteria from his previous years' course-surveys. Plus, he also reported that his own feelings of professional efficacy were enhanced.

Of course, expert teachers would not interpret this anecdotal evidence as suggesting that they or any other teacher should perform this activity every 15 minutes during a lecture, but they would concur that incorporating these types of short, motivational events are stimulants to learning.

5. **Challenging students.** Effective instructors *challenge students' thinking*[14] by raising controversial issues; by adding

an opposing view or another perspective to an argument, by provoking further cognition with questions; such as: "What might have happened if...?"; by forcing learners to analyze their own assumptions and biases; by challenging them to evaluate the accuracy of others' *and* their own beliefs and perspectives; by requiring them to "break" the traditional mold for solving problems and to examine problems from new perspectives; or by having them explain *and* defend their position on an issue in pairs, triads, or small groups (or doing the same thing, except to have them deliberately argue for the opposing position—in order to force them to experience a "contradictory" stance).

6. **Using arousal**. Proficient instructors enhance their presentations by capitalizing on the *arousal value*[15] of a variety of motivational techniques. Some of these are: suspense (e.g., deliberately delaying the presentation of a solution in order to build interest); novelty (e.g., the professor enters the class wearing a T-shirt with the question "Why?" printed on the front, and "Why not?" on the back. She uses these questions in her motivational set); surprise (e.g., after students try unsuccessfully to solve a problem, the instructor solves it in an unusual way); unexpected events (e.g., request students to generate possible examination questions that may actually be selected by the professor); complexity (e.g., the teacher presents a seemingly difficult problem—but shows students how to break it down into manageable steps); ambiguity (e.g., the instructor raises a real-world issue that cannot be resolved using conventional methods, and requests students to grapple with alternative solutions); incongruity (e.g., learners are exposed to a number of contradictory positions regarding an issue, where none are perfect); curiosity (e.g., the teacher presents an idea or event from the course and questions students as to the reasons behind it); or discovery (here, good instructors try to replace the traditional "lab" type investigation, where students conduct an inquiry that is often meaningless to their life's experiences, with one that relates to real-world problems).

Other arousal-creating activities that effective instructors incorporate into their interactive teaching are: having students who possess a unique skill to teach the skill to the group; deliberately teaching students helpful information-retrieval skills (e.g., the use of mnemonic devices and memory strategies, such as the traditional "Every Good Boy Deserves Fudge" for the notes on a music staff); using familiar material when giving examples, so as to help students apply what they have previously learned; and minimizing the appeal of competing motivational systems, such as rewarding group interaction and discouraging uncooperative behavior.

The latter is accomplished in part by reducing any negative consequences of group participation by positively reinforcing the following: involving student leaders, not permitting sarcasm or belittling remarks, increasing the physical and psychological comfort of group-work, gearing group assignments to the interests and development level of members, and identifying— with genuine public reinforcement—members who do participate well.

7. **Promoting transfer.**[16] Expert teachers are proficient at helping learners to become active in transferring the "course-acquired" knowledge to real-world situations.

Over the span of my career as a second-language teacher, I witnessed a dramatic change in teaching methodology for second-language acquisition, from the traditional grammar/translation approach (in which learners scarcely *used* the listening and speaking portion of the target language in authentic settings, but concentrated on often tedious reading and writing exercises) to the current communicative approach (in which students begin functioning in the aural/oral facets of *applying* the language—by progressive steps—in actual, real-life settings. The reading/writing aspects do not predominate).

Similarly, experienced instructors at the undergraduate level realize that a key motivational device in their courses is to structure learning activities to represent, as much as possible, the actual conditions that prevail outside of the classroom. For many disciplines in the professional schools, such as medicine, dentistry, nursing, veterinary medicine, teaching, architecture, or computer science, this transfer process is easier to operationalize than it is for certain other disciplines.

Yet, *all* students can be provided with at least some experience in applying their newly acquired knowledge to real-world situations.

Techniques that exemplary instructors have used to accomplish this goal are: making provision for students to practice sub-skills, before combining the sub-skills into one holistic process; permitting practice on related cases or problems that are somewhat different from the ones learners initially experienced; providing accurate feedback to them as they practice; identifying the pragmatic benefits of knowing the material (e.g., knowledge of trigonometrical functions will help one navigate, measure distances, and estimate heights of structures); giving learners conceptual models that captures the essence of a subject—or having students attempt to construct and defend a model; and requiring them to find where and how they, themselves, could apply their new knowledge in their own life-experiences.

8. **Sustaining motivation.**[17] Human beings become temporarily satiated when their needs, drives, and motives are satisfied. Thus, it would be impossible for instructors to maintain continually high levels of cognitive stimulation with all students over extended periods of time. Moreover, it would also be unwise to attempt to do so, because once any of these stimuli become over-used and commonplace, their effectiveness diminishes.

Having established this fact does not mean, however, that simply because students may be initially motivated to engage in learning through the incorporation of a particular arousing technique, that instructors should cease all subsequent motivational efforts. On the contrary, the research literature[18] identifies a variety of ways that effective teachers employ to maintain student interest and attention on a regular basis.

One of these key techniques is: to continue to vary the instructional stimuli (e.g., good teachers continue to vary their speech and voice patterns, use movement, model enthusiasm, and add unpredictable elements to the teaching/learning process). A second is to switch communication media (e.g., combine auditory and visual stimuli in aesthetically pleasing and well-paced formats, using print materials, overheads, charts, chalkboard, 35 mm slides, video cassettes, 16 mm motion pictures, or audio recordings).

A third technique is to continue to introduce change-of-pace activities, periodically (e.g., a 15 minute mini-lecture, a 5 minute "think-pair-share" activity in which individual students first write down their personal answer to a question given to the class or their response to a common issue or problem). Then, each person shares his/her response with a partner—modifying it afterwards if desired; and finally each pair prepares to share the response either with another pair or two pairs, or else with the entire class when called upon.[19]

After this think- pair-share activity, instructors could implement a 3 minute independent-study segment; a second 15 minute mini-lecture; a second 5 minute "think-pair-share" event; and a 5 minute student-centered summary, reflection, and conclusion segment.

A fourth motivational activity is for instructors to continue to make use of relevant and appropriate humor—either intentionally planned or spontaneous. Both the research literature[20] and instructors' own personal experience have indicated that student attention and interest are increased by teachers' incorporation of humor, that humor helps reduce anxiety in a group, that it appears to foster student creativity, and that teachers can learn to apply humor.

A fifth means of sustaining interest is that effective instructors are able to maintain their demonstration of enthusiasm in their teaching (e.g., using movement, voice, pausing, gesturing, and interest in the subject). A sixth way is to pose oral questions at relevant junctures for the purposes of: emphasizing key points, providing for student practice and application of knowledge, gaining student attention, providing respondents' and audience self-awareness (of their own level of knowledge), allowing momentary diversion from the regular agenda, and conducting a review or summary.

* * * * *

In the above section I have shown that skilled instructors are able to transform the traditional lecture into an interactive approach that motivates students to engage in a variety of active learning experiences.

Distinctive Demonstrations[21]

Definition and purposes. A second category of teacher-directed approaches—and one that could also be classified as one type of interactive lecture, according to the description given in the previous section—is the demonstration. It is defined as an instructional method in which a learner views a real or life-like example of the skill or process to be learned. Its goal is for the learner to imitate a physical performance or adopt the attitudes of the person modeling a particular skill.

The demonstration method has been a part of the educational and training aspects of human experience for centuries. However, in the case of undergraduate education, what do effective instructors do in conducting their demonstration lessons that go beyond the conventional "Watch me, and copy what I do" approach? How do they arrange and present the event in order to enhance learners' motivation to be engaged in the activity and to master it? Skilled teachers employ certain strategies to achieve these goals, some of which are presented below.

Accenting the Strengths and Reducing the Limitations of Demonstrations

1. **Planning and structuring.** Just as exemplary teachers carefully prepare and create a clear organizational framework for all of their instructional tasks, they incorporate similar planning and structuring procedures in presenting a demonstration. Thus, they bring to bear a variety of instructional behaviors (such as those previously described in this manual), as they prepare and deliver the demonstration.

In sum, they: clearly state the objectives of the session and the rationale for learning; use a motivational set; present the new skill or information in "bite-size segments," in which students practice each of these sub-units; provide learners with feedback on their progress; ask key questions; make clear transitions and appropriate summaries; and have learners practice the entire skill—or apply the new knowledge—in life-like situations.

2. **Matching students' development level.** Exemplary instructors do not over-emphasize the perfection of their own demonstration of the skill; but rather, they concentrate on re-structuring the performance of the specific skill, task, or cognitive process into discrete and understandable stages or steps in order for students first of all to observe and examine

each step, successively; and then to try performing and perfecting each one.

For instance, in my own teaching and supervisory work in French-as-a-second-language (FSL) programs, I found that the best FSL instructors were not necessarily individuals or who were highly skilled in the four language skills of comprehension, speaking, reading, and writing the target language. Rather, many of the most effective teachers were people who were not necessarily francophones, but who had to learn French the same way their students were having to learn it—through considerable persistence, trials, and errors.

Native speakers, on the other hand, often were not aware of the linguistic difficulties encountered by non-native speakers of the language: the former possessed extensive knowledge and practical linguistic experience, by virtue of having "grown up" in the language, but this knowledge is often completely unfamiliar to the latter.

Thus, some teachers who were first-speakers of the target language never had to experience the efforts and frustrations of progressing through the often painful, incremental steps of language acquisition. They would occasionally become perplexed and impatient at students for not being able to grasp and/or to perform some of what they perceived to be "simple nuances" of pronunciation, grammar, or idiom—especially in the speaking and listening skills.

Effective instructors are well aware of such dangers, and therefore they take extra care in avoiding these errors. They recognize that being a well-versed specialist in a particular field may blind one from realizing that novices in the subject may not understand how the content-knowledge and skills have been constructed and how they fit together.

Moreover, expert teachers break the demonstration of a skill into incremental steps, making use of all the structuring behaviors described earlier. They teach each sub-skill with a style that matches the particular development level of the learners in performing that task.[22] For instance, if the student is at a low development level for that specific skill (i.e., having both low competence in it, and low confidence to attempt it), the instructor (or coach, or trainer, or teacher) will use a style characterized by a high degree of direction (i.e., "telling") and a high degree of encouragement to compensate for the low development levels of the learner at that stage.

Then, as the learner's level of development in performing the sub-skills progresses (i.e., they gain more competence and confidence), the instructor synchronizes his/her leadership style with that level, by gradually reducing the initial amount of supervisory direction and support, because as the learner progresses, he/she does not require as much of this guidance.

Thus, exemplary teachers adjust their demonstration strategies to meet the developmental readiness level of the learners; they are not trapped into thinking that "a one-size-fits-all" instructional approach is effective.

3. Maintaining motivation. Whether expert instructors demonstrate performing a gymnastics maneuver in Physical Education, executing a laboratory procedure in Biochemistry, participating in a formal telephone conversation in Spanish, or performing a blood-glucose level test in Medicine, they typically exhibit the following characteristics in their demonstrations for the purpose of keeping learners motivated: (a) they prepare and structure the presentation (according to guidelines described in earlier sections of this manual); (b) they tailor their teaching style to match the readiness level of the learners to perform that skill; (c) they define and explain any new concepts or objects; (d) they begin each stage of the demonstration by summarizing what is to be done, and then they re-explain it as they do it; (e) they perform each sub-skill slowly with exaggerated and/or deliberate movements—and pertinent comments; (f) they have each participant practice the sub-skill, and they provide brief but clear feedback on each learner's performance (they eventually have students practice the task at "normal speed" so as to embed it back into its authentic setting); (g) when correcting learners' mistakes, they reflect the foundational ethical and motivational principles emphasized in earlier parts of this handbook by *not* stressing the mistake nor dwelling on reasons for it—but rather by patiently demonstrating the correct skill again, and by clearly re-explaining necessary procedures accompanying it.

Then, they encourage students to make further attempts, and similarly provide feedback—always being sensitive to the learners' feelings and confidence-levels, and always being aware of their own tone of voice in the coaching process. Good teachers are not offensive in their professional demeanor, nor do they discourage students who may lack skill or confidence or both.

Occasionally, an instructor may have a graduate teaching assistant or a student perform a demonstration.[23] In such cases, effective instructors are as careful—and generally more so—in working closely with the assistant to incorporate all of the above procedures to ensure that a "distinctive demonstration" occurs. Sometimes the assistant will be "the silent partner," while the teacher provides the narrative commentary about the task by explaining, pointing, gesturing, re-explaining, and focusing students' attention on various components of the demonstration.

Of course, *the* key distinctive mark of an effective demonstration is clarity. If clarify is lacking then "...some students may learn no more from watching your demonstration than they would from watching a magician perform a baffling trick."[24]

Dynamic Discussions[25]

A third sub-set of teacher-directed methods is the classroom or whole-group discussion. I have categorized it as a teacher-centered approach because the instructor plans, prepares, and conducts it—although, eventually, some teachers are able to prepare students to conduct large-group discussions on their own, with minimal teacher intervention.

Definition. A discussion is defined[26] as the interchange of ideas among two or more people by means of oral communication and listening.

Purposes. Skilled instructors incorporate discussions into their courses: to enhance students' thinking skills; to promote learners' ability to support their assertions and to defend and refute arguments logically; to examine other perspectives; to provide a venue for modifying attitudes; to gain insights from interacting with other participants; and to have students to construct new personal meanings through a process of cooperative inquiry.

Strengths. It must be noted at the outset that some educators and students do not subscribe to large-class discussions,[27] because they believe them to be cumbersome and a waste of valuable time that would be better spent "covering" the course content. Others feel that because only "verbal students" participate, the majority of students profit little from class discussions. However, skilled instructors are able both to minimize these potential deficiencies, and to capitalize on the strengths of the discussion method—as has been identified in the pertinent research literature.

Some of these key strengths are that discussions:[28] (a) provide a valuable diversion from the "regular agenda" (assuming the activity is well prepared); (b) provide a venue where students' views, attitudes, values and beliefs can be publicly expressed, examined, challenged, defended, and/or modified through the social interaction process; (c) are more effective than lectures in promoting students' higher level cognitive thinking (i.e., analysis, synthesis, and evaluation), and in changing in students' attitudes and solidifying public decisions and commitment; (d) foster students' self-initiated and extemporaneous reasoning and speaking abilities (their capacity "to think on their feet" or "argue from their seat"); (e) force participants to abide by the group-rules (e.g., using active listening, not interrupting, not dominating, respecting minority views, or not making inhibiting or offensive remarks); (f) lead participants to become more flexible in their views and to attempt new syntheses of their growing accumulation of knowledge; and (g) permit the instructor's incorporation of the effective oral-questioning skills (described in Chapter 3) in order to stimulate and challenge students' cognitive and emotional states.

Limitations.[29] As is the case with all teaching methodologies, there are potential weaknesses with the discussion approach. However, exemplary instructors are not only aware of these limitations, but they often tap their own repertoire of accumulated skills and experiences to adjust the activities and procedures in order to reduce, or even eliminate altogether, these possible deficiencies. They use their creative energies to devise strategies to bypass the problems; for, after all, the difficulties often arise because of misuse or misapplication by instructors—not because of inherent blemishes in the approach, itself.

Some of these potential problems, and sensible solutions that experienced instructors have applied to resolve them, are summarized below.

1. Discussions may deteriorate into informal chats dominated by a clique of vocal members or into simple question-answer recitations dominated by the professor. The first problem is eliminated if the instructor initially sets and enforces the ground rules that ensure that no individual or sub-group monopolizes the conversation, and that everyone is granted equal opportunity to contribute.

When dealing with dominating members, effective instructors may ask them privately to avoid monopolizing. They may also suggest ways to curb their behavior, such as: counting to ten before saying anything; waiting until two or three other people speak before re-entering; having group-members rotate organizational roles; raising the problem with the whole class to seek solutions; or finally removing the person from the group.

The second difficulty is not actually problematic, unless the question-answer format lasts too long. In fact, this approach is effective initially if students are unfamiliar with the group-discussion format because it uses structured questioning procedures, to which each person can get accustomed before launching into more sophisticated levels of the discussion process. In fact, once learners are experienced with the discussion approach, teacher questions may actually inhibit the process, because these questions may be perceived as solidifying instructor dominance.[30]

A consequence of dominant members monopolizing is that other members will often remain silent. This, too, is prevented when instructors explicitly state and follow through with the relevant procedures and rules for the discussion. In the case of naturally reticent individuals, moreover, effective instructors gradually involve them by means of sensitive and tactful application of appropriate questioning, positive reinforcement, and nurturing of the "inviting" group atmosphere.

2. Opponents of the discussion approach claim it results in "the blind leading the blind," or "the pooling of ignorance" or "a waste of tuition fees to have to listen to non-experts express unfounded opinions." To deal with these potential problems, effective teachers—as part of the ground rules for discussion— require that participants first have the necessary background content and group-process skills from which to develop the conversation.

Thus, instructors select topics based on required readings or from fields with which learners have some familiarity—but for which they have not yet fully developed their conceptualizations and their articulation of these. Also, the topics should be of a controversial nature, compared to more factual subjects often addressed under the shorter question-answer, recitation-discussion format. (These have their place in serving as lead-up activities to more complex discussions). The topic of discussion should explore debatable issues where interpretation, divergence, subjectivity, opinion, and personal values are central elements.

A basic purpose of the discussion method, in fact, is developmental: participants are to take a position, defend it with evidence, respond to counter-arguments and refutations against their position and launch reasoned or re-adjusted arguments in support of it. Naturally , this takes time and effort—compared to the relatively efficient presentation of ideas via the lecture-format. However, the positive results of undergraduate students experiencing intellectual growth and desirable attitude change through this vehicle of social and cognitive interaction are well documented.[31]

3. Discussions can bog down, get sidetracked, become irrelevant, slow, unproductive boring, and frustrating. Yes, this is true; but so can any other teaching method—unless the instructor prepares well, especially for learners who are inexperienced in participating effectively in discussions. In order to prevent these negative eventualities, proficient instructors employ several strategies.

One strategy is that they clearly connect the discussion topic to one or more of the course objectives so that participants see the reason for the activity. A second approach is that they carefully explain the rationale for the ground rules (i.e., respecting the right of others to hold views, and being able to criticize others' positions without attacking the people).

Third, they begin discussion activities with undergraduate students in short, well-structured formats, such as brainstorming with the whole class (i.e., the teacher invites everyone to contribute suggestions about a topic, and the teacher writes the ideas on the board or overhead. Ground rules here are: do not judge the ideas—other than not permitting any offensive or obscene comments; build on others' suggestions; and accept suggestions in any order. Then, the instructor helps the group re-arrange the items into categories, and helps them—through questioning—to reach tentative conclusions about the subject. Before progressing to more advanced levels of discussion, in which the teacher plays a less directive role, the early discussion experiences are purposefully designed and controlled by the instructor).

A fourth approach is that skilled instructors not only explain the ground rules to beginning classes, but they consistently monitor students' compliance with these rules during the first few discussion sessions—providing for both positive and corrective feedback. (The latter—in keeping with the fundamentals of creating a pleasant yet business-like working climate—is provided briefly, objectively, but supportively.)

A fifth technique to increase group motivation in discussions is that expert teachers choose interesting topics, often presented in the form of a question rather than a statement, in order to stimulate student interest and participation (e.g., "Should students' end-of-term evaluations of their professors be signed?" or "Should new instructors in post-secondary institutions be required to take some type of 'teacher-preparation' work, prior to beginning to teach?").

They also gear the discussion process to the development level of the learners in the group, because undergraduates often require help starting the discussion. Thus, proficient instructors may begin with a short anecdote and ask for comments; or they may ask for a volunteer to share what happened when they experienced a certain incident; or they may present a short case to the whole class and have pairs of students discover the problem or issue and how to solve it.

Because undergraduates tend to avoid adversarial, competitive, or hostile discussion scenarios, their instructors are careful to maintain an inviting climate and not to reduce students' self-esteem. To do this, they skillfully help build participants' confidence to participate and their competence in thinking, reflecting, active listening, forming arguments and counter arguments, and in clearly articulating their positions.

4. Undergraduate students do not typically participate actively in class: recent research[32] indicates that only about 6%

of class time is spent in student participation, and that approximately half of students report participating "infrequently" or "almost never"; and yet nearly 97% of students state that all classes should provide for some type of student involvement.

Although great variations exist among instructors, those who are exemplary reverse these non-participation trends by consistently employing the following techniques: posing oral questions, asking for clarification or student responses, accepting/praising/repeating student answers, or using students names when posing questions or administering feedback.

Current research[33] also indicates that less than a third of undergraduate students make nearly ninety percent of classroom comments, and that most students feel that speaking up in class is most suited to those vocal individuals who tend to take the responsibility for carrying the dialogue. The majority refrain from contributing because (a) they feel their contributions may not be well structured, (b) they feel unknowledgeable in the subject-field, (c) they had not done the required homework, or (d) the class is too large and they would be embarrassed.

Skilled instructors attempt to counteract these trends by implementing the techniques identified in this handbook. They ensure that their own rhetoric (e.g., "All questions are welcome."; "Learning involves making errors."; "Don't be timid...give it a try") consistently matches the reality of their daily practice and attitude toward all group-members. In short, they balance their supportive encouragement with the challenge and probing of student responses—all conducted in a spirit of trust and genuine acceptance.

Realistically, many effective professors do not incorporate the discussion method all of the time: they often employ the lecture method—but they add discussion at key junctures to create motivation in their sessions.

5. To conduct large-group discussions properly requires much energy, and it is intellectually exhausting and often emotionally disturbing. It requires instructors to have high levels of preparation, knowledge, confidence, and patience to make discussions successful—yet, excellent teachers accomplish these goals.

They persist, despite the rather disconcerting findings of current research on classroom participation[34] in post-secondary education that reveals: (a) more classroom interaction is initiated by students than it is by instructors, (b) students feel that instructors are less proficient at conducting discussions than they are at basic teaching, (c) students rate themselves as participating less than their instructors rate them, and (d) instructors pose few higher-order thinking questions in their classes.

These findings suggest that the majority of faculty-members could give more attention to incorporating discussion-type activities in their teaching. Moreover, for individuals just beginning their teaching career, accomplishing this task might be easier than for their more seasoned colleagues, who may find such a change more difficult to manage. The key in either case would be to start with a small improvement that is controlled and directed, to assess its effect, and then to proceed according to the results, making adjustments as necessary.

Implementing Dynamic Discussions: A Distillation of Findings[35]

In this section I summarize how exemplary instructors structure and conduct effective classroom discussions.

1. **Establish ground rules.** Good instructors set basic procedural guidelines for member conduct during discussion, such as: active listening, no rudeness, and logical argument.

2. **Set clear goals.** They provide explicit objectives, instructions, and a time-limit (for initial discussion activities).

3. **Know when to intervene.** Effective instructors intuitively discern when to pose a question, to request an elaboration, to review the group's progress, or to proceed to the next point.

4. **Handle hinderers.** Skilled teachers deal with individuals who block the group's progress (e.g., ensuring that monopolizers do not dominate, dealing with irrelevant issues later, defusing hostile situations, redirecting digressions or trivialities, and encouraging quiet students to contribute).

5. Maintain flexibility. Effective instructors vary their degree of direction according to the context: they adjust their control, and sometimes permit an open discussion if the situation warrants it.

* * * * *

In Part 1 of this chapter, I described how effective teachers implement three common teacher-centered methods: lively lectures, distinctive demonstrations, and dynamic discussions. I illustrated how these instructors strive to prepare and present a variety of interesting learning activities for each of these approaches in order to arouse and maintain students' motivation to learn.

In Part 2, I explore how skilled faculty-members prepare and arrange several stimulating student-centered learning experiences.

Part 2: Student-Centered Approaches

Like teacher-centered approaches, student-centered methodologies are also planned and implemented by the instructor, but they are incorporated in such a manner as to permit greater student choice and ownership than is the case for the more closely controlled teacher-directed methods examined in Part 1. Moreover, I have indicated throughout this manual that good teachers characteristically blend *both* categories of activities into integrated, holistic sessions designed to sustain learners' interest and to help them engage in meaningful and relevant learning experiences.

Furthermore, the three teacher-centered approaches described in Part 1 had components of student-centered tasks in them; and, in Part 2, the student-directed strategies, correspondingly, have certain teacher-directed aspects to them. Ultimately, instructors are charged with the obligation to organize the classroom environment to enhance learning. In the final analysis, they are still responsible for, and in charge of, directing the course work—even when some of the learning experiences might be designed as "learner-centered."

In this section, I describe some of the ways that excellent instructors implement five recognized student-centered methods. I employ the same organizational framework used in Part 1 that provides each method's definition and purpose, and its strengths and limitations, along with some of the stimulating strategies instructors apply in its implementation. These five methodologies are small-group work, cooperative learning, discovery/inquiry activities, panels and debates, and drama activities.

Small-Group Activities[36]

Definition and purposes. A small-group activity consists of a team of learners (usually numbering three to seven people) working to accomplish a certain task. The goals to be attained typically are: (a) to examine a controversial issue via the discussion method and to generate a set of tentative conclusions; (b) to complete a class-project, in which members divide the task into sections, assign one of the tasks to each student, and then compile the individuals' work into a final product; or (c) to solve a problem, examine a case-study, conduct an inquiry or laboratory investigation, participate in a debate or panel, or engage in a role-play, simulation, or other group activity incorporating drama. (I describe these activities later in this section.)

As I emphasized in earlier sections of this manual, any categorization of these methods will produce considerable overlap between and among the various approaches. It is evident that "small-group work" actually includes elements of the discussion approach, as well as encompassing the other four "student-centered" strategies. Likewise, certain aspects of the discussion approach blend into most of the other instructional methods; while "lecturing," technically, occurs with all of the methods—when, for instance, teachers introduce a new activity or topic; or when they explain or describe the ground-rules, expectations, and assessment procedures for a small-group assignment.

However, for analytical and reflective purposes, I follow the classification scheme initially established for this manual, even though in the daily routines of teaching-practice thinking in terms of such a categorization may be artificial.

Strengths.[37] The advantages of using small-group activities are similar to many of those identified for the discussion method in Part 1, above. In addition to those benefits, small-group work provides for: (a) fostering the democratic ideal of pooling individuals' talents and knowledge for the good of the collectivity; (b) enhancing individuals' social and interpersonal skills; (c) promoting problem-solving abilities; (d) empowering participants with increased choice and decision-making (within reasonable limits); (e) balancing the opportunity to let participants apply their unique abilities to achieving the goal (and gain approval, thereby) with the ethical responsibility of each member to undertake occasionally a task for which he/she may not have an affinity; (f) permitting the open exchange and examination of a variety of perspectives in a more informal forum than that of a whole-class discussion; (g) increasing students' overall *active* participation (e.g., in reasoning, speaking, and giving feedback) compared to their more passive behavior during pure lecture segments; (h) providing "real-world experience" of having to engage seriously in the conflict-resolution process to deal with differences that inevitably arise during interpersonal activities; and (i) increasing participants' depth of understanding of the course content, thus promoting positive attitudes toward the subject and ultimately leading to enhanced motivation to learn.

Limitations.[38] As I indicated in previous sections of this handbook, competent instructors are well aware of the potential problems that may arise with any teaching method—including the discussion-approach. However, such teachers are skilled at adapting the procedures to compensate for such difficulties: this skill is, in part, what helps distinguish them as exemplary professionals.

Some of the deficiencies of the small-group approach that experienced teachers manage to curtail have already been described in the previous section on the discussion method. Others are summarized below.

1. To reduce the possibility of small-group tasks becoming unproductive "gab-sessions," or of deteriorating into boring time-wasters, effective instructors arrange for the groups to engage in specific activities guided by explicit procedures and time-limits. Such activities may start with short pair-share exercises, where participants prepare an individual solution, discuss it with a peer, formulate a "joint-response," and describe it to the larger group.

As students become more familiar with the collaboration process, instructors may choose to assign longer and more complex projects to groups. However, in doing so, they ensure that the groups' success is experienced in incremental steps.

2. To help eliminate the occasional resistance to change arising among some students and faculty-members toward the use of small-group work (because they say it is a "time-waster"), exemplary instructors consistently advocate the benefits of group activities, emphasizing that some conflict is normal whenever human beings interact. They also stress that future employers, for example, desire to hire candidates who not only possess specialized content knowledge, but who also have demonstrable skills in team-inquiry processes, in interpersonal communication, and in dealing constructively with others as they seek to solve often-chaotic problems.[39] Instructors thus identify practical and relevant reasons for students to practice these group-processes.

Another reason why some instructors dislike the small-group approach may be their previous negative experiences with it: it may have been ineffective at best, or disastrous at worst. All instructors have probably encountered some such dismal results; however, expert teachers attempt to correct any deficiencies they observe and try again later with a readjusted version—often simpler, shorter, and faster—in order for all participants (including the instructor) to gain some success, and to experience the subsequent sense of accomplishment and satisfaction that results from reaching a group goal.

3. Critics are correct when they assert that "the reality" of small-group activities with undergraduates does not always match "the ideal."[40] They accurately point out: (a) that intellectual pitfalls may often be present (e.g., that both teachers and students often seek to bias a discussion in their favor; that groups or alliances within groups may label non-conforming members as deviants, and unduly pressure them to accept a contrary view; or that individuals may voluntarily or non-voluntarily withhold critical information from the group); and (b) that social barriers may be present (e.g., that some members may over-contribute, some under-contribute, or that minority-group members may participate less than other members).

Experienced instructors do not deny or ignore such problems, but they confront these difficulties early. For instance, they seek to eradicate the intellectual problems by persisting in their challenge of members to view issues from outside of their own mind set; to examine consciously their internalized assumptions; and to realize that no one needs training to serve one's own immediate interests, but that everyone must seek for clarity, evidence, reasoned judgment, and understanding of alternative perspectives—not solely for the purpose of enhancing one's status, but of genuinely seeing others' points-of-view.

These teachers also actively deal with the psycho-social pitfalls that may arise in group-work by patiently yet seriously confronting the non-participation issue by employing questioning skills, reinforcing involvement, providing continued encouragement, raising the status of minority group-members, re-arranging the groups, and modeling expected behavior themselves. They work at not reacting negatively if a student criticizes them or their ideas. They try not to be overly protective of their own egos and self-esteem at the expense of facing the confrontation squarely. They attempt not to take the criticism personally but to take it seriously—in that the person(s) levelling the critique may well have a legitimate reason for complaint.[41]

Implementation guidelines.[42] Taking into consideration all of the methods and strategies just described for the small-group approach, I synthesize this information into a set of practical guidelines that proficient instructors employ in organizing and implementing small-group activities for the purpose of increasing students' motivation to learn. I emphasize, too, that these guidelines may also be applied generally to the four other student-centered approaches described later in this chapter, because all of them incorporate substantial aspects of small-group activity.

1. The small-group method has been used successfully by effective teachers in some fashion for all subjects; however, admittedly certain courses may be more or less suited for this approach. For instance, one Chemistry professor irately demanded how he was to incorporate role-playing into his organic chemistry classes![43]

The critical point in all effective teaching, however, is not how well or poorly each instructor implements instructional variety, per se, but rather how he/she creates optimum learning activities for participants. There is no single technique or approach that guarantees the achievement of this goal; however, exemplary instructors seem to be constantly on the lookout for effective ways to sustain learner interest and motivation in the courses for which they are responsible.

Thus, in the case of the angry Chemistry faculty-member, he could perhaps institute a brief paired-activity similar to the one initiated by the Physics professor described in Chapter 4 of this handbook. Or, he might consider adapting to his situation what another Chemistry professor practices to arrange group-work in his courses.[44]

The latter lets students form groups of four or five people, to whom he distributes (near the end of most class-periods) two or three examination-like problems based on the day's material. The groups solve the problems, and the professor grades their answers and returns them the following day. He found that after some initial resistance to the activity, most students seemed to benefit from the task. The anecdotal evidence indicated that both of these group efforts paid demonstrable dividends in higher student interest and achievement.

2. Simply putting students into groups will not produce automatic success. In fact, doing so will in all probability guarantee that the potential weaknesses of the discussion approach and small-group methods described earlier in this Chapter will materialize. Experienced instructors, anticipating the possibility of such problems arising, are *proactive* in designing, implementing, and monitoring procedures that will tend to prevent these difficulties from emerging.

First, they select motivating topics, issues or questions that are directly related to one or more of the course objectives. Second, they organize the activity so that participants (either in pairs, triads, or groups of four to seven members) will have the necessary background information and/or group skills to complete the required task in a relatively short time-frame. Third, they provide the entire class with precise instructions and directions of what is to be done, how the member-roles are to function (e.g., recorder, encourager, chairperson, and so forth), and how the process/product will be assessed.

Fourth, these instructors teach—and re-teach as necessary, just as they would present any topic or concept in the course—the fundamental group-procedures and social rules that everyone is expected to follow (e.g., active listening, no interrupting or monopolizing, everyone contributing, demonstrating respect, critiquing ideas not people, no one shirking responsibilities, administering sanctions by the group for non-compliance, and having access to the professor for guidance, clarification, and certain resources).

Fifth, skillful teachers circulate and monitor the progress of each group (and individuals in it), providing feedback—both positive and negative, if required. The positive reinforcement typically outweighs the latter, and both kinds tend to be given briefly, specifically, and genuinely—with the corrective feedback being administered in an objective but non-threatening manner.

* * * * *

Because most of the strengths, possible problems, and motivational strategies identified for both the discussion and the small-group methods also apply to the next four small-group approaches, I refer the reader to those previous descriptions found earlier in this chapter.

In the following sections, I summarize how effective instructors apply certain motivating strategies to incorporate the four student-centered approaches that employ small-group activities within a whole-class framework. These activities are cooperative learning, panels/debates, dramatics, and other projects.

Cooperative Learning[45]

Definition and purposes. Although some educators make a distinction between "cooperative" and "collaborative" (CL) learning approaches, most practicing instructors are less concerned about semantic or conceptual differences between them. They typically regard the CL approach as one type of small-group activity, in which members work together to assist one another learn or to cooperate in creating a final product, such as a project, a report, or a presentation.

The purpose of the cooperative/collaborative groups is not simply to reach a solution or "get *the* answer to a problem," but to have *all* group-members help each other search for and grasp the meaning of a process or event. A characteristic feature of the CL approach—distinguishing it from regular small-group work—is the mutuality, rather than the individuality, of the goal activity: the *whole* group is responsible for assisting all members to learn (or to perform or to create) the specified product. Thus, the group's goal is based on the achievement of each member.

Typically consisting of four to seven members of mixed abilities, CL groups have two basic aspects: the task dimension (i.e., to complete an assignment, or to understand and solve a problem) and the reward dimension, in which individuals receive personal credit only if the group succeeds. Thus, members are motivated to be responsible for their follow-members' learning.

Strengths. Although the bulk of research on CL has been conducted at the K-12 level, there has been a recent increase in research on the effects of small-group learning at the post-secondary level. The majority of the findings of all of this research, however, has been consistently favorable.[46]

There tends to be an increase of group-members' positive attitudes toward both the subject-material and their team-members, as well as an extension of learners' use of higher-order thinking skills. There is also evidence of more positive psychological well-being among participants (e.g., higher levels of self-efficacy and self-esteem), and of a more productive and supportive whole-classroom learning climate.

Limitations.[47] As stated in previous sections of this manual, some professors and students reject any type of small-group activity, believing that it is simply not constructive. Reasons they cite for this are that: dominant members rule while quiet ones are passive; not all students cooperate; the topic may not be relevant; the final result may not be useful; students are accustomed to individual learning, and they may see collaboration as unnatural and "forced"; if "more able" students are to teach less able ones, what happens when a group is formed without the former being present?

Furthermore, some students see it as slowing their individual pace and interfering with their own progress; participants often do not have the necessary background to sustain intelligent discussion on a topic; there is the emergence of simple logistical problems, such as the problem of setting a meeting time and place suitable for all members—when they must meet outside of class-time; and the fact that it is a time-consuming exercise.

Implementation. Proponents of CL readily recognize that the approach will fail if instructors do not ensure that certain basic conditions are met—similar to the experience of keeping to a diet. These five essential elements are described below.

1. **Positive interdependence.** Individuals succeed only when all members do. A member's work benefits the whole group, and the whole group's product benefits the individual. Specific roles are assigned, but mutual dependence is mandatory in order to achieve the common goals and the joint reward.

2. **Individual and group accountability.** Each member has a key task to perform, and the final product is incomplete without it.

3. **Promotive interaction.** Members must communicate in order to promote each individual's effectiveness by describing, explaining, questioning, discussing, defending, and assessing each other's work; and by supporting, encouraging, and assisting one another.

4. **Interpersonal and group processing skills.** If members do not possess and exercise these essential skills, instructors must teach and model them; and must have students practice them while being given feedback. Students must be able to work cooperatively, communicate clearly, employ acceptable social skills, follow shared decision-making and leadership principles, and exercise conflict-management skills, as required.

5. **Content knowledge.** Participants must possess sufficient subject-matter background to engage in the discussion or task in question.

Effective instructors must monitor each group's progress and intervene when necessary to help groups to maintain both the "task" and the "team" processes.

It is understandable that when some instructors—especially those who are new to teaching—realize the considerable effort required by students and themselves to incorporate CL activities effectively, they retreat from the prospect. Admittedly, it is time-consuming, it requires preparation and active monitoring, and it requires perseverance![48]

However, a solution to this concern, and one enacted initially by many excellent instructors, is to start with a small group-project. They may launch a short but interesting group activity related to the course, and in which groups will be motivated and successful. Then, as participants gradually become accustomed to "the roles and rules" of the method, effective instructors—if they so desire—may increase the complexity of the task. Some professors, on the other hand, will continue to utilize their proven "brief but powerful" CL activities, with which previous classes have been motivated and satisfied. In such cases, instructors may make minor adaptations to the tasks from year to year.

Some examples. One successful but simple collaborative writing-activity given to pairs of students to make sense of reading assignments is a notebook-exchange strategy.[49]

Students do an assigned reading out of class; and then on a page in a notebook, consisting of four or five columns, they write three to six excerpts from the reading that they feel are important, helpful, or confusing.

In the next column beside each excerpt they write a brief comment, explanation, or question about it. They then exchange the notebook with a partner; and both students read each other's excerpts and comments, and in turn write a comment in the third column pertaining to each excerpt, or previous comment, or both.

Notebooks are then returned to their original owners, who read the three columns, and finally write a concluding comment in the fourth column, based on the interchanges and their reflections on them.

Benefits of this task, reported by professors who use it, were that students helped each other make sense of the readings and the central concepts therein; and that participants—in discovering what either satisfied or puzzled their partners—also gained personal insights about their own understanding of the material.

A second example of an uncomplicated collaborative learning activity[50] related to class readings has proven to be effective. In this strategy, the whole class is divided into sub-groups of four or five students each. A set of identical readings are assigned to each group, so that each member of that group has the same reading. Each of the other sub-groups receives a set of identical readings (one for each member), but the set is different from the other groups' sets.

Each student is to read his/her article and prepare to present an oral summary of it for the next class-period. Then, sub-groups are re-arranged so that each new group consists of students who have read and summarized a different article—each student with a separate reading.

Next, each student in every group is given the same package of questions related to all the articles. Consequently, because only one person in each sub-group knows the answers for each article's questions, each person becomes a valuable information-resource for their fellow-members. Therefore, the participants must collaborate in sharing their research with each other: the entire group depends equally on each participant.

Panels and Debates[51]

These two student-centered approaches could also be classified as types of small-group activities, because typically there are from three to seven participants directly involved in the activity, with the remainder of the whole group participating indirectly in the role of judges or evaluators, or more casually as observers.

Because panels and debates are usually organized to be publicly conducted, they are more structured than other small-group or CL activities. The latter tend to function in a more informal atmosphere.

Panels. Panel discussions are similar to small-group discussions except that the speakers are grouped together so that they are visible (and audible) to the audience.

Each panel-member, in order, gives an oral presentation of a few minutes' duration. There is a moderator or chairperson who presides and who introduces and thanks each speaker. The panelists' presentations amount to mini-lectures, in which they express their views and opinions on a specific topic. Often the panelists are selected for their divergence of perspectives, in order to provide contrast and to add interest for the audience and panelists, alike.

After the initial presentations the moderator may request the panelists to exchange comments, or to field questions from the audience, or to engage in an open discussion among the panelists and the audience. Occasionally, the panel may take the role of questioners or interrogators of a guest, as well.

The *advantages* of a panel discussion are that: it presents several perspectives on a subject; it arouses interest; it promotes broader understanding of issues; and—for the panelists —their preparation, public presentation, and active participation often bolster their own motivation and enthusiasm for both the topic and the panel-process.

Its *drawbacks* are that: (a) considerable preparation is required: for the instructor to organize it; for the panelists to prepare and present their talks and to respond to questions; for the observers to listen, to reflect, to question, and to synthesize the arguments; and for the chairperson to be alert to judge when and how to intervene; and (b) the audience may not possess enough competence and confidence in the subject to participate adequately in the question/answer/discussion portion, or may not possess the necessary interpersonal skills to make the activity effective.

Many of the specific strategies that effective instructors employ to increase participant motivation in the panel activity are similar to those used for all small-group work. They are described in earlier sections of this manual. Additional strategies that competent instructors use for panels are: (a) to ensure that the selected topic will increase participants' intellectual and emotional involvement; (b) to ensure that the observers and audience will have an active role to fulfill during and/or after the presentation (e.g., to fill out an evaluation form, or to complete an assignment on a hand-out); to have panelists prepare strong (and/or provocative) arguments; (c) to provide the presenters with an opportunity, not only to respond to questions from other panelists and the audience, but to add or clarify information, and to present a summary statement; and

(d) to ensure that the moderator effectively fulfills his/her role (i.e., to involve the whole group, to keep the proceedings on track and on schedule, to prevent arguments from escalating between any two participants, to prevent the panel activity from deteriorating into a casual chat session, and after the discussion to provide both the presenters and the observers with assessment comments from the professor).

Debates. A debate, like the panel discussion, is a formal and staged oral presentation involving two individuals or teams that discuss a controversial topic issue from the pro and con positions. Each side presents polarized or contrasting views—the positive and negative biases surrounding the subject.[52]

The debate operates according to clear rules that specify the procedures of the presentations (e.g., each speaker has a brief time-limit to present an initial argument; there are no interruptions permitted; each side alternates to present their position, then to make counter-arguments to refute their opponents' points). Each team ends by presenting summary statements.

As with the panel discussion, the moderator of the debate must ensure that debaters abide by the organizational structures. The audience also may be required to conduct formal observations and evaluations on the proceedings, and to provide feedback to the participants, later.

The debate method shares most of the same *strengths* characterizing the panel-discussion approach, but it also provides increased opportunity for debaters to develop their extemporaneous listening, reasoning, analytical, and speaking skills. Participants not only have to demonstrate improved alertness and intellectual agility to discern flaws in their opponents' arguments, but they must increasingly sharpen their skills of bolstering and defending their own team's position by presenting sound evidence and using keen logic. Good debaters are also able to confront differing viewpoints without attacking the person(s) holding such positions.

Disadvantages of the debate approach are similar to those of the other small-group approaches, but one that is unique to it is that in the real world an issue is seldom purely dichotomous: truth is rarely as simplistic as the debate process makes it out to be. Consequently, experienced instructors advise participants of these limitations, while at the same time, encouraging them to capitalize on the cognitive advantages that accrue by simply experiencing the process of the debate process.

Another potential limitation of which effective instructors advise participants is the danger of being so cognitively and emotionally attached to a single polarized viewpoint—as is the case in the debate competition—that individuals may become close-minded. Thus, skilled teachers emphasize—particularly in the debriefing period after the debate session—that a key purpose of the debate process is to promote reflection and modification of opinion among participants and observers, alike.

An example of how effective instructors incorporate one type of debate into their courses is one that has proven successful with large classes. The teacher first selects a dichotomous question related to the course content, then divides the large class into two sections—perhaps separated by an aisle in the lecture theatre.

The instructor then sets some basic ground rules, such as: a one-minute time limit per speaker; the speaker is to stand up and present his/her position in a well-projected voice; no interruption of presenters is permitted; each side is permitted five different speakers to make initial arguments—in alternating order; and after all ten speakers finish, then each side is permitted to begin the refutation process.

Also, some audience-members are randomly selected to judge the quality of the debate using evaluation forms prepared earlier by the instructor and distributed just before the event. The balance of the audience receives another handout with several questions for which they write answers during the debate. These questions relate both to the subject-matter issues being argued and to the debate process, itself. Thus, *all* members of the class are engaged in some portion of the debate.

At the conclusion of the debate, the instructor conducts a debriefing session, in which the evaluators present their findings, some of the audience-members share their data, and the debaters describe some of their thought-processes, insights, and emotional reactions they experienced. Finally, the instructor reiterates the purpose of the activity, highlights its strengths and deficiencies, positively reinforces the efforts of all participants, and comments on the content issue, itself.

When instructors skillfully implement some of these student-centered strategies into their coursework, the result is in an increase in student interest in the subject.

Drama in Teaching, Role-Plays, and Simulations[53]

Dramatics. A third category of student-centered techniques that exemplary instructors occasionally incorporate into their classes is the use of some type of drama activity. Although certain subjects may lend themselves more than others to this approach, proponents of the use of drama in teaching assert that it can be utilized *in at least some form* with any subject in all disciplines.[54]

One of these forms may simply be the incorporation of relevant humor, or an interesting anecdote in the motivational set, or having a small-group to present a short dialogue to enhance student interest in the topic of the day.

Drama in teaching does not necessarily entail the full-scale production of a theatrical play by a class—although such activities are possible and effective—but rather it means the implementation of certain instructor and/or student activities, events, or experiences within the teaching/learning process that accentuates the affective domain of human life (i.e., the emotional aspect that touches our feelings and sentiments).

Thus, some educators believe that "theatre" means to see or view an event, while "drama" means to do or live through an event, in which people experience the humanizing process of "being in someone else's shoes."[55] The latter can be incorporated into any subject.

Because effective learning is multisensory in nature, good teachers constantly seek to use a variety of measures that will accelerate, deepen, and stimulate the quality of student learning. Dramatics help achieve this. "Motivation" is, in fact, a derivative of the same Latin root for "emotion," which means "to move;" thus, effective teachers add motivational components to their instruction that will cause learners to feel what it may be like to do or think via others' experiences. I have emphasized this principle throughout this handbook.

Not only this, but the very essence of successful teaching is a performing art: instructors on a routine basis must act a part, improvise, initiate purposeful acting, be "on stage" in real life, and compete with other media and personnel who are also vying for students' attention.

> Whether teachers themselves perform or concentrate upon getting students to perform, both are engaged in devising ways of translating passive acts of teaching and learning into performance...the teacher's performance remains essential to most teaching and learning.[56]

During my own career in education over the past four decades—whether in my teaching of *all* age-groups, in my administration and career counselling roles, or in my conference and seminar presentations—I have found that the incorporation of dramatics in *all* of these areas has consistently produced participant motivation in the subject area under consideration, and has provided greater professional satisfaction in my work.[57]

For instance, I have used full-fledged plays (complete with costuming, lighting, sound-effects, music and props) to motivate my teen-aged French-as-a-second-language students (who were in "compulsory" classes, and some of whom hated French). These French/English bilingual theatrical pieces were co-designed with students, and had such titles as "The Boy Who Wanted to be a Mountie". (This play was the history of a lad, who all the way through his home- and school-life expressed a desire to become a member of the R.C.M.P., and who had his wish realized—but who encountered bitter-sweet experiences en route. Incidentally, I also found that this age of students was consistently the most difficult to motivate.)

With respect to adult learners, in my courses on the use of instructional media in teaching, I found that the occasional incorporation of drama also played a key part in arousing and sustaining adult student motivation to engage in the course.[58] One example was a creative task devised by some of my colleagues and I that was assigned to groups of four or five prospective teachers, in which they were given a camcorder and a one-and-a-half hour time limit to produce a one-to-two minute television commercial advertising a university course of their choice. Groups were to "invent" a class to be offered on campus and, on the basis of the commercial, to try to attract students to enrol in it.

Invariably—according to the final course evaluations submitted by the students in these courses—class-members were not only stimulated and satisfied by the opportunity to create their own commercial, but the success of such activities seemed to transfer to the whole course, in general, causing participants to engage in all of the learning experiences with a certain enthusiasm and vigor—in comparison with some of the other university-level courses I have taught[59] that did not incorporate a drama component.

Role-plays.[60] A role-play is a short skit enacted by two or more individuals that portrays a typical real-world situation. There is not generally a formal script, although actors are given a brief description of the scenario and the role they are to fill. They therefore improvise and react spontaneously, as the character they are playing would probably behave in real life.

At an appropriate point, the instructor may stop the skit and involve the players *and* the audience in a discussion and analysis of the actions, feelings, and thoughts that occurred.

The purposes of role-plays are: to have students experience the emotions and feelings that arise in a situation, which they may have only known cognitively; to have them gain a fuller understanding of the cognitive processes required in a situation; to explore new fields; to help them prepare for potentially emotional incidents that they may meet later in their careers; to force them "to pass through" the actual event within the safety of a classroom; to provide them with increased confidence, if and when they do later encounter a similar incident.

Advantages of the role-play approach are that: (a) students become actively involved in a realistic situation; (b) it can break down cultural or social barriers, by having individuals experience "the other person's feelings"; it can compress time in order to present the key events and concepts intended; (c) it can be used to examine a problem-situation in virtually any subject having to do with human relationships; (d) it can involve many people, in both the acting and in the discussion it generates; and (e) it permits participants to rehearse their behavior in a safe setting that provides some reality, and yet permits some new ideas to be tried without fear of making errors.

Limitations of the role-play strategy are: the reluctance, discomfort, or embarrassment that may accompany many initial efforts incorporating drama; its time-consuming preparation and debriefing; and its lack of effectiveness unless actors have some background information to help them improvise how the character they are playing would typically behave in the scenario.

As was the case with the other student-centered methods described in this handbook, however, competent instructors work at preventing most of these potential difficulties from arising by carefully ensuring that: (a) the emotional climate is respectful and secure; (b) the purpose of the activity, its relevance to the course, and the procedures to be followed by players, audience, observers, and evaluators are all clearly understood; (c) the actors are chosen sensitively; and (d) the whole-class debriefing period is thorough and beneficial.

Examples of role-plays are: participating in an interview, enacting a business transaction, conducting a telephone conversation, counseling a supervisee, supervising a worker, negotiating a contract, hiring or firing an employee, or participating in a dialogue.

Simulations.[61] A simulation is similar to a role-play, but is typically longer and more complex. One of its purposes is to prepare participants for a future "actual" position in their work or career. It represents a real-world situation as closely as possible, and it helps people experience the consequences of their actions.

In a simulation, the learner becomes actively engaged in applying previously learned material. Being an artificial situation with authentic characteristics, it excludes the possibility of serious risk that could be present with an actual incident.

Benefits of the simulation approach are that: (a) it motivates participants and observers; (b) it enhances cognitive and skill development in problem-solving and decision-making situations, and helps reduce prior negative attitudes related to such areas; (c) it reduces complicated processes into manageable portions that can be practiced; (d) it can be used to assess participants' application of knowledge and performance; (e) it sensitizes individuals to the values and experiences of others; and (f) the "self-feedback" it provides is often very valuable.

Possible *disadvantages* of simulations are that: they are more time-consuming and complicated than role-plays; their effectiveness depends on how "real" they can be made, and on how meaningful the concluding discussion is for participants;

players and observers must know the subject well, in order to gain maximum benefit from the activity; and such simulations will not produce successful results unless both instructor and participants are willing to invest considerable effort: "they are not a soft option...they take more time than preparing a lecture."[62]

Thus, simulations are more rare than other forms of student-centered methods in adult education, but where they are employed, effective instructors implement the following guidelines:

1. They recognize that simulation activities function most effectively in courses that study where crisis decisions must be made, or where best solutions on issues must be selected (e.g., business administration, collective bargaining, counseling/therapy sessions, health sciences problems, teacher/student or employer/employee relations, or any type of training simulation that involves problem-resolution or crisis-intervention).

2. They ensure that participants know the procedures to be followed: how to identify and analyze the issues involved (and their underlying assumptions); how to formulate, pose, and answer questions about these areas; how to find and weigh evidence; how to ensure equitability, justice, and ethical conduct; and how to mount a strong defense of decisions.

3. They conduct the debriefing session carefully, permitting participants to explain how they arrived at their decisions, and encouraging others to inquire and probe regarding some of the details of their thinking.

4. They follow a clear format that includes such steps as: (a) providing a clear introduction and background to the whole group regarding the activity; (b) dividing the class into several groups, each receiving one role to play and a specific task to follow; (c) forming new groups composed of individuals representing each one of the different role-tasks; (d) instructing each new group to work through the inevitable conflict to arrive at a best decision; and (d) to spend time in the large group investigating the decision process—exploring individuals' and small-groups' planning and strategic procedures, discussing

difficulties that arose, and reporting what information was useful and what was missing.

Particular examples of simulation experiences that proficient instructors have incorporated into their courses are: in Business Administration simulating a corporation's board of directors' meeting where a range of interests are prominent; in Education simulating a faculty council deciding on who to hire for dean; in Communications simulating a student-council meeting deciding how to make policy concerning individuals on campus with disabilities; in Chemistry simulating an undergraduate class "playing" various elements in chemical reactions, and how they combine into compounds; in Educational Administration, simulating a school-board meeting to formulate policy on the use of prayer and Bible readings in schools; or in Psychology, simulating a group-therapy session for troubled adolescents.

Research[63] has indicated that transfer of learning positively occurs when teachers have effectively combined several of these student-centered strategies: simulation, role-play, modeling appropriate behaviors by the instructor, and small-group assignments (accompanied by specific feedback for these groups). The effect of any one of these activities on transfer was much less than was the synergistic result of combining several of them.

Other Strategies

A fourth grouping of student-centered experiences that successful teachers occasionally incorporate into their coursework consists of small-group projects, discovery and inquiry activities, and problem-solving sessions.[64]

Again, the purpose of implementing these activities is not simply to use variety, per se, (although such a reason is not invalid), but in order to enhance students' motivation to increase their knowledge and/or skills in the subject, to cater to the range of learning styles and development levels that are inevitably present in any group of undergraduate learners, and to help instructors avoid becoming stagnant in their own professional teaching practice.

Many of those activities can be done individually or collaboratively: competent instructors intersperse these learning activities throughout the term's work—in areas where they see them fitting best.

Projects. Projects may take the form of assigned tasks, papers, reports, readings, case studies or presentations that students are to complete with respect to various parts of the course. A key purpose of such projects is to permit learners to delve into an area of interest in the content more intensively.

The *advantages* of such projects are: that students can study a specific area more thoroughly; that they can experience a change-of-pace from the regular course routines; and that—if it culminates in an oral presentation or demonstration in front of the large-group—students will experience both the discomfort and the subsequent satisfaction of publicly presenting some of their work.

Potential *hazards* of the project method are that: it may consume more of the students' time and effort than it is worth (i.e., in terms of percentage of the course grade); and the provision of feedback may not be appropriately timed for maximum student benefit—particularly if it is not given until the end of the term.

To help eliminate these trouble spots, experienced instructors do three things: (a) they ensure that the project has clear instructions, that it is task-oriented, and that the task is straight-forward; (b) they provide a time-limit and clarify the criteria and expectations by which it will be evaluated; and (c) they make themselves available to answer questions, to clarify points, and to provide periodic formative (i.e., ongoing) assessment of students' progress.

Discovery, inquiry and problem-solving. Effective instructors design independent or small-group projects, or shorter assignments, that take the form of discovery or inquiry activities or problem-solving sessions.

These types of activities present a relevant or interesting problem that students are requested to resolve, through specifically defining the problem, designing procedures for seeing solutions, searching for data, analyzing the data and creating probable solutions, verifying these solutions, and reaching plausible conclusions or generalizations.

Occasionally, the instructor's motivational set for a class-period might be stated as a puzzling question posed to the class that is to answered by students during the session by their engagement in a combination of teaching and learning activities.

When the instructor states the objectives for a particular lesson, he/she will *not* state what the learners are "going to learn"—since students are expected to "discover" the learning outcomes by the end of that period. Yet, the objectives should always be stated clearly and concisely at the beginning of every class-session—as emphasized in Chapter 3. Therefore, when stating the objectives for an inquiry or discovery session with a group of TAs, for instance, an effective instructor may say something like this: "Today, you will discover, by conducting this series of investigation activities, the similarities and differences between using 16mm film and VHS video as motion media in your teaching, and you will discover their respective advantages and disadvantages."

For example, in this scenario, the instructor will have prepared several "stations" in the communications laboratory. Each station has a stack of printed questions on handouts and is equipped with short "teaching" episodes recorded either on a 16mm film or a video-cassette that: (a) tells students how to load, view, and unload the respective machines, and (b) helps answer the print questions, some of which require individual TA reflection about their own teaching context.

Thus, as pairs or small groups of students proceed from station-to-station at timed intervals, they are not only learning how to operate the various types of media equipment, but they may also collaborate on the higher order cognitive categories of Bloom's Taxonomy.

Hence, the original objectives or question presented as the initial motivational set in this session gradually unfolds as the students complete the inquiry and "discover" the responses or resolve the problem.

Effective instructors are careful to mix the levels of questions in the inquiry exercise so as to require students to articulate their understanding of processes, to apply immediately their newly acquired knowledge, to analyze carefully, and to synthesize and assess their (and their partners') reasoning.

Further, they ensure that students know that the problem-solving or inquiry activity is not only connected clearly to the course goals, but they explicitly explain the purpose of the investigation and how it will benefit students (e.g., to succeed in the present course, or to lay a foundation for future courses in the discipline, or to be more skilled in their chosen career.)

Instructors who are effective at incorporating these inquiry activities into their courses identify the following *advantages* of the method: it is motivating for learners; students participate and use complex thinking; they employ a variety of resources (including each other, if group-work is involved); and it often promotes spontaneous and open-ended thinking and the creation of new ideas.

Two potential *limitations* are that to plan, prepare, monitor, and debrief the activity requires substantial time and effort. That is why many expert teachers incorporate this problem-solving approach selectively—not all of the time. They believe in its potency, but they also realize that employing any single teaching methodology will never guarantee effective results all the time: other strategies must be incorporated in order to capitalize on each one's respective benefits.

Traditional "laboratory investigations" generally do not generate genuine curiosity among students—rather they often become routine exercises for getting the right answers and a good "lab mark." On the other hand, exemplary instructors—at least some of the time—attempt to prompt students to raise some authentic questions that they would like to address or have addressed in class.

Sometimes, these teachers—in order to generate such questions—will request students to write down and submit, anonymously, questions like: "What puzzles you most about this topic?" or "What gave you the most difficulty in the lab (or reading, or lecture)?" or "What unfulfilled expectation can you report from this activity?" or "What was the 'muddiest' point for you in my presentation, today?"

Instructors then collect, collate, and analyze these questions, and address the major concerns during the next class-period.[65]

* * * * *

In this chapter I have described several methodologies that effective instructors incorporate into the teaching/learning process. Although most teachers use teacher-directed approaches much of the time (e.g., the lecture) proficient practitioners do not abuse or misuse it. On the contrary, they skillfully apply interactive elements to their presentations; and they thoughtfully employ a variety of student-centered activities at strategic points, both in their daily classes and also at key points throughout the term.

I have indicated throughout this chapter that the key reason they do so is not to give themselves" a break from teaching, while the students do group work," but rather to help quench the seemingly endless desire among effective teachers: (a) to make the course more interesting; (b) to increase learner motivation to develop their knowledge and skills; (c) to balance students' learning with their feeling of acceptance and support; and (d) to ground whatever instructional decisions they make in the foundational principles of effective instruction and ethical values (that were described in Chapter 1 of this handbook).

In Chapter 5 I attempt to tie the three essential instructional strands together (i.e., objectives, activities, and evaluation) by summarizing key strategies that exemplary instructors apply in assessing students' learning progress.

References

1. See, for example, Gage and Berliner (1992) and Notterman and Drewry (1993).

2. See Notterman and Drewry (1993) and Slavin (1994).

3. See Freiberg and Driscoll (1992), Jarvis (1995), Katz and Henry (1993), and McCown et al. (1996).

4. See Gage and Berliner (1992) and Jarvis (1995).

5. See Cashin (1990), Good and Brophy (1995), and Winzer (1995).

6. See, for example, Davis (1993), Jarvis (1995), McCown et al. (1996).

7. See Freiberg and Driscoll (1992), Good and Brophy (1995), and Jarvis (1995).

8. See Brookfield (1991), Davis (1993), and Lazar (1995).

9. See Freiberg and Driscoll (1992), Gage and Berliner (1992), Lambert et al. (1996) and Tierney (1996).

10. See Creed (1993), Davis (1993), and McCown et al. (1996).

11. See Davidson and Ambrose (1995), Dembo (1994), Katz and Henry (1993), "Lecturing myths" (1994), and Weimer (1998).

12. See Eble (1988), Good and Brophy (1995), and Marchese and Pollack (1993).

13. This anecdote was circulated orally at the fourth national Conference on the Training and Employment of Graduate Teaching Assistants, Chicago, November 11-13, 1993. See also McCown et al. (1996).

14. See Davis (1993), Stice (1987), and Weimer (1993, 1996d).

15. See Eble (1988), Frederick (1987), and Gage and Berliner (1992).

16. See Gage and Berliner (1992), Lambert et al. (1996), and McCown et al. (1996).

17. See Brooks (1987), Lambert et al. (1996), and Weaver and Cotrell (1987).

18. See, for example, Eble (1988), Gage and Berliner (1992), Good and Brophy (1995), and Winzer (1995).

19. See Bender et al. (1994), Frederick (1987), McCown et al. (1996), and Weaver and Cotrell (1987).

20. See Bender et al. (1994), Cashin (1990), Eble (1988), and Weaver and Cotrell (1987).

21. See Good and Brophy (1995); Heinich, Molenda, and Russell (1993); and Jarvis (1995).

22. See, for example, Ralph (1994a) and Ralph and Yang (1993).

23. See, for example, Bender et al. (1994) and Knapper (1987).

24. See Good and Brophy (1995, p. 275).

25. See, for example, Freiberg and Driscoll (1992), Gage and Berliner (1992), and Leinhardt (1995).

26. See Brookfield (1991), Freiberg and Driscoll (1992), and Gunter et al. (1995).

27. See Brookfield (1991), Gage and Berliner (1992), Huston (1997), and Waldron and Moore (1991).

28. See Dunkin and Barnes (1986), Gage and Berliner (1992), Kraft (1990), and Weimer (1990a, 1990b, 1990c).

29. See Jarvis (1995), Orlich et al. (1994), and Weimer (1993).

30. See, for example, Dillon (1983) and Freiberg and Driscoll (1992).

31. Dunkin and Barnes (1986) provide a good synthesis of some of these research findings.

32. Nunn (1996) gives a condensation of some of this research.

33. See Nunn (1996).

34. See the entire issue of *The Teaching Professor, 10* (7).

35. See Davidson and Ambrose (1995), Eble (1988), and McCown et al. (1996).

36. See, for example, Gage and Berliner (1992) and McCown et al. (1996).

37. See Abbott, Wulff, and Katiszego (1989); Jarvis (1995); Kraft (1990); and Waldron and Moore (1991).

38. See Gage and Berliner (19992), Huston (1997), Lazar (1995), and Weimer (1990a, 1990b, 1990c).

39. See Kraft (1990); Nyquist, Abbott, and Wulff (1989); and Weimer (1990a, 1990b, 1990c, 1993).

40. See Gage and Berliner (1992), Kraft (1990), Sternberg (1987), and Weimer (1990a, 1990b, 1990c, 1993, 1996a).

41. See, for example, Ralph (1995d, 1996a, 1997a).

42. See Elliott et al. (1996) and Orlich et al. (1994).

43. This incident is described in Palmer (1993, p. 9).

44. See Lazar (1995) and Morse (1995).

45. See, for example, Bruffee (1995), Guskey (1996), Slavin (1994), and Weimer (1997a, 1997b, 1997c).

46. See "New source" (1994), Raffini (1993), and Weimer (1996a,1996b, 1997a, 1997b, 1997c).

47. See, for example, Angelo, Seldin, Weimer, and Dotolo (1995); Hartz (1995); Jarvis (1995); and Lazar (1995).

48. See Angelo et. al. (1995) and Weimer (1996b).

49. See "New source" (1994).

50. See Weimer (1993, p. 58).

51. See, for example, Bender et al. (1994), Jarvis (1995), Orlich et al. (1994), and Waldron and Moore (1991).

52. See Bender et al. (1994) and Frederick (1987).

53. See, for example, Eble (1988), Frederick (1987), Gappa-Levi (1996), and Ralph (1997c).

54. See, for example, Eble (1988), Kelly (1976), and Ralph (1982, 1989, 1994d).

55. See Kelly (1976).

56. See Eble (1988, p. 13).

57. See Ralph (1982, 1989, 1995b).

58. See Ralph (1997c).

59. See Ralph (1995d, 1997a).

60. See Baughman (1974), Brookfield (1991), Jarvis (1995), and Waldron and Moore (1991).

61. See Brookfield (1991); Frederick (1987); Heinich, Molenda, and Russell (1993); and Jarvis (1995).

62. See Brookfield (1991, pp. 122-123).

63. See Freiberg and Driscoll (1992, p. 338).

64. For project work see Hyerle (1996) and Jarvis (1995). For discovery/inquiry activities see Barell (1991) and Katz and Henry (1993). For problem-solving ideas see Baron (1987) and Knapper (1987). For group-work see Angelo (1991a, 1991b) and Yamane (1997).

65. See, for example, Angelo (1991a), Angelo et al. (1995), and Mosteller (1989).

Chapter 5

ASSESSING LEARNERS' PROGRESS

In this chapter, I summarize essential evaluation strategies and practices that effective instructors employ to assess students' learning in their courses. However, before describing these methods, I first present definitions and key guidelines for conducting student evaluation—within which these teachers ground their various assessment practices. These basic guiding-premises are, themselves, also rooted in the fundamental principles of effective teaching and professional ethics that were presented in Chapter 1.

Some Key Definitions[1]

In this handbook, I use "assessment" and "evaluation" interchangeably, because they both refer to determining how well students are progressing in their learning. (Some educators, however, reserve the term evaluation for judgments made about the quality of instruction, the curriculum, the program, and the institution.)

"Grading" refers to the process of categorizing students into percentage, letter, or pass/fail grades—according to the assessment data.

An "examination" or "test" is a task, activity, or question (or set of questions) in which learners engage in order to demonstrate their level of accomplishment in meeting specified learning objectives.

The key purposes of assessment are: (a) to provide feedback to students and the instructor on the students' learning progress in achieving the course objectives—and consequently, on the effectiveness of the entire teaching/learning process; and (b) to help guide future decisions about the process—both on the part of the instructor and the student.

Assessment practices encompass several dimensions: formal (e.g., "official" examinations) and informal (e.g., anecdotal and observational data); formative (e.g., how learners continue to develop) and summative (e.g., how learners have developed);

norm-referenced (e.g., how students compare with each other) and criterion-referenced (e.g., how they compare to pre-established objectives); and teacher- (the instructor conducts all the evaluation), and self- and peer-evaluation (students evaluate their own and each other's work).

The five guidelines that successful instructors typically incorporate into their evaluation practices are described below.

Part 1: Five Basic Guidelines of Assessment[2]

1. Congruence of Evaluation With Objectives and Activities

As I have noted throughout this handbook, effective instructors ensure that the procedures and activities utilized to evaluate students' learning progress demonstrate consistency with both the learning objectives of the course, and the various teaching/learning tasks and activities in which learners engage in the class. These teachers are adamant that all three components of the instructional process must be parallel: "the tests of performance" must reflect what students have been doing and learning throughout the term. Practicing anything other than this arrangement is not only indefensible, but it is unprofessional and unethical.

This is illustrated in Figure 5.1.

2. Integration of Evaluation and Learning

All assessment activity should be an integral part of the learning process—not isolated nor independent from it. Exemplary teachers insist that whether the assessment activity is of the formative (i.e., providing ongoing, cumulative feedback to learners on their performance to help them develop their knowledge and skills) or of the summative type (i.e., typically providing them with formal feedback on their achievement at key junctures in the course, such as at mid-term or term-end), they both must reflect the natural and logical extension of what students have been practicing and learning throughout the course.

An effective assessment activity makes an effective teaching/learning activity, and vice versa: nearly any task used for one may be used for the other.[3]

3. Utilization of Both "Traditional" and Authentic Assessment

Proficient instructors recognize the deficiencies of the conventional method of student evaluation (i.e., the end-of-term marathon of several 3-hour written final examinations, for which students cram, regurgitate, then forget). Although—by virtue of the administrative bureaucracy by which higher-education operates—it is unlikely that these traditional procedures, as we know them, will be eliminated.

However, skilled instructors adjust the evaluation process, so that students are not trapped into demonstrating what they do not know, but given the opportunity to show what they do know. Exemplary instructors: explicitly describe the evaluation criteria and standards early in the term; ensure that students

Figure 5.1. Effective instructors ensure congruency between learning objectives, activities, and assessment.

understand exactly what they are to learn or be able to do for each class-session and for each evaluation task; gather a variety of evaluation data for each learner, in order to arrive at a cumulative and composite picture of his/her learning accomplishments; and clearly identify for learners their particular strengths and weaknesses—and how they could improve the latter.

They employ both print-based evaluations (e.g., term papers, reports, examinations, quizzes, and other written assignments) and performance-based or authentic assessments.

Authentic assessment,[4] a recent term that refers to what many educators from a variety of fields have long practiced (e.g., in the arts, industrial and technological training, second-language acquisition, health sciences education, teacher training, preparation for social work/counselling/ psychotherapy, education in the animal and crop sciences, training in physical education, or preparation in architecture, engineering, and other professional schools and colleges), refers to the process of evaluating how well learners perform realistic tasks that require a transfer of their newly acquired knowledge and skills to different situations.

These "authentic" tasks being evaluated would reflect, as closely as possible, the actual conditions that learners would encounter as they would apply their skills in real-world contexts. In particular, they would have to make wise and informed judgments on how to adjust their performance according to unique situational factors. Thus, traditional evaluation tasks and tests are somewhat analogous to drills in athletics, scales in music, or exercises in second-language learning; whereas performance tasks and tests are like actual sports games, real music recitals, or authentic conversations with native speakers of the target language.[5]

Assessing this type of authentic activity provides a more reliable picture of what the student actually knows and is able to do, concerning the subject in question. In this light, the traditional written examination that often seeks to measure students' low-order thinking, memorization of facts, and solving of "textbook-type" problems, is found wanting.

In the field of second-language acquisition, for instance, (an area in which I have had experience as a student, a teacher, and an administrator), the current emphasis on authentic learning *and* evaluation activities illustrates how productive such a philosophy can be. Instead of assessing students' mastery of second-language grammar rules and ability to read, write, and translate (skills which are commendable and needed for specific situations), effective teachers immediately have students—at whatever age they may be—to begin to use (listen, speak, read, and write) the target language to communicate in lifelike situations.

Of course, beginning learners are not fluent at first, but through successive approximations and continual practice (with appropriate feedback), students acquire more sophistication in their usage of the target language. That is not to say that learners do not spent time on the traditional "pattern and drill exercises," but the emphasis is on constructing and practicing meaningful and relevant conversation to meet realistic objectives: talking on the telephone, going shopping, going to the dentist, travelling, or ordering a restaurant meal.

Thus, proficient instructors who implement principles of authentic learning and assessment in their courses—for any subject—ensure that *both* the learning activities *and* the evaluation tasks are similar: students *do* what will be *tested*, and they are *tested* on what they have *done*.

4. Combination of Low- and High-Ordered Cognition

Skillful instructors ensure that they create learning and evaluation activities for students, which blend both low-order thinking with high-order cognitive skills. Learners obviously need a grasp of the basic facts and concepts fundamental to any field of knowledge; but they also must be challenged, prompted, and stimulated to progress in their development.

As I have described earlier in this handbook, effective teachers are skilled at tactfully balancing both the "task" dimension, with the "support" aspect in providing motivational activities for students in their courses. Moreover, these activities must be seen by students as being relevant, interesting, and helpful to them, in their personal lives.

5. Establishing Fairness and Excellence in Assessment

Exemplary instructors build a reputation among students and faculty-peers, alike, that their instructional techniques (including their assessment instruments and processes) are both interesting and fair. They design both the learning and the evaluation strategies for *validity* (i.e., the extent that the activities assess what they are supposed to assess: or, again, that the objectives, the tasks, and the evaluations are all aligned) and for *reliability* (i.e., accuracy and consistency of results covering a range of similar activities over time).

Because these instructors emphasize authentic learning and evaluation, then both the daily assignments *and* the periodic "tests" concentrate on the same type of learning experiences. Thus, in this context, "teaching to the test" is a concept that is not to be abhorred, but to be pursued.

When students understand that the three components of instruction—the objectives, the learning tasks, and the evaluation of learning—are so intimately integrated, and that each one mutually affects, and is affected by, the others; then they typically concur that the instructor, the course, and the assessment process offer activities that are both relevant and challenging, and equitable and satisfying, as well.

It becomes clear to everyone involved that the assessment tasks assist in guiding their learning, as much as they do in judging it.

Some Examples of Authentic Assessment[6]

Authentic assessment is also known as alternative assessment, direct assessment, process testing, and performance assessment. It seeks to evaluate learners' actual display or demonstration of the skills and the knowledge internalized in a course—as articulated by the course or class-period's objectives: if the course is about singing and playing musical instruments, the evaluation should not be conducted with multiple-choice questions; if about repairing computers, the test should not be an essay-type; if about administering CPR, the assessment should not be paper and pencil exam; if about developing literary discrimination, the assessment should not test students' lower-order knowledge of details of Shakespeare's plays; if about diagnosing and treating orthodontic patients in dentistry,[7] the final examination should not be entirely of a sit-down reading and writing type held in a gymnasium with 700 other students.

However, I hasten to add two key points to this discussion. The first is the fact that the objectives of certain courses and programs may concentrate on students' reading, writing, logic, reasoning, analytical, synthesis, and evaluation abilities. In this type of program, the learning objectives, the course activities, and the assessment strategies may *all* be best conducted via reading/writing activities and instruments—rather than, for instance, in the physical-education gym where volleyball referees are engaged in a workshop and clinic on their officiating skills.

The second point I re-emphasize is that in many courses, good instructors use a combination of authentic and traditional assessment strategies. Incorporating this blended plan is, in itself, a motivating feature of the course for students—because it allows them the opportunity to have a range of assessment activities included in their final grade, rather than having to depend on only one or two "readings" of their achievement. Not only that, but some effective instructors are also skilled in constructing pen-and-paper tests that do measure higher-order cognitive processes, as well. (Some examples are provided in Part 2 of this chapter.)

* * * * *

Using the above guidelines and principles of sound assessment as a foundation, effective instructors construct a variety of evaluation activities and instruments to use in their courses. In Part 2 of this chapter, I summarize basic strategies and practices they follow in this construction process, and I provide some specific examples of these instruments, as well.

Part 2: Assessment Strategies and Practices

Exemplary instructors outline in the course syllabus on the first day of class the standards, criteria, and tasks by which learners will be evaluated. They are explicit about: what students are to learn and be able to do; how they will be required to demonstrate their achievement of these objectives; what expectations the instructor has for this performance; and how it will be evaluated and graded.

Typically, good teachers implement a variety of types of assessment tasks throughout the term; and as emphasized in Part 1 of this chapter, they will create a blend of authentic performance events and traditional types, such as term papers or other written tasks, individual and group projects, formal examinations, short quizzes, oral presentations, student "clinical" demonstrations, laboratory investigations, performances, or portfolios (i.e., collections of students' work collected over a period of time) — some of which are described elsewhere in this manual.

For analytical and reflective purposes, I organize the assessment strategies and activities into three categories: performance tasks, longer written activities, and shorter written tasks. Before describing how experienced instructors create and implement these strategies, I present five keys to the incorporation of effective learning and assessment tasks, which themselves are based on the foundational principles described both in Chapter 1 of this manual and in Part 1 of the present chapter.

Keys to Implementing Effective Learning and Assessment Activities[8]

1. **Clarity of purpose.** Experienced teachers explicitly link all class assignments, readings, practical or clinical experiences, evaluation tasks, and other coursework to the course's goals and to the particular class period's learning objectives. They clearly explain the rationale behind, and the directions for, each task —and specifically how it will be evaluated with respect to concrete criteria, standards, expectations, and worth—both in terms of grade or point value and of the accrued benefits of learning it.

2. **Variety of samples.** Good instructors not only divide the material to be learned into manageable segments but they require learners to practice the specific skills, or put the knowledge to immediate use by applying it to new situations or transferring it to novel circumstances. Furthermore, the teachers arrange these application sessions in order that learners will encounter a range of experiences that will both solidify and yet challenge their developmental levels. Students will use both

lower order (i.e., knowledge and comprehension) and higher order thinking skills (i.e., application, analysis, synthesis, and evaluation) in an assortment of relevant and meaningful learning tasks.

3. Appropriate feedback. Individuals do not learn simply by practicing; they must also receive feedback about their progress. In keeping with the basic principles emphasized throughout this manual, proficient instructors ensure that learners are provided with positive reinforcement and constructive criticism relevant to their performance of the skills being learned.

As explained in previous sections, this feedback may take the form of: (a) oral praise, gestures, facial expressions, nods, smiles or other body language; (b) formal written comments and/or grades; (c) peer-evaluation given orally or by check-list or rating scale form; or (d) through students' own self-reflection and self-appraisal.

Effective instructors do not respond with too much nor too little observational and evaluatory data: they endeavour to provide concise and accurate commentary in order to assist learners to develop their competence and confidence in the learning task.

Effective feedback meets that following criteria: it guides, not blames; it describes an individual's personal progress, not how far there is left to go; it is specific, not general; it is generally welcomed by learners, not ignored; it describes a student's level of accomplishment, not merely a simplistic comparison with "the average"; and it ascertains the quality of the performance, not the difficulty level of the task.[9]

4. Evaluation as motivation. Experienced instructors capitalize on the motivating power of assessment, testing, and grading. Both research[10] and anecdotal evidence reported by most educators confirm that, in general, testing and the expectations resulting from the grading process positively affect the study habits of learners, and improve their performance.

When students know that the assessment tasks are relevant both to the course and to their personal lives, and when they know that the instructor has shown professional credibility and personal authenticity in his/her teaching, then they do

not see the evaluation activities as threatening or meaningless—but rather as an opportunity to demonstrate what they
have learned or are able to do. Effective assessment experiences
should thus lead to feelings of success among learners.[11]

5. **Sensible, sensitive decisions.** Instructors who are
deemed as expert practitioners base their instructional and
evaluatory decisions on the principle of fairness and impartiality. Not only do they appraise samples of students' performance
in an equitable manner, but their assessment standards are set
so that all participants can achieve satisfactory results with a
reasonable effort.

If students perceive that "This prof is easy" they feel that
they are not really working to their potential. On the other
hand, if standards are consistently too difficult, then all but the
most persistent learners may become frustrated, discouraged,
and resentful. Yet, "grade inflation" by instructors does not
necessarily motivate learners.

Good instructors are not reluctant to provide honest feedback to students for low performance or shoddy work. They help
students to learn from their errors; they use assessment and
grading to inform learning (and teaching); and they administer
criticism succinctly and positively—without demeaning the
learner.

I now describe how proficient instructors implement some
typical strategies in the three assessment categories.

Performance Tasks[12]

One category of learning and assessment activities that
respected instructors implement in their teaching are authentic
or performance tasks. As explained in previous sections of this
book, these types of activities focus on students' application of
higher order thinking skills to resolve problems from real-world
contexts.

In these tasks—whether practiced by students as they
internalize the new knowledge and skills embedded within
these activities, or whether these tasks are performed after
students have had considerable experience using them—learners demonstrate their learning under the conditions (or as

similar as possible to them) in which the newly acquired knowledge and skills are normally applied.

These performance-tasks, practicum-sessions, clinical-experiences, apprenticeships, internships, articling experiences, or in-service training sessions have been incorporated in various ways in many disciplines: the health sciences, agriculture and the animal sciences, education, counselling, social work, law, business administration, and industrial and technological training. They are also used in professional-development workshops and initiatives to help new instructors at the post-secondary level develop their teaching competence (for which purpose I have written this manual).

Thus, there is nothing necessarily new nor profound in this process of authentic assessment; but I stress that effective teachers of *all* disciplines are well able to apply it, in at least *some* form, in their courses.

Certainly, some of these authentic tasks may not be restricted to non-pencil-and-paper activities (e.g., recitals, sports events, exhibits, expositions, displays, demonstrations, simulations, oral presentations, role-plays, dramas, interviews, dialogues, debates, panels, speeches, micro-teaching, training-sessions, counseling sessions, doing a procedure, or creating/inventing/ producing an object/process/event). They may well include *some* of the traditional learning and evaluation methods that can be used by students to demonstrate what they are able to *do* and what they have learned—particularly, if the course focuses on such skills (e.g., mathematics, design, logic and reasoning, reading/writing/ composing, or preparing for discussion/debate/argument).

Furthermore, exemplary instructors recognize that the implementation of the three strategies is often an integrated process: that "performance" may include traditional print and other media; and, as well, that the psychomotor and visual dimensions are often a part of the conventional written assignments and tests.

Whether instructors implement the performance task as a learning or as an evaluation experience, they make certain that the following criteria are met:

1. **Realistic encounters.** The task addresses actual questions or concerns that are faced by professionals in the field or

by individuals in their daily living. An example from a French-as-a-second-language course is for students to watch and to understand a French movie and to be able to participate in a meaningful discussion of it using French that reflects the developmental level at which they are.

2. **Life-like contexts.** Authentic learning and assessment tasks should be conducted—to the extend that is feasible—in an actual situation representative of the realistic conditions that normally occur. An example from the field of medical education would be to have a medical intern-resident to display her actual teaching skills, and to have her supervisor and/or peers observe (and assess) her performance (according to pre-established criteria that she and her colleagues have been studying in an instructional-improvement workshop).[13]

This teaching episode could be with a five-year-old patient and his family-members, as the resident explains the patient's recuperation process and discusses what the child and the family will do during the recovery period.

3. **Complex problems.** Authentic learning deals with non-routine issues that are often ambiguous, complex, open-ended, and "messy"—unlike many of the rather artificial questions that traditional "in-class" assignments or textbook problems address. An example from the field of Business Administration could be a group-project to provide a set of alternate solutions for the board of directors of a local business organization to consider as they seek the resolution of an actual issue regarding their future corporate expansion. (Such authentic projects are regularly assigned to groups of students by a university's faculty of commerce instructors in conjunction with local business and industrial firms, who formally apply to a campus-based program in order to receive professional assistance in resolving actual dilemmas that they encounter in the routines of business life.)

4. **Clear standards.** Exemplary instructors who routinely incorporate authentic learning tasks into their courses explicitly describe how each task will be assessed, so that all people involved know precisely what is expected, what criteria will be

used to judge the process and/or product, and how it will be graded.

Effective instructors provide and explain the specific sets of indicators, check-lists, rating scales, and assessment forms that will be used to evaluate students' progress. They also provide for student practice in using the instruments, in order to help participants both to give and to receive feedback.

Not only this, but these teachers also make provision for negotiating (within institutional guidelines) certain aspects of the course tasks—according to the unique context of individual students. The students, therefore, have opportunity for a degree of input and "ownership" in the process.

An example from the field of Communications could be the opportunity for students to present, individually, a brief "microteaching" episode in front of their small-group, in which they teach a mini-lesson of 10-minutes duration that is recorded on video-tape, and in which the person's peers serve as students participating in the lesson.

One of the small-groups from the whole class would sit at the back of the room and evaluate this teaching/learning session, using assessment forms selected by the person doing the microteaching. (The skills shown on these forms would have been previously studied and practiced by all students in the large class. This series of evaluation instruments might provide assessment criteria or check-list ratings for such skills as "presenting," "questioning," "responding," "creating climate," and so on—as described earlier in this manual.)

At the conclusion of the microteaching, the participants who played the role of "students" would give either oral or written feedback to "the teacher" on his/her performance, and the evaluators from the back would likewise provide the practitioner with assessments of the "teacher's" performance. Finally, the individual would perform a self-appraisal of his/her microteaching after considering this peer-feedback, the video-recording of his/her performance, and his/her own feelings about the entire process.

5. **A collaborative effort.** In these types of alternative learning and assessment tasks, successful instructors demonstrate their openness to interact with the learner. Thus, the learners would be prepared to defend and justify their decisions

and actions about their performance in the task, and the instructors would provide learners with appropriate feedback before, during, and after the activity. One purpose of the latter might be to assist novice practitioners to adjust planned procedures to meet unforeseen contingencies that arise within the context of the actual situation.

An example of such collaboration is from the discipline of Counseling Psychology, in which a student is doing a "practicum" by co-counseling with her supervisor in a series of group-counseling sessions with a group of junior-high school aged students. Two of these students' classmates had recently died in a car accident, and the two counsellors are attempting to help the group work through the grieving process.

Between counselling sessions the practicum student and her supervisor not only discuss and plan their upcoming counselling sessions and procedures, but they feel free to question each other and respond to why or why not they said certain things in the sessions; or to explore how and why they would conduct an intended activity with the group the next day.

6. A flexible process. Unlike the traditional examination situation authentic assessment tasks provide opportunity for ongoing evaluator/evaluatee communication, and the possible adjustment of a final assessment if circumstances warrant, or if the appraiser happened to be negligent in a part of his/her judgment.

Because of the flexibility built into these learning and evaluation situations, such adjustment is possible — without sacrificing any of the integrity of the process or the credibility of the participants, and without requiring the participants to endure a lengthy, formal appeal process through the institutional bureaucracy.

The example in the previous section illustrates how this principle of flexibility may operate.

7. A variety of samples. When effective instructors use authentic learning and assessment tasks in their teaching, they combine them with an assortment of other appropriate activities that are congruent with the foundational principles underlying effective and ethical teaching and motivation of learning. Thus, rather than basing their assessment of students' learning achievement on one or two major writing tasks (e.g., the final exam and a term paper), instructors not only recognize that students have multiple strengths, but they also ensure that students have opportunity to practice and apply their developing knowledge and skills in diverse contexts, under varying conditions, and through assorted activities.

Sometimes, instructors will have students collect a series of assignments and products they have completed over the term —along with evidence of students' reflection on their learning in this area—and have them produce a "portfolio" or a "process folio."[14]

A portfolio is a multimedia collection of finished samples of a student's work that focuses on documentation of the scope of his/her achievements and their quality. A process folio, on the other hand, reflects the ongoing learning and creating activities that the learner has undertaken. It would contain such items as first drafts of writing or other tasks, documentation of difficulties (and the resolution of them), other works-in-progress, and evidence of the students' reflection on his/her progress in the course.

Both folios or kits would also contain evidence of students' self-evaluation of their own performance, and they could also include documentation received from other individuals that attest to some facet of the students' accomplishments in the course.

If instructors incorporate folio evaluation into their courses, they also plan so that students would engage in these tasks from the beginning of the course and throughout its duration, and with progressively developing sophistication. Throughout this process, instructors would also observe and assess consistent trends and patterns in students' performance and responses— rather than observing solely for discrete measurements of single events. This process further emphasizes "a shift from a snapshot metaphor to the cinematic metaphor."[15]

* * * * *

In summary,[16] the *advantages* of performance tasks are that: (a) they permit instructors to take into consideration the diversity of student talents and abilities; (b) they focus on meaningful, relevant, and motivational activities; (c) they provide for development and refinement of students' task-specific competence and confidence; and (d) they require increasing levels of student self-appraisal skills.

Disadvantages of authentic learning and assessment activities are that: (a) they are time-consuming to devise, prepare, and conduct; (b) they require careful planning and plentiful resources, in terms of organizational and logistical arrangement, space and equipment, materials and support services, personnel, and persistent effort by all participants; (c) they require explicitly stated instructions, procedures, and assessment criteria—together with provision for flexible and sensitive adjustment; and (d) they necessitate detailed observation and assessment procedures and instruments to ensure thorough and fair evaluation.

Many effective teachers are willing to expend this degree of energy on some of their coursework activities in order to enhance students' internalization of the new material, and to help improve their own instructional practice.

Longer Written-Projects (e.g., Term Papers and Essays)[17]

A second category of learning and assessment activities consists of tasks of the more traditional nature: those for which students compose a written response or create a document. It may take the form of an essay, a term-paper, or any language composition using the medium of the printed (or handwritten) words. This writing task may be done "in class," in "out-of-class" time, or in a formal examination situation; it may stand alone or may be part of a larger assignment or project; and it may be used for student self-reflective purposes, or for submission to the instructor to be formally assessed and graded for the course.

In the case of formal assessment of longer written material —whether as a course assignment or as an examination question —effective instructors follow these guidelines: the writing task is clearly described; the assessment criteria and grading scheme are fully explained; students understand the relevance of the assignment, and how it connects to the course's learning objectives (and to its meaning outside of the class); and practical suggestions (e.g., resources to be used) and an example of a model piece are provided for students' reference.

Good instructors ensure that the longer writing tasks require students to demonstrate higher-order thinking process: the lower-order skills can be measured using objective-type tasks. In testing situations, instructors give several shorter essay questions rather than a single long one, because the former can sample a wider range of student thinking and creativity. Moreover, instructors would ensure that each question has one major focus, not several; and that the questions reflect the key learning objectives of the course.

The *strengths* of well-designed longer writing tasks are that they:

1. assess learners' higher levels of cognition, self-expression, organizational abilities, and writing skills;
2. are valuable for formative assessment purposes, in that students can gain insight into their writing and thinking strengths and deficiencies, and learn to improve the latter;
3. are relatively easy to construct; and
4. can provide more information about what a student has learned, than that provided by multiple-choice or short-answer tasks.

The *weaknesses* of these longer writing tasks (and how effective teachers seek to eliminate them) are described below.

1. Scoring is time-consuming and often notorious for being unreliable. To compensate for these limitations, effective instructors prepare answer-keys for each response, showing the values to be given for the various components of the answer. Also, they attempt to assess the papers without knowing the writers' names; and for examinations, they arrange to grade the same question for everyone at one time, rather than completing each students' entire exam before going on to the next paper in the stack.

To improve scoring reliability for term papers, many competent instructors read all papers twice: the first, reading is done fairly quickly in order to classify each paper into one of three or four categories (excellent, good, weak, and poor); and the second reading is to be more precise and to provide specific feedback.

Since students' writing-skills are important, some instructors give two grades on a written assignment: one for language mechanics, grammar, and neatness; and one for the content and logical presentation. They then mathematically combine the two grades, depending on the course and its objectives (e.g., an equal weighting, or an offset scale, such as 3:2, 2:3, 4:1, and so on).

To reduce the problem of tedium in scoring, expert instructors ensure that they explicitly inform students of the expected length of the writing, of the necessity to be concise, and of the number of points to be awarded for each piece—and how these points, in turn, will be awarded.

They also use a model answer to guide their grading—but they may at times incorporate a global or holistic evaluation scheme. (Here, instructors read a response and—by virtue of their accumulated experience—are able to generate a relatively reliable overall score for the response. They may still use an appropriate model or overall scale (e.g., 5 would mean "this is publishable", 3 would mean "equivalent to what a normal 3rd year student produces", and so forth).

2. Longer writing assignments may be misused if they concentrate on low-level cognitive tasks (e.g., recall of memorized facts); or if they attempt to assess students' performance or demonstration skills through writing—rather than to evaluate their actual doing of the task (e.g., having medical students write an essay on "starting an I.V." versus observing them as they perform the actual procedure).

Experienced instructors, therefore, use a variety of evaluation practices, but they ensure that these assessment techniques match the skill and knowledge being examined.

3. Longer written-tasks are limited in that they sample a reduced range of the course's objectives, because they tend to be more intensive than extensive in scope—compared to short answer activities or multiple-choice tests that can sample a greater number of objectives and topics. This disadvantage can be eliminated when instructors use a variety of assessment tasks throughout the term. At the same time, however, they are careful not to assign too many diverse tasks, nor ones that are too lengthy. For instance, with tests, assigning several shorter

essays will sample students' learning more adequately, and thus yield a more reliable score,[18] than evaluating only one essay.

4. Reliability of grading essays and papers may be contaminated by such extraneous factors as: "the halo-effect" (i.e., a student's reputation or personality may influence the evaluator's assessment); the writer's penmanship and language mechanics; the grader's biases; and the general inconsistency of assessments even done by the same evaluator.

Some poorly constructed essay items are shown in Appendix C.

As I mentioned earlier, effective instructors not only are aware of these potential limitations, but they are proactive in taking measures to prevent them from arising. They first establish the grading criteria and values for each piece and they abide by them consistently as they assess each paper, regardless of other impinging conditions. If they are in doubt about a marginal grade, they will seek a second opinion from a colleague; or, if that is not possible, they will tend to err on the side of leniency.

Shorter Written-Tasks[19]

In this third category of learning and assessment activities, I categorize such tasks and objective tests as the supply type (i.e., short-answer or completion), and the selection type (i.e., multiple-choice, matching, and binary types—True/False, Yes/No, or Right/Wrong).

Short-answer or completion.[20] These types of questions lend themselves to measuring students' knowledge and recall abilities, of the what? who? when? and where? variety. They require a single-word response, a longer phrase, or occasionally a brief answer of two or three sentences; and they are conducive to assessing students' knowledge of definitions, terms, facts, and basic concepts. However, expert instructors are also able to construct short-answer questions that demand higher-order thinking.

When incorporating short-answer questions, skilled instructors are careful to: (a) relate the questions to the learning objectives; (b) use clear, concise language; (c) construct the question to ensure that there is one correct response; (d) avoid trivial items; (e) place the blanks near the end of the sentences, use no more than two blanks per item, and make the blanks the same length; (f) avoid verbatim quotations from textbooks; (g) avoid giving clues or cues, and only omit key words (that form the answers to go in the blanks); (h) accept sensible, alternative responses; (i) and develop a large bank of possible questions to use as alternate questions from year to year, so that students cannot pass the information from one class to another.

Advantages of short-answer questions are that: they are easier to construct than the multiple-choice type and are easier to score than essay responses; they can provide insight into students' thinking skills, but are better for assessing low-order skills; they assess students' recall and supply skills, rather than mere recognition skills; and they provide more reliability and objectivity in scoring than do essay questions.

Disadvantages arise when instructors fail to construct the items according to the guidelines listed above.

Matching.[21] Matching questions are designed so that there are more responses (typically labelled with letters on the right-hand side of the page) than there are premises or questions (generally labelled with numbers on the left-hand side), in order to require students to apply their skills of reasoning and logic.

Usually, ten to fifteen stimulus items are listed on the left-side of a single page, with the fifteen to twenty responses listed on the right side. (Students should not be distracted by having to turn pages repeatedly as they search for answers). Teachers also arrange the questions in a logical order (e.g., alphabetical or chronological), and they ensure that the material being tested is of a homogenous nature.

The *advantages* of matching-type questions are that they: measure low-order knowledge, are relatively easy to construct and score, and assess learners' skills to discriminate and associate terms. *Disadvantages* are that: students can tell others of the questions, and the items do not assess higher order cognitive processes.

Thus, this question-type has limited usefulness because it focuses on discrete facts, rather than on complex or subtle types of knowledge and understanding.

That is not to say that humans do not need to master essential facts: where would we be, if we could not acquire the fundamental basics of knowledge in any field? Similarly, effective teachers make use of these objective-types of questions and tasks in their courses. They may or may not incorporate them in formal examinations, however; but they occasionally employ them for "an informal test," say, (a) at the beginning of a class—as a motivational set—to arouse attention, or to check learners' prior knowledge before a presentation; or (b) at the end, to provide a "post-test" of the learners' grasp of the material just presented.

Binary-type questions.[22] Binary items have only two choices: true/false, yes/no, right/wrong or +/-. Although there is little diagnostic value to such items, these types of questions are occasionally used by experienced instructors for introductory, review, or motivational purposes—as were the matching questions, above.

Binary questions may penalize divergent thinkers, who often are able to conceive of a case when something is not true (or false); thus, good instructors construct them to be entirely true or entirely false. They avoid double negatives in the wording; and for items that are absolutely true, they avoid including adverbs like "occasionally," "usually," or "seldom". For items that are unequivocally false, they avoid words, such as: "all," "none," or "never".

Good binary items are rather difficult to write but they are easy to score; and instructors can use them to cover much basic subject-matter in a short time. Because guessing can be a problem, some experienced teachers compensate by varying the responding or scoring procedures.

For instance, they sometimes instruct respondents to "correct a statement if it is false;" or, when scoring the items, they may attempt to offset the apparent simplicity of the questions by subtracting the number of the student's incorrect responses from his/her number of correct ones. However, this can be quite severe in that, for a 10-item test, 7 correct responses minus 3 incorrect ones yields a score of only 40 percent.

Thus, some instructors moderate this technique, somewhat, by subtracting one-half the number wrong from the number right. Therefore, for the person whose raw score was 7 out of 10, his/her final score would be 7 - 1 1/2 = 5 1/2. In other words, effective teachers are able to arrange the conditions so that sheer guessing is discouraged, and so that students will have to know the material.

In addition to following the above guidelines when constructing binary items, skilled instructors also ensure that the following criteria are met:

1. They write short, simple declarative sentences, or "If... then..." sentences.
2. Each item has one main idea and only one definite response.
3. They attribute statements of opinion to a source that is provided within the statement.
4. They avoid broad generalities or trivialities, and they avoid ambiguities.
5. They make all items approximately equivalent in length.
6. They use an equivalent number of binary (e.g., true and false) items.
7. They ensure that false statements appear plausible to individuals who are not familiar with the material.

Multiple-choice.[23] This item is the most versatile and commonly used objective-type question. Skilled instructors use it for assessing both lower- and higher-order cognitive skills. Multiple-choice type questions have been held in disrepute because critics decried their inability to assess other than trivial knowledge, but such is not the case. As with short-answer and completion items, competent teachers are able to construct multiple-choice items to assess comprehension-, application-, analysis-, synthesis-, and evaluation-level skills.

As was the case for all of the assessment tasks described to this point in the handbook, effective instructors compose multiple-choice questions according to established criteria, as described below:

1. They link each question to the learning objectives of the course.

2. They use: clear language, a common format, grammatical consistency, and standard length of items; and they place the bulk of the information for the question in the stem (i.e., the initial portion of the item).

3. They focus the question on a general rule or major concept, not on minor exceptions; and they make the options or responses plausible to anyone not having studied the content.

4. They tend to avoid: giving cues or clues either within the question, itself, or in other questions; overusing "all of the above" or "none of the above;" giving personal opinion; using verbatim, textual quotations; using the negative (but if they do, they underline it); or using "always" or "never" or employing trick questions. (Confusing or convoluted phraseology measures reading ability more than content understanding.)

5. They employ either a direct-question stem or an incomplete-statement stem. Also, they use the same number of alternative responses—of approximately the same length—for each question; and they arrange these alternatives in a logical order. Plus, they group questions on a specific topic together.

6. They typically construct the stem (i.e., the major component) first, then they write the correct response, followed by the distracters (i.e., the incorrect answers)—which, again, will seem plausible to the uninformed. The stem contains they key information and the problem, while the alternatives are clear and concise. Irrelevant material is omitted.

7. Instructors not only base the questions on the learning objectives for the course (i.e., What students are to *learn* or *be able to do*), but they set the number of questions to reflect the proportion of time spent on each topic. They also adjust the complexity of the questions to match students' developmental level: yet, they include a few to which almost everyone can respond correctly, as well as a few that will stretch the best students' cognitive abilities.

In general, however, exemplary instructors guard the balance between "too difficult and too easy," so that any student who exerts a reasonable effort in their work will achieve satisfactory results.[24]

Major *strengths* of multiple-choice questions are that they: (a) assess all levels of cognitive abilities, (b) sample the entire range of the course material, (c) are easy to score, (d) provide diagnostic information about students' level of understanding of specific topics; (e) permit a relatively rapid and accurate reading of students' comprehensive understanding of an entire course, and (f) provide an efficient and effective way of assessing the learning of a large number of students.

Four *limitations* of multiple-choice questions are identified below.

1. They do not assess students' ability to express, present, and defend their ideas, nor to demonstrate what and how they are able to create, compose, perform, or argue. Multiple-choice tasks focus on recognition of correct responses rather than on their production. (However, some students answer multiple-choice questions by, first of all, covering up all of the responses and then figuring out the correct answer by processing the information provided in the stem. After generating their correct response, they subsequently examine the given responses—as a verification to corroborate their own solution.)

2. They are difficult and time-consuming to construct. (In fact, some researchers[25] believe that a multiple-choice question that takes students' one minute to answer and teachers one second to score will take teachers one hour to design!).

3. They may not accurately assess learners' *actual* attitudes toward the course, because respondents may answer these types of questions in the way they think the instructor would want, or the way that would put themselves in the best light.

4. They are criticized as: being trivial, measuring only factual knowledge, promoting narrow thinking and "tunnel vision" (i.e., one correct answer), relying on memorization, and concentrating on "the basics." (Although effective instructors acknowledge that many of these misuses have occurred, they have also demonstrated that such weaknesses are not necessarily inherent in the item-type itself, but in the questionable manner with which some instructors have implemented it.)

The issue, therefore, is not whether or not to use multiple-choice—or any of the other objective-task or test items—but it is when and how to use them!

Because of the organizational and administrative policies and procedures that regulate the operation of post-secondary educational institutions, all instructors must determine a final grade for every student in their courses. How do effective teachers accomplish this task?

To answer this question, and as a means of distilling the description of the strategies and practices identified in this present chapter, I present a synthesized list of key principles that effective instructors use to guide their grading procedures.

1. **Recognition of complexity.** All teachers acknowledge that the process of combining the results of students' achievement for a disparate number of learning objectives in a course is a complicated task. Moreover, some instructors become quite cynical about the whole process: "Grading outstrips both intercollegiate athletics and intramural sports as the most frequently played game on the college campus."[27]

However, despite the challenges they encounter in seeking to arrive at an accurate grade that represents a learner's level of achievement in a course, exemplary instructors align and integrate their grading procedures with their planning and instructional processes, as well as with their core personal and ethical values about the entire teaching enterprise. I have emphasized this key premise throughout this handbook.

2. **Linking evaluation and objectives.** The cardinal rule of teaching to which excellent instructors adhere is to align the evaluation practices with the learning objectives and the teaching/learning experiences in a course — as explained in Chapter 3 of this manual. What students do and practice to achieve the intended objectives during the term of the course is congruent with what they do during the assessment activities: in fact, the two components may occasionally be one and the same task.

Competent instructors insist on and maintain this critical connection, and they explicitly describe and explain this principle to students. Thus, students are informed on the first day of class, orally and in the printed course syllabus, precisely what the course assignments and examinations will be like, what criteria will be used to judge each task, and how the grading procedures will function.

3. Validity of procedures. Proficient instructors ensure that their evaluation procedures and grading scheme adhere to the criterion of validity; that is, that the task (and its subsequent grade) measures what it is intended to measure. Thus, all assessment tasks are directly related both to the objectives and the content of the course. The tasks should also be predictive of the students' achievement and performance on similar types of skills or knowledge.

4. Consistency of assessment. Experienced instructors give careful attention to the reliability of their assessment and grading of students' learning over time. They seek to eliminate any contextual factors that might bias or distort the objectivity of their judgment.

To do this they: provide clear, concise directions and instructions about all course activities; they establish and explain the expectations and assessment standards by which these activities will be evaluated; and they gather data from multiple sources using a variety of methods, media, and measurements to provide a more comprehensive, composite, and reliable picture of a students' learning progress.

Too, effective teachers recognize that reliability of grading is enhanced when students are given the opportunity to submit or perform several smaller assignments or tasks than to base the grade on one or two larger tasks.

5. Computation of grades. As I emphasized in previous sections, instructors are expected to abide by the policies of their institution with respect to grading—even though they may have philosophical differences with these policies.

For instance, many post-secondary institutions use a *norm-referenced system* in recording and reporting final grades. This system assumes that students' grades will follow a normal distribution of the bell curve, and that a student's rank within the distribution—not his/her absolute score—will determine the final grade.

On the other hand, some instructors reject this system on the grounds that each student's standing is compared to other students' results—rather than being compared to his/her own past achievement record, or to some absolute standard, or pre-established set of criteria. A *criterion-referenced system* assesses students' work, against an agreed-upon standard or criterion—despite how well other people in the group do. In this system, a students' absolute score—not their relative score—determines their performance level.

Some institutions regulate grading practice stringently. For instance, some department heads may state:

> Your class average for all the sections in this course should typically range from 70% to 75%. Some students will be higher or lower. Check with the instructors of the other sections to make sure your syllabuses and exams are fairly similar, and that your class averages are fairly close.
>
> Other than that, students will start complaining of unfairness between and among sections...

By abiding by the constraints in a case such as this, instructors do have the security of living within the status quo and the "traditions" of their colleagues. The system is familiar to professors, students, and administrators, alike; and if one keeps the class average "within bounds," then the evaluation process should go smoothly.

However, if an instructor wishes to use criterion-referenced assessment, then he/she may possibly experience difficulty in attempting to persuade students, peers, and administrators to agree with that process.

Effective instructors, though, often use a *combination* of the two methods.[28] For instance, they may first use a norm-referenced approach to grade specific assignments or tests. For example, they would initially sort the papers into three basic categories, such as: weak, satisfactory, and above average; then, within each of these three groupings, they would further rank the assignments, holistically, as to first, second, third, and so forth. Third, instructors would assign grades to the papers according to these ranked placements in each category, by assigning the grade of, say, 72% to the middle-ranked papers (to comply with the department head's advice in the above example), and then proceeding from there with the others' grades according to their respective rankings.

After calculating similar norm-referenced assessments for a number of learning tasks, the instructors would then combine these sub-grades into an overall grade for each student in the course using a criterion-referenced approach. For instance, they would examine *each* of these "sub-set scores" in comparison to the specific learning objectives that were stated for the course, and would determine how well each student performed in relation to each criterion. This analysis would result in the overall final grade.

6. Importance of feedback. Although effective teachers comply with the regulations for assigning final grades within their institutions, they use the evaluation data for other key purposes. One is to provide feedback to learners to guide their learning, and the second is for instructors to use this feedback to improve their own teaching.

More important than a number or a letter on a transcript, is the evaluatory feedback that the assessment procedures provide. The formative assessment process (i.e., the ongoing, continuous feedback given for students' successive engagements in a variety of learning activities throughout the term) identifies learners' strengths and weaknesses (and suggestions to ameliorate the latter) in their performance of various learning tasks.

It also provides information to faculty-members, as to how they might adjust the program to accommodate revealed needs of students. For instance, a class's poor performance on a specific learning or assessment task would probably not provoke this response (overheard in a faculty lounge) from exemplary instructors:

> What's wrong with this bunch? I think I inherited a "bad crop" from last year...I've told them, and they should know better—they're nineteen years old, after all...they were supposed to show all of their work and calculations on this test to get part marks...

Rather, an effective instructor might respond like this (in class, in the-period following the test):

> Many of you lost points because you did not show your work or calculations. Perhaps you did not understand the instructions. Although you may be disappointed with your test-

grade today, I'm certain you will remember for next week's quiz.

Now, as an example of what I mean, let's look at question number four. You compare what you wrote with this model of the solution that I am going to work through with you on the overhead...

Thus, effective instructors attempt to provide students with helpful feedback regarding all the tasks in which they participate; and as they do, they focus more on students and their ultimate learning, and less on their grades. In fact,[29] researchers report that there is a weak correlation between grades earned and later success in life.

* * * * *

In Chapter 5, I have presented a synthesis of practical assessment practices that good instructors employ to build and maintain learning motivation among their students.

As was described, they do not reject traditional evaluation processes and strategies, but they are conscientious about implementing them in such a way that students' personal interests and educational needs are addressed.

Furthermore, in their repertoire of evaluation activities, experienced instructors also incorporate authentic-assessment tasks that engage students' in actual performances or demonstrations of certain skills and practices they may need in their later careers, occupations, and personal lives.

Above all, exemplary teachers work at ensuring that the assessment activities are clear, relevant, meaningful, realistic, and useful to the participants. Learners achieve this goal with reasonable effort, provided that the overall teaching/learning climate is positive and productive, and provided that both the instructional and content aspects are implemented with competence, precision, and fairness—a critical theme emphasized throughout this handbook.

References

1. See Anderson, Major, and Mitchell (1992); Lowman (1987); McMillan (1988); and Pratt (1994).

2. See "American Association" (1992), Freiberg and Driscoll (1992), Gage and Berliner (1992), Posner (1995), and Ralph (1997b).

3. See Gardner (1993), Pratt (1994), and Sternberg (1997).

4. See Cronin (1993), Herman et al. (1992), Perrone (1991), Ralph (1997b), Wiggins (1993), and Worthen (1993).

5. See Gage and Berliner (1992).

6. These illustrations are adapted from Frazee and Rudnitski (1995), Posner (1995), Pratt (1994), Ralph (1997b), and Sternberg (1997).

7. See Ralph and Konchak (1996).

8. See Biehler and Snowman (1993), Freiberg and Driscoll (1992), Lowman (1987), and Wentz and Yarling (1994).

9. See McCown et al. (1996).

10. See Freiberg and Driscoll (1992), Gage and Berliner (1992), Lowman (1987), and Ralph (1982, 1989).

11. See Gage and Berliner (1992).

12. See footnote 2, above. Also see Angelo et al. (1995), Borich (1994), Dembo (1994), and Gardner (1993).

13. See, for example, Ralph (1996b).

14. For descriptions and explanations of these "folio" documents see Borich (1994), Gage and Berliner (1992), Gardner (1993), Good and Brophy (1995), and McCown et al. (1996).

15. See Posner (1995, p. 240).

16. See McCown et al. (1996).

17. See, for example, Lorber (1996), Notterman and Drewry (1993), Slavin (1994), and Weimer (1993, 1998).

18. See Pratt (1994, p. 122).

19. See, for example, Freiberg and Driscoll (1992), Good and Brophy (1995), Lorber (1996), and Slavin (1994).

20. See, for example, Biehler and Snowman (1993), Dembo (1994), Gage and Berliner (1992), and Weimer (1993).

21. See, for example, Anderson et al. (1992), Frieberg and Driscoll (1992), Lorber (1996), and Notterman and Drewry (1993).

22. See Frazee and Rudnitski (1995) and McCown et al. (1996).

23. See, for example, Anderson et al. (1992), Biehler and Snowman (1993), Clegg and Cashin (1990), Dembo (1994), and Nottermand and Drewry (1993).

24. See Eble (1988) and Good and Brophy (1995).

25. See Clegg and Cashin (1990).

26. See Gage and Berliner (1992), Lewis (1992), McMillan (1988), Weimer (1993), and Winzer (1995).

27. See Pollio and Humphreys (1988, p. 85).

28. See, for example, Lewis (1992) and Virginia Polytechnic (1991).

29. See Pollio and Humphreys (1988, p. 92) and Sternberg (1997, p. 20).

EPILOGUE

My purpose in preparing this handbook was to present a set of key principles and practices that effective instructors at the post-secondary level have been shown to apply in order to increase learning motivation in their courses. I synthesized this information from both a survey of the research-literature on this subject, and from a review of the practical experience gained by some of my colleagues and myself during our educational careers. I employed a visual (see Figure 1.5) to represent in graphic form the major components of effective teaching and how these aspects are interrelated.

I showed that successful practitioners who teach in a wide variety of subjects or settings base their instructional decisions and strategies on several foundational principles that emerge from three sources. These sources that have been well-reported in the literature are: the teaching effectiveness research, the field of motivation of learning, and the human relations element.

In the five chapters of this handbook I distilled what pertinent educational research and personal experience have identified to be practical and relevant strategies that good instructors incorporate to stimulate students' interest in learning. I provided a condensation of essential practices and activities that exemplary instructors incorporate in their planning and implementation of both the managerial and the instructional aspects of the teaching/learning process. I also summarized major components of the instructional phase; and I emphasized the congruency between and among the instructional objectives, the learning activities, and the assessment tasks.

I now conclude this handbook by first posing a key question and then by offering responses to it. The question is: "What implications can new instructors who have not had prior teacher preparation (or ones who do have prior teaching experience but who wish to improve their present instructional skills) derive from the information presented in this manual?" In other words, "So what?"

To reply I present five implications that relate directly to how interested individuals may gain some worthwhile suggestions from this handbook to apply in their own instructional context.

In fact, four things may occur as a result of individuals reading a book such as this, or attending a conference, or participating in a workshop on instructional improvement.

1. They may receive reinforcement by having some of their own current practice substantiated, and they may consequently sense a warm glow of satisfaction, saying, "Hey, I do that, already!"

2. They may discover something new that is applicable to their particular situation, saying, "Hey, that is a technique I think will work for me."

3. They may get discouraged or resentful about "experts" advocating idealistic notions without any practical reality, by saying, "Hey, what do they know about how difficult my situation is...!" or

4. They may not be aware of their own instructional strengths and weaknesses, or they may not desire to improve, saying, "Hey, who cares?"

(It is my hope that individuals using this handbook will react in the first two ways just described.)

1. Effective Teaching is Important

One implication I draw from the contents of this handbook is that the act of teaching is important. Despite the belief of some educators that any emphasis on instruction is misplaced, and that teachers of undergraduate, or any adult students, must focus only on students' learning, I believe that effective learning by all students will simply not occur without good teaching.

Although it is true that a few students will learn well independently—despite what the instructor does or does not do—the majority of learners will progress in their achievement more efficiently and effectively when they work with exemplary instructors.

However, in many institutions of post-secondary education, neither the administrative and faculty reward-system nor the organizational climate seem genuinely to support instructional improvement. Thus, as a given, many beginning instructors are expected to teach well without receiving any sustained, substantial assistance.

It is my view, and that of other writers,[1] that the teaching enterprise is critical to the ongoing success of all undergraduate programs, and of higher education in general.

2. Effective Teaching is Complex

Although in this handbook I have examined several generic instructional skills and practices—applicable to any subject and teaching situation—I also recognize that teaching is more than performing a prescribed set of techniques.[2]

I have argued that it is, indeed, a complex orchestration of skills, methods, materials, and media designed to enhance learning. However, to underrate the significance of the various instructional competencies (such as structuring, presenting, questioning, or responding), by intimating that they are merely mechanical and trivial behaviors that reduce the art and craft of teaching to a recipe is unwarranted and untenable.

All of these generic skills are essential to good teaching, but they are not sufficient to guarantee continued and sustained effectiveness, just as is the case in performing any complex process in any professional career or occupation. When one considers individuals who excel in their particular field of endeavour—whether as a surgeon, a lawyer, an athlete, an engineer, a merchant, a pilot, a social worker, or a minister, it is clear that their competence includes more than isolated skills, drills, repetitions, or discrete behaviors. Yet, none of them could be successful unless they had first mastered and internalized the fundamental, prerequisite skills and knowledge of their field—and upon which they build and develop increasingly sophisticated expertise.

Hence, I accentuate my emphasis on practicing the basic teaching competencies: I believe that they should become key components of effective instructors' professional repertoire. Of course the implication, here, is that good teaching can be learned, practiced, developed, and improved. It does take concerted, conscientious, sustained effort.

3. Effective Teaching Blends Both Task and Human Dimensions

In this handbook I have attempted to side-step the polarization question of whether good instructors should be more task-oriented (i.e., focused on structure, objectives, techniques, learning assignments, and management), or more human oriented (i.e., emphasizing interpersonal communication, encouragement, collaboration, and support). I regard such an issue as a non-question and a false dichotomy: both dimensions are required—but not always in equal proportions.[3]

As I argue in a second handbook[4] for supervisory personnel that complements this present manual, and that may be used in conjunction with it, effective leaders (whether supervisors, instructors, coaches, trainers, or managers) purposefully vary their supervisory styles in order to synchronize their leadership behavior to match the particular developmental level of the people for whom they are responsible in the supervisor-supervisee relationship.

For example, as I have also indicated in this present volume, if a learner's development level was low (i.e., having both low competence and low confidence in performing a certain skill), then the person in the supervisory role would reciprocate by adjusting his/her leadership style to help meet the learner's developmental needs. This would be done by providing both *high task* response to meet the learner's *low competence* level (e.g., telling, showing, directing), and *high support* behavior to meet the learner's *low confidence* level (e.g., providing encouragement, reinforcement, or praise).

However, according to the contextual factors within each situation, the leader would adjust the degree of his/her task and human responses.

The implication, here, is that effective teachers enhance their ability to carry out this process through reflective practice and experience.

4. Effective Teaching is More than Subject-Matter

I have maintained in this handbook that exemplary instructors possess and apply three essential sources of professional knowledge and skills, and that a lack of any of them seriously hinders or even destroys their teaching effectiveness. The first source is familiarity with and currency in the subject-matter being taught—not just the specific course, but a solid grounding in the whole discipline, including the concepts and skills learned both in prerequisite courses and in later courses.

The second source is the generic pedagogical skills such as described in this handbook: classroom management and organization, planning and structuring, presenting skills, motivation of learning, oral questioning and responding, and evaluation and assessment skills. The third source of knowledge accessed by effective instructors, and one not fully examined in this volume—nor in any other single book, because of the sheer volume entailed to do justice to the subject— is called Pedagogical Content Knowledge (PCK).[5]

PCK is a specialized and unique body of knowledge possessed only by "experienced experts" who have taught a subject for a considerable time. This exclusive area of professional knowledge and skills not only combines the general content knowledge of the subject-matter and the generic pedagogical skills, but it includes a distinctive component. This consists of an instructors' awareness of such things as: knowing where students typically have difficulty with a particular concept or skill, and how to compensate for this; knowing what examples and non-examples to give students in order to clarify their understanding; being aware of when to speed up or slow down the instruction; knowing how much practice to provide before moving on; or understanding—and correcting—students' misconceptions, misperceptions, and common mistakes in understanding specific course material.

Instructors must draw upon *all* three of these knowledge sources in order for them to have consistent instructional success. However, the implication of this truth for beginning instructors is that not only is the goal of exemplary teaching possible to attain, but that it also requires sustained effort and practice to achieve and maintain it.

5. Effective Teaching Requires Effort

I draw a significant implication from the content of this handbook at the risk of being misrepresented as resorting to clichés and platitudes. Although this implication is not new nor profound, it is crucial for the process of instructional improvement. It is that effective teaching—as described in this manual—is neither solely a talent nor gift with which one is born; and neither does it unfold automatically the longer one teaches. Rather, it is an integrated combination of knowledge and skills that one learns and continues to develop through deliberate, reflective practice.

I have summarized the essential teaching skills in this handbook. Anyone desiring to improve these teaching skills could be overwhelmed with the number of techniques to practice. Experienced teachers and the research literature on effective teaching, however, suggest practical ways to initiate this task of professional development. Some of them are:

- **Begin small.** Rather than attempting to make a total change at one time, or to learn everything simultaneously, it is easier and more beneficial to add one technique or adjust one approach at a time. To proceed in progressive steps seems more advantageous than endeavoring to undertake comprehensive changes.

- **Be systematic.** By first ascertaining at what level of understanding learners are, through informal surveys, un-graded questionnaires, or un-signed tests,[6] and then by sharing this data with the class and adjusting their instructional activities accordingly, proficient teachers are able to add a motivational dimension to their coursework that may have been previously lacking.

- **Converse with peers.** Most instructors who are interested in professional improvement find difficulty in attempting to accomplish it independently. Cognitive development psychologists tell us that individuals learn as they construct personal meaning from their interactions with new knowledge and skills encountered through interpersonal dialogue, and often in social contexts.

  Instructors experience mutual benefits through collaborative efforts such as: team teaching, peer assessment, cross-college collaboration, mentoring, participating in teaching seminars and workshops, attending instructional conferences (at the local, regional, national, and international levels), or engaging in informal conversations about teaching with peers and administrators.

- **Participate in initiatives.** In an increasing number of institutions, newly hired faculty-members and graduate teaching assistants are expected either to provide evidence of having taken a previous course in instructional development or to enrol in one prior to the commencement of teaching (e.g., a summer seminar or orientation workshop). Although such a step is commendable, the difficulty of simply "taking one course" is that instructional development — like any type of learning — does not happen via a one-shot effort.

In fact, researchers[8] in the field of professional development have found that workshop participants typically require up to 25 practice-sessions implementing a new instructional skill before it is transferred into an internalized component of their personal teaching repertoire. Not only that, but teachers will not even bother sustaining their practice of a technique in their regular instructional contexts unless they are personally convinced of its benefit to them in their unique situations.

6. Effective Teaching Requires Personal Motivation[9]

A final implication of the fact that good instruction requires deliberate time and effort is one that is at the heart of this handbook: the issue of individual motivation. Just as learners, who are not motivated to engage in their coursework, will not demonstrate acceptable progress, similarly, instructors who are not intrinsically motivated to engage in enhancing their teaching will show little improvement.

Yet, some may ask, how can new teachers be motivated when they have little time nor incentive to participate in such efforts?

Thankfully, positive signs of institutional change are occurring; department heads and administrators at the post-secondary level are meeting these needs by providing time, resources, and support to help instructors desiring to build and/or refine their teaching skills.

I offer this handbook to serve as one of those resources.

References

1. See Cohen and Seaman (1997), Davis (1993), Eble (1988), Gibbs (1995), Kennedy (1995), Lambert et al. (1996), Plater (1995), and Wise (1996). See also Ralph (1995a, 1995c).

2. See, for example, Brandt (1997), Ducharme (1995), Nord (1990), Palmer (1993), Ralph (1994e), and Yelon (1996).

3. See, for example, Ralph (1993b, 1993c, 1994c, 1996a, 1998b).

4. See Ralph (1998b).

5. See Shulman (1987). See also Glatthorn (1997) and Good (1990).

6. See Angelo (1991b) and Murray (1987).

7. See Angelo (1991a), Eble (1988), Palmer (1993), Plater (1995), Ralph (1996b), and Shulman (1993).

8. See Showers, Joyce, and Bennett (1987).

9. See Fullan (1991, 1994), Ralph (1996a), Schmoker (1997), and Stipek (1988).

Bibliography

Abbott, R., Wulff, D., & Katiszego, C. (1989). Review of research on TA training. In J. Nyquist, R. Abbott, & D. Wulff (Eds.), *Teaching assistant training in the 1990s* (pp. 111-124). San Francisco: Jossey-Bass.

Ahluwalia, D., & McCreary, M. (n.d.). *Teaching students with disabilities: A guide for faculty*. Saskatoon, Saskatchewan: University of Saskatchewan.

Albright, M., & Graf, D. (1992). Instructional technology and the faculty member. In M. Albright & D. Graf (Eds.), *Teaching in the information age: The role of educational technology* (pp. 7-15). San Francisco: Jossey-Bass.

Amabile, T. (1989). *Growing up creative: Nurturing a lifetime of creativity*. New York: Crown.

American Association for Higher Education. (1992, December). *Principles of good practice for assessing student learning*. Washington, DC: AAHE Assessment Forum.

American Psychological Association. (1994). *Publication manual of the American Psychological Association*. (4th ed.). Washington, DC: Author.

Ames, R., & Ames, C. (1984). Introduction. In R. Ames & C. Ames (Eds.), *Research in motivation in education: Vol. 1. Student motivation* (pp. 1-11). Toronto, ON: Academic.

Anderson, D., Major, R., & Mitchell, R. (1992). *Teacher supervision that works: A guide for university supervisors*. New York: Praeger.

Angelo, T. (1991a). Introduction and overview: From classroom assessment to classroom research. In T. Angelo (Ed.), *Classroom research: Early lessons from success, New directions for teaching and learning,* no. 46. San Francisco: Jossey-Bass.

Angelo, T. (1991b). Ten easy pieces: Assessing higher learning in four dimensions. In T. Angelo (Ed.), *Classroom research: Early lessons from success, New directions for teaching and learning,* no. 46. San Francisco: Jossey-Bass.

Angelo, T. (1993). A "teachers dozen." *American Association for Higher Education Bulletin, 45*(8), 3-7, 13.

Angelo, T., Seldin, P., Weimer, M., & Dotolo, L. (1995, March). Enhancing and evaluating college teaching and learning. In P. Haskins (Moderator), *College teaching and learning video-conference.* Site: Saskatoon, SK: University of Saskatchewan.

Armstrong, D., & Savage, T. (1994). *Secondary education: An introduction* (3rd ed.). New York: Macmillan.

Aronson, J. (1987). Six keys to effective instruction in large classes: Advice from a practitioner. In M. Weimer (Ed.), *Teaching large classes well* (pp. 31-37). San Francisco: Jossey-Bass.

Barell, J. (1991). *Teaching for thoughtfulness.* New York: Longman.

Baron, J. (1987). Evaluating thinking skills in the classroom. In J. Baron & R. Sternberg (Eds.), *Teaching thinking skills: Theory and practice* (pp. 221-247). New York: Freeman.

Barr, R., & Tagg, J. (1995). From teaching to learning: A new paradigm for undergraduate education. *Change, 27*(6), 12-25.

Baughman, M. (1974). *Baughman's handbook of humor in education.* West Nyack, NY: Parker.

Beachem, K. (1996). Teaching needs personal style. *The teaching Professor, 10*(10), 3.

Beidler, P. (Ed.). (1986). *Distinguished teachers on effective teaching.* San Francisco: Jossey-Bass.

Bender, E., Dunn, M., Kendall, B., Larson, C., & Wilkes, P. (Eds.). (1994). *Quick bits: Successful strategies by award winning teachers.* Bloomington, IN: Indiana University.

Berkowitz, P. (1995a). Learning to be better teachers. *University Affairs, 36* (8), 12-13.

Berkowitz, P. (1995b). Judging performance. *University Affairs, 36*(6), 6-7.

Biehler, R., & Snowman, J. (1993). *Psychology applied to teaching* (7th ed.). Boston: Houghton Mifflin.

Bloom, B., Englehart, M., Furst, E., Hill, W., & Krathwohl, D. (1956). *Taxonomy of educational objectives. Handbook 1: Cognitive domain.* New York: McKay.

Bonwell, C. (1996). Research watch: Building a supportive climate for active learning. *The National Teaching & Learning Forum, 6*(1), 4-7.

Borich, G. (1994). *Observation Skills for Effective teaching* (2nd ed.). New York: Merrill.

Brandt, R. (1997). On using knowledge about our brain: A conversation with Bob Sylvester. *Educational Leadership, 54* (6), 16-19.

Brookfield, S. (1991). *The skillful teacher: On technique, trust, and responsiveness in the classroom.* San Francisco, CA: Jossey-Bass.

Brookfield, S. (1995). *Becoming a critically reflective teacher.* San Francisco: Jossey-Bass.

Brookfield, S. (1996). Teacher roles and teaching styles. In A. Tuijnman (Ed.), *International encyclopedia of adult education and training* (2nd ed.). (pp. 529-534). New York: Elsevier.

Brooks, R. (1987). Dealing with details in a large class. In M. Weimer (Ed.), *Teaching large classes well* (pp. 39-44). San Francisco: Jossey-Bass.

Browne, M., & Keeley, S. (1990). Achieving excellence: Advice to new teachers. In M. Weimer & R. Neff (Eds.), *Teaching college: Collected readings for the new instructor* (pp. 39-44). Madison, WI: Magna.

Bruffee, K. (1994). Making the most of knowledgeable peers. *Change, 26*(3), 39-44.

Bruffee, K. (1995). Sharing our toys: Cooperative learning versus collaborative learning. *Change, 27*(1), 12-18.

But I made a 9 in psychology. (1996, November). *University Affairs, 37*(9), 5.

Case, R., Harper, K. , Tilly, S., & Wiens, J. (1994). Stewart on teaching versus facilitating: A misconstrued dichotomy. *Canadian Journal of Education, 19* (3), 287-298.

Cashin, W. (1990). Improving lectures. In M. Weimer & R. Neff (Eds.), *Teaching college: Collected readings for the new instructor* (pp. 59-63). Madison, WI: Magna.

Chance, P. (1986). *Thinking in the classroom: A survey of programs.* New York: Teachers College.

Cheney, L. (1994). Taking steps to build support for change. *Change, 26*(3), 45.

Chiarelott, L., Davidman, L., & Ryan, K. (1994). *Lenses on teaching* (2nd ed.). New York: Harcourt Brace.

Clegg, V., & Cashin, W. (1990). Improving multiple-choice tests. In M. Weimer & R. Neff (Eds.), *Teaching college: Collected readings for the new instructor* (pp. 125-131). Madison, WI: Magna.

Clipperton, R., & Leong, C. (1985). *Language awareness and humor comprehension in skilled and less skilled readers* (Research Center Report No. 134). Regina, SK: Saskatchewan School Trustees Association.

Cohen, F., & Seaman, L. (1997). Research versus "real-search." *Phi Delta Kappan, 78*(7), 564-567.

Cornett, C. (1983). *What you should know about teaching and learning styles* (Fastback No. 191). Bloomington, IN: Phi Delta Kappa Foundation.

Creed, T. (1993). "The" seven principles...not! *American Association for Higher Education Bulletin, 45*(8), 8-9.

Cronin, J. (1993). Four misconceptions about authentic learning. *Educational Leadership, 50*(7), 78-80.

Daloz, L. (1986). *Effective teaching and mentoring: Realizing the transformational power of adult learning experiences.* San Francisco: Jossey-Bass.

Daloz, L., Keen, C., Keen, J., & Parks, S. (1996). Lives of commitment. *Change, 28*(3), 10-15.

Danielson, C. (1996). *Enhancing professional practice: A framework for teaching.* Alexandria, VA: Association for Supervision and Curriculum Development.

Davidson, C., & Ambrose, S. (1995). Leading discussions effectively. *The Teaching Professor, 9*(6), 8.

Davis, J. (1993). *Better teaching, more learning.* Phoenix, AZ: Oryx.

Day, H., Berlyne, D., & Hunt, D. (Eds.). (1971). *Intrinsic motivation: A new direction in education*. Toronto, ON: Holt, Rinehart and Winston.

de Charms, R. (1984). Motivation enhancement in educational settings. In R. Ames & C. Ames (Eds.), *Research on motivation in education: Vol. 1. Student motivation* (pp. 275-310). Toronto, ON: Academic

Dembo, M. (1994). *Applying educational psychology* (5th ed.). New York: Longman.

Dillon, J. (1983). *Teaching and the art of questioning* (fastback No. 194). Bloomington, IN: Phi Delta Kappa Foundation.

Dillon, R. (1986). Issues in cognitive psychology and instruction. In R. Dillon & R. Sternberg (Eds.), *Cognition and instruction* (pp. 1-12). New York: Academic.

Dillon, R., & Sternberg, R. (Eds.). (1986). *Cognition and instruction*. New York: Academic.

Doyle, D. (1997). Education and character: A constructive view. *Phi Delta Kappan, 78*(6), 440-443.

Draves, W. (1988). *How to teach adults in one hour*. M Manhattan, KS: Learning Resources Network.

Driscoll, M. (1994). *Psychology of learning for instruction*. Boston: Allyn and Bacon.

Ducharme, E. (1995). The great teacher question: Beyond competencies. In K. Ryan & J. Cooper (Eds.), *Kaleidoscope: Readings in education* (7th ed., pp. 23-29). Boston: Houghton Mifflin.

Dunkin, M., & Barnes, J. (1986). Research on teaching in higher education. In M. Wittrock (Ed.), *Handbook of research on teaching* (3rd ed., pp. 754-777). New York: Macmillan.

Eble, K. (1988). *The craft of teaching: A guide to mastering the professor's art* (2nd ed.). San Francisco: Jossey-Bass.

Eby, J. (1992). *Reflective planning, teaching, and evaluation for the elementary school.* New York: Merrill.

Edgerton, R. (1996). Learning, teaching, technology: Putting first things first. *American Association for Higher Education Bulletin, 49*(1), 3-6.

Elliott, S., Katochwill, T., Littlefield, J., & Travers, J. (1996). *Educational psychology: Effective teaching, effective learning* (2nd ed.). Dubuque, IA: Brown & Benchmark.

Evans, N. (1994). *Experiential learning for all.* London: Cassell.

Frazee, B., & Rudnitski, R. (1995). *Integrated teaching methods.* Boston, MA: Delmar.

Frederick, P. (1987). Student involvement: Active learning in large classes. In M. Weimer (Ed.), *Teaching large classes well* (pp. 45-56). San Francisco: Jossey-Bass.

Freiberg, H., & Driscoll, A. (1992). *Universal teaching strategies.* Boston: Allyn and Bacon.

Fullan, M. (1991). *The new meaning of educational change* (2nd ed.). New York: Teachers College.

Fullan, M. (1994, March). *Harnessing the forces of educational reform.* Paper presented at the 49th annual conference of the Association for Supervision and Curriculum Development, Chicago, IL.

Fuller, F., & Bown, O. (1975). Becoming a teacher. In K. Ryan (Ed.), *Teacher education: The 74th yearbook of the National Society for the Study of Education: Part II* (pp. 25-52). Chicago: University of Chicago Press.

Gage, N., & Berliner, D. (1992). *Educational psychology* (5th ed.). Toronto: Houghton Mifflin.

Gagne, R., Briggs, L., & Wager, W. (1992). *Principles of instructional design* (4th ed.). New York: Harcourt Brace Jovanovich.

Gappa-Levi, L. (1996). TA forum: Isn't teaching drama? *The National Teaching & Learning Forum, 5*(4), 8-9.

Gardiner, L. (1997). Producing dramatic increases in student learning: Can we do it? *The National Teaching & Learning Forum, 6*(2), 8-10.

Gardner, H. (Ed.). (1993). *Multiple intelligences: The theory in practice.* New York: Basic

Garmston, R. (1994). The persuasive art of presenting: Presenting to groups experiencing change. *Journal of Staff Development, 15*(1), 66-68.

Gibbs, G. (1995). Promoting excellent teaching is harder than you'd think. *Change, 27*(3), 17-20.

Gingell, S. (1997). An open secret for a good day in class. *Vox, 20,* 2-4. (Available from the University of Saskatchewan Faculty Association, College of Education, 28 Campus Drive, Saskatoon, SK, S7N 0X1).

Glatthorn, A. (1997). *Differentiated supervision.* Alexandria, VA: Association for Supervision and Curriculum Development.

Good, T. (1990). Building the knowledge base of teaching. In D. Dill and associates (Eds.), *What teachers need to know: The knowledge, skills, and values essential to good teaching* (pp. 17-75). San Francisco: Jossey-Bass.

Good, T., & Brophy, J. (1995). *Contemporary educational psychology* (5th ed.). White Plains, NY: Longman.

Gunter, M., Estes, T., & Schwab, J. (1995). *Instruction: A models approach* (2nd ed.). Boston: Allyn and Bacon.

Guskey, T. (1996). Reporting on student learning: Lessons from the past—prescriptions for the future. In T. Guskey (Ed.), *Communicating student learning* (pp. 13-24). Alexandria, VA: Association for Supervision and Curriculum Development.

Guskin, A. (1994). Restructuring the role of faculty.*Change, 26*(5), 16-25.

Gustafson, K. (1996). Instructional design: Models. In A. Tuijnman (Ed.), *International encyclopedia of adult education and training* (2nd ed., pp. 503-509). New York: Elsevier Science.

Hartz, G. (1995). Introductory courses: 10 no-no's. *The Teaching Professor, 9*(6), 1-2.

Haycock, K. (1996). Thinking differently about school reform. *Change, 28*(1), 12-18.

Heinich, R., Molenda, M., & Russell, J. (1993). *Instructional media and the new technologies of instruction* (4th ed.). New York: Macmillan.

Herman, J., Aschbacher, P., & Winters, L. (1992). *A practical guide to alternative assessment.* Alexandria, VA: Association for Supervision and Curriculum Development.

Hidi, S., Renninger, K., & Krapp, A. (1992). The present state of interest research. In K. Renninger, S. Hidi, & A. Krapp (Eds.), *The role of interest in learning and development* (pp. 433-446). Hillsdale, NJ: Laurence Erlbaum.

Hopkins, W., & Moore, K. (1993). *Clinical supervision: A practical guide to student teacher supervision.* Madison, WI: Brown & Benchmark.

Hoyle, E., & John, P. (1995). *Professional knowledge and professional practice.* London: Cassell.

Huston, J. (1997). The details of discussion. *The Teaching Professor, 11*(2), 3.

Hyerle, D. (1996). *Visual tools for constructing knowledge.* Alexandria, VA: Association for Supervision and Curriculum Development.

Jarvis, P. (1995). *Adult and continuing education: Theory and practice* (2nd ed.). London: Routledge.

Katz, J., & Henry, M. (1993). *Turning professors into teachers.* Phoenix, AZ: Oryx.

Kelly, E. (1976). *Dramatics in the classroom: Making lessons come alive* (Fastback No. 70). Bloomington, IN: Phi Delta Kappa Educational Foundation.

Kennedy, D. (1995). Another century's end, another revolution for higher education. *Change, 27*(3), 8-15.

Knapper, C. (1987). Large classes and learning. In M. Weimer (Ed.), *Teaching large classes well* (pp. 5-15). San Francisco: Jossey-Bass.

Knowles, M. (1990). *The adult learner: A neglected species* (4th ed.). Houston, TX: Gulf.

Kohn, A. (1997). How not to teach values: A critical look at character education. *Phi Delta Kappan, 78*(6), 428-439.

Kounin, J. (1970). *Discipline and group management in classrooms.* New York: Holt, Rinehart and Winston.

Kraft, R. (1990). Group-inquiry turns passive students active. In M. Weimer & R. Neff (Eds.), *Teaching college: Collected readings for the new instructor* (pp. 99-104). Madison, WI: Magna.

Kruse, J. (1988). *Classroom activities in thinking skills.* Philadelphia, PA: Research for Better Schools.

Kuh, B. (1997). Creating "seamless" learning environments. *The Teaching Professor, 11*(2), 7.

Labouvie-Vief, G. (1992). A neo-Piagetian perspective on adult cognitive development. In R. Sternberg & C. Berg (Eds.), *Intellectual development* (pp. 197-228). Cambridge, UK: Cambridge University.

Lambert, L., Tice, S., & Featherstone, P. (Eds.). (1996). *University teaching: A guide for graduate students.* Syracuse, NY: Syracuse University Press.

Langrehr, J. (1988). *Teaching students to think.* Bloomington, IN: National Education Service.

Latham, A. (1997). Asking students the right questions. *Educational Leadership, 54*(6), 84-85.

Lazar, A. (1995). Do students study together? *The Teaching Professor, 9*(9), 3-4.

Lecturing myths. (1994, Fall). *Instructional Strategies Series Newsletter, 3*(3), 2-3. (Available from the Saskatchewan Professional Development Unit, P.O. Box 1108, Saskatoon, SK, S7K 3N3).

Leinhardt, G. (1995). What research on learning tells us about teaching. In K. Ryan & J. Cooper (Eds.), *Kaleidoscope: Readings in education* (7th ed., pp. 265-270). Boston: Houghton Mifflin.

Lewis, K. (1992). *Teaching pedagogy to teaching assistants: A handbook for 398T instructors* (3rd ed.). Austin, TX: University of Texas at Austin, Centre for Teaching Effectiveness.

Lim, B. (1996). Students' expectations of professors. *The Teaching Professor, 10*(4), 3-4.

Lorber, M. (1996). *Objectives, methods, and evaluation for secondary teaching* (4th ed.). Boston, MA: Allyn and Bacon.

Love, P., & Love, A. (1996). The interrelatedness of intellectual, social, and emotional influences on student learning. *The National Teaching & Learning Forum, 5*(5), 8-10.

Lowman, J. (1987). Giving students feedback. In M. Weimer (Ed.), *Teaching large classes well* (pp. 71-83). San Francisco: Jossey-Bass.

Malcolm, J. (1995, May). The competence of worker bees: The implications of competence-based education for educators of adults. In M. Collins (Ed.), *Proceedings of the International Conference on Educating the Adult Educator: Role of the University* (pp. 61-71). Canmore, Alberta, Canada.

Marchese, T., & Pollack, B. (1993). Deep learning, surface learning. *American Association for Higher Education Bulletin, 39*(7), 10-13.

Marken, R. (1997). A really good day in the classroom. *Vox, 20,* 4-6. (Available from the University of Saskatchewan Faculty Association, College of Education, 28 Campus Drive, Saskatoon, SK, S7N 0X1).

McCabe, D., & Trevino, L. (1996). What we know about cheating in college. *Change, 28*(1), 28-33.

McCandless, B. (1967). *Children: Behavior and development.* New York: Holt, Rinehart Winston.

McCown, R., Driscoll, M., Roop, P., Saklofske, D., Kelly, I., Schwean, V., & Gajadharsingh, J. (1996). *Educational psychology: A learning-centered approach to classroom practice* (Canadian ed.). Scarborough, ON: Allyn and Bacon.

McMillan, J. (Ed.). (1988). *Assessing students' learning.* San Francisco: Jossey-Bass.

McNeely, S. (1995). *Instructor's toolbox to accompany Good & Brophy contemporary educational psychology* (5th ed.). White Plains, NY: Longman.

Moore, R. (1984). *Master teachers* (Fastback No. 201). Bloomington, IN: Phi Delta Kappa Educational Foundation.

Morse, J. (1995). A yes for group work. *The Teaching Professor, 9*(9), 3-4.

Mosteller, F. (1989). The "muddiest point in the lecture" as a feedback device. *On Teaching and Learning: The Journal of the Harvard-Danforth Center, 3,* 10-21.

Murray, H. (1987). Acquiring student feedback that improves instruction. In M. Weimer (Ed.), *Teaching large classes well* (pp. 85-96). San Francisco: Jossey-Bass.

New source for collaborative learning. (1994, Summer). *The Quarterly Newsletter from the National Center on Postsecondary Teaching, Learning & Assessment, 3*(2), 1-2.

Nord, W. (1990). Teaching and morality: The knowledge most worth having. In D. Dill and associates (Eds.), *What teachers need to know: The knowledge, skills, and values essential to good teaching* (pp. 173-198). San Francisco: Jossey-Bass.

Nothing succeeds like success. (1994, October). *University Affairs, 35*(8), 28.

Notterman, J., & Drewry, H. (1993). *Psychology and education: Parallel and interactive approaches.* New York: Plenum.

Nunn, C. (1996). Discussion details. *The Teaching Professor, 10*(7), 5.

Nyquist, J., Abbott, R., & Wulff, D. (1989). *Teaching assistant training in the 1990s.* San Francisco: Jossey-Bass.

Old-fashioned teacher wins professor of the year award. (1996, August/September). *University Affairs, 37*(7), 8.

Orlich, D., Harder, R., Callahan, R., Kauchak, D., & Gibson, H. (1994). *Teaching strategies: A guide to better instruction* (4th ed.). Lexington, MA: D.C. Heath.

Palmer, P. (1993). Good talk about good teaching: Improving teaching through conversation and community. *Change, 25*(6), 8-13.

Paul, R. (1987). Dialogical thinking: Critical thought essential to the acquisition of rational knowledge and passions. In J. Baron & R. Sternberg (Eds.), *Teaching thinking skills: Theory and practice* (pp. 127-148). New York: Freeman.

Perrone, V. (1991). Introduction. In V. Perrone (Ed.), *Expanding student assessment* (pp. vii-xi). Alexandria, VA: Association for Supervision and Curriculum Development.

Peters, A. (1996). Jolly good fellows. *University Affairs, 37*(8), 18.

Peters, J. (1995, May). Good question! Collaborative learning and the intentional stance. In M. Collins (Ed.), *Proceedings of the International Conference on Educating the Adult Educator: Role of the University* (pp. 269-274). Canmore, Alberta, Canada.

Plater, W. (1995). Future work: Faculty time in the 21st century. *Change, 27*(3), 22-33.

Pollio, H., & Humphreys, W. (1988). Grading students. In J. McMillan (Ed.), *Assessing students' learning* (pp. 85-97). San Francisco: Jossey-Bass.

Poole, W. (1994). Removing the "super" from supervision. *Journal of Curriculum and Supervision, 9*(3), 284-309.

Popham W. J. (1998). Farewell, curriculum: Confessions of an assessment convert. *Phi Delta Kappan, 79*(5), 380-384.

Posner, G. (1995). *Analyzing the curriculum* (2nd ed.). New York: McGraw-Hill.

Pratt, D. 91994). *Curriculum planning: A handbook for professionals*. New York: Harcourt Brace.

Raffini, J. (1993). *Winners without losers*. Boston: Allyn and Bacon.

Ralph, E. (1982). The unmotivated second-language learner: Can students' negative attitudes be changed? *The Canadian Modern Language Review, 38*(3), 493-502.

Ralph, E. (1989). Research on effective teaching: How can it help L2 teachers motivate the unmotivated learner? *The Canadian Modern Language Review, 46*(1), 135-146.

Ralph, E. (1993a). Beginning teachers and classroom management: Questions from practice, answers from research. *Middle School Journal, 25*(1), 60-64.

Ralph, E. (1993b). Enhancing Aboriginal teacher education: One promising approach. *Canadian Journal of Native Education, 20*(1), 44-62.

Ralph, E. (1993c). Sensitive, sensible practicum supervision: A contextual application in Saskatchewan. *The Alberta Journal of Educational Research, 39*(3), 283-296.

Ralph, E. (1994a). Beginning teachers as effective classroom managers: How are they?...Managing? *McGill Journal of Education, 29*(2), 181-196.

Ralph, E. (1994b). Enhancing the supervision of beginning teachers: A Canadian initiative. *Teaching & Teacher Education, 10*(2), 185-203.

Ralph, E. (1994c). Helping beginning teachers improve via contextual supervision. *Journal of Teacher Education, 45*(5), 354-363.

Ralph, E. (1994d). Middle and secondary L2 teachers: Meeting classroom management challenges. *Foreign Language Annals, 27*(1), 89-103.

Ralph, E. (1994e). On assembling the pieces: What do retired educators tell us? *Action in Teacher Education, 16*(2), 62-72.

Ralph, E. (1994f). Teaching to the test: Principles of authentic assessment for second language education. *Mosaic, 1*(4), 9-13.

Ralph, E. (1995a). Are self-assessments accurate? Evaluating novices' teaching via triangulation. *Research in Education, 53* (May), 41-51.

Ralph, E. (1995b). Motivating parents to support second-language programs. *Mosaic, 2*(4), 1-7.

Ralph, E. (1995c). The transfer of knowledge from practicum to practice: Novice teachers' views. *Brock University, 5*(1), 6-21.

Ralph, E. (1995d). Toward instructional improvement: Reflections and insights on a Canadian journey. *The Journal of Graduate Teaching Assistant Development, 2*(3), 125-133.

Ralph, E. (1996a). Contextual supervision: Matching supervisory styles with learners' needs. *The Canadian Administrator, 35*(3), 1-11.

Ralph, E. (1996b). Improving teaching through cross-college collaboration: Reflections on a Saskatchewan experience. *McGill Journal of Education, 31*, 297-318.

Ralph, E. (1997a). Improving both GTA and instructional developer effectiveness. *The Journal of Staff, Program & Organization Development, 14*(3), 145-157.

Ralph, E. (1997b). Teaching to the test: Principles of authentic assessment for second language education. In A. Mollica (Ed.), Teaching languages (pp. 249-257). Welland, ON: Soleil. (Reprinted from Edwin G. Ralph, (1994), "Teaching to the Test: Principles of Authentic Assessment for Second Language Education," *Mosaic, 1*(4), 9-13.)

Ralph, E. G. (1997c). The power of using drama in the teaching of second languages: Some recollections. *The McGill Journal of Education, 32*(3), 273-288.

Ralph, E. (1998a). *Developing novice teachers oral-questioning skills.* Manuscript submitted for publication.

Ralph, E. (1998b). *Developing practitioners: A handbook of contextual supervision.* Stillwater, OK: New Forums Press.

Ralph, E. (1998c). *Oral-questioning skills of novice teachers: ...Any questions?* Manuscript submitted for publication.

Ralph, E., & Konchak, P. (1996). Implications for improving teaching in the health sciences: Some Canadian findings. *Quality in Higher Education, 2*(1), 45-55.

Ralph, E., & Yang, B. (1993). Beginning teachers' utilization of instructional media: A Canadian case study. *Educational & Training Technology International, 30*(4), 299-318.

Reigeluth, C. (1996). Instructional design: Guidelines and theories. In A. Tuijnman (Ed.), *International encyclopedia of adult education and training* (2nd ed., pp. 497-503). New York: Elsevier Science.

Rhem, J. (1997). Video review: Two looks at large classes. *The National Teaching & Learning Forum, 6*(2), 11.

Rockwood, H. (1996). Studying style [Review of the book *Teaching with style: A practical guide to enhancing learning by understanding teaching & learning styles*]. *The National Teaching & Learning Forum, 5*(5), 10-12.

Rogers, C., & Freiberg, H. (1994). *Freedom to learn* (3rd.). NewYork: Merrill.

Scherer, M. (Ed.). (1997-1998). Reading for equity [entire issue]. *Educational Leadership, 55*(4).

Schmoker, M. (1997). Occupational knowledge and the in evitability of school improvement. *Phi Delta Kappan, 78*(7), 560-563.

Schon, D. (1995). The new scholarship requires a new epistemology: Knowing in action. *Change, 27*(6), 26-34.

Sergiovanni, T. (1992). *Moral leadership: Getting to the heart of* school improvement. San Francisco, CA: Jossey-Bass.

Sims, S., & Sims, R. (1995a). Learning and learning styles: A review and look to the future. In R. Sims & S. Sims (Eds.), *The importance of learning styles* (pp. 193-210). Westport, CT: Greenwood.

Sims, R., & Sims, S. (1995b). Learning enhancement in higher education. In R. Sims & S. Sims (Eds.), *The importance of learning styles* (pp. 1-24). Westport, CT: Greenwood.

Shils, E. (1983). *The academic ethic* (The report of a study group of the International Council on the Future of the University). Chicago, IL: University of Chicago Press.

Showers, B., Joyce, B., & Bennett, B. (1987). Synthesis of research on staff development: A framework for future study and a state-of-the-art analysis. *Educational Leadership, 45*(3), 77-87.

Shulman, L. (1987). Knowledge and teaching: Foundations of the new reform. *Harvard Educational Review, 57*, 1-22.

Shulman, L. (1993). Teaching as community property: Putting an end to pedagogical solitude. *Change, 25*(6), 6-7.

Shulman, J., & Colbert, A. (Eds.). (1988). *The intern teacher casebook*. Eugene, OR: Far West Laboratory for Educational Research and Development.

Slavin, R. (1994). *Educational psychology: Theory and practice* (4th ed.). Boston: Allyn and Bacon.

Smith , D., & Sanche, R. (1992). Saskatchewan interns' concerns at three stages of a four-month practicum. *The Alberta Journal of Educational Research, 38*(2), 121-132.

Sternberg, R. (1987). Questions and answers about the nature and teaching of thinking skills. In J. Baron & R. Sternberg (Eds.), *Teaching thinking skills: Theory and practice* (pp. 251-259). New York: Freeman.

Sternberg, R. (1994). Triarchic theory of human intelligence. In R. Sternberg (Ed.), *Encyclopedia of human intelligence: Vol. 2* (pp. 1087-1091). New York: Macmillan.

Sternberg, R. (1997). What does it mean to be smart? *Educational Leadership, 54*(6), 20-24.

Stewart, D. (1993). Teaching or facilitating: A false dichotomy. *Canadian Journal of Education, 18*(1), 1-13.

Stewart, D. (1994). Teaching undiminished: A reply to my critics. *Canadian Journal of Education, 19*(3), 299-304.

Stice, J. (Ed.). (1987). *Developing critical thinking and problem-solving abilities*. San Francisco: Jossey-Bass.

Stipek, D. (1988). *Motivation to learn: From theory to practice*. Englewood Cliffs, NJ: Prentice-Hall.

Svinicki, M. (1992). Assertiveness and the college instructor. In K. Lewis (Ed.), *Teaching pedagogy to teaching assistants: A handbook for 398T instructors* (3rd ed., pp. 64-70). Austin, TX: University of Texas at Austin, Center for Teaching Effectiveness.

The landscape: Where's the beef? College seniors evaluate their undergraduate experience. (1994). *Change, 26*(5), 29-32.

Thomas, A. (1988). The new world of continuing education. In T. Barer-Stein & J. Draper (Eds.), *The craft of teaching adults*. Toronto, ON: Culture Concepts.

Thomas, A. (1996, December). A matter of meaning. *Canadian Learning, 2*, 4.

Thirty years of cheating. (1996, April). *The Teaching Professor, 10*(4), 6.

Tierney, E. (1996). *How to make effective presentations*. Thousand Oaks, CA: Sage.

Torrance, E., & Myers, R. (1973). *Creative learning & teaching*. New York: Dodd, Mead.

University of Saskatchewan. (n.d.) *University teaching and learning: An instructional resource guide for graduate student teachers at the University of Saskatchewan*. Saskatoon, SK: University of Saskatchewan, Extension Division, Author.

University of Saskatchewan. (1997-1998). *The Internship Manual*. Saskatoon, SK: University of Saskatchewan, College of Education.

Vale, N. (1995). Size doesn't count. *University Affairs, 36*(6), 40.

Virginia Polytechnic Institute and State University. (1991). *Virginia Tech GTA handbook*. Blacksburg, VA: Research and Graduate Studies Division.

Vojtek, R. (1994). Twenty-five years in organization development: A conversation with Richard Schmuck and Philip Runkel. *Journal of Staff Development, 15*(1), 46-50.

Waldron, M., & Moore, G. (1991). *Helping adults learn: Course planning for adult learners*. Toronto: Thompson.

Weaver, R., II, & Cotrell, H. (1987). Lecturing: Essential communication strategies. In M. Weimer (Ed.), *Teaching large classes well* (pp. 57-70). San Francisco: Jossey-Bass.

Weber, E. (1997). Resolving small group conflicts. *The Teaching Professor, 11*(2), 4.

Weil, M., & Joyce, B. (1978). *Information processing models of teaching: Expanding your teaching repertoire.* Englewood Cliffs, NJ: Prentice-Hall.

Weimer, M. (1990a). *Improving college teaching: Strategies for developing instructional effectiveness.* San Francisco: Jossey-Bass.

Weimer, M. (1990b). Successful participation strategies. In M. Weimer & R. Neff (Eds.), *Teaching college: Collected readings for the new instructor* (pp. 95-96). Madison, WI: Magna.

Weimer, M. (1990c). What can discussion accomplish? In M. Weimer & R. Neff (Eds.), *Teaching college: Collected readings for the new instructor* (p. 97). Madison, WI: Magna.

Weimer, M. (1993). *Improving your classroom teaching: Vol. 1.* London: Sage.

Weimer, M. (1996a). Active learning: Quantity, extent, depth count. *The Teaching Professor, 10*(10), 1.

Weimer, M. (1996b). Cooperative learning and communication: Evidence of results. *The Teaching Professor, 10*(10), 5.

Weimer, M. (1996c). The ethics of teaching. *The Teaching Professor, 10*(10), 2.

Weimer, M. (1996d). Student motivation not a desperate situation. *The Teaching Professor, 10*(10), 7.

Weimer, M. (1997a). Cooperative learning & problem solving. *The Teaching Professor, 11*(1), 2.

Weimer, M. (1997b). Problem-based learning models. *The Teaching Professor, 11*(1), 4.

Weimer, M. (1997c). What makes a good teacher? *The Teaching Professor, 11*(1), 1-2.

Weimer, M. (Ed.). (1998). *The teaching professor, 12*(1) [entire issue].

Wentz, P., & Yarling, J. (1994). *Student teaching casebook for supervising teachers and teaching interns.* New York: Merrill.

Wiggins, G. (1993). Assessment: authenticity, context, and validity. *Phi Delta Kappan, 75,* 200-214.

Wiles, J., & Bondi, J. (1991). *Supervision: A guide to practice* (3rd ed.). New York: Merrill.

Winzer, M. (1995). *Educational psychology in the Canadian classroom* (2nd ed.). Scarborough, ON: Allyn and Bacon.

Wise, A. (Ed.). (1996). Quality teaching for the 21st century [entire issue]. *Phi Delta Kappan, 78*(3).

Worthen, B. (1993). Critical issues that will determine the future of authentic assessment. *Phi Delta Kappan, 74,* 444-454.

Yamane, D. (1997). Group projects: Problems and possible solutions. *The Teaching Professor, 11*(2), 5.

Yelon, S. (1996). *Powerful principles of instruction.* White Plains, NY: Longman.

Appendix A

1. Introduction

Title: "The Use of Projected Visuals in Presentations"

Learners: Twenty adult learners from business, industry, goverment, education, and health-care fields; a range of ages, training, and background. All have voluntarily enrolled to enhace their presenting skills by learning to incoporate instructional media.

Course: Held one evening per week for 13 weeks; 2 1/2 hours per session.

2. Brainstorming

The "What?" and "How?" to teach this unit:

Content Ideas	Method/Process Ideas
The overhead projector	Lecture
Overhead transparencies	Independent study
35 mm slides	Projects
Filmstrips	Portfolios
Opaque projection	Presentations
Making/Preparing visuals	Skits/Dramas
Selecting visuals (rent, purchase, borrow)	Laboratory work
Operating/maintaining equipment	Demonstration
Tips/Pitfalls for each	Discussion
	Panels/Debates

3. Concept Map:

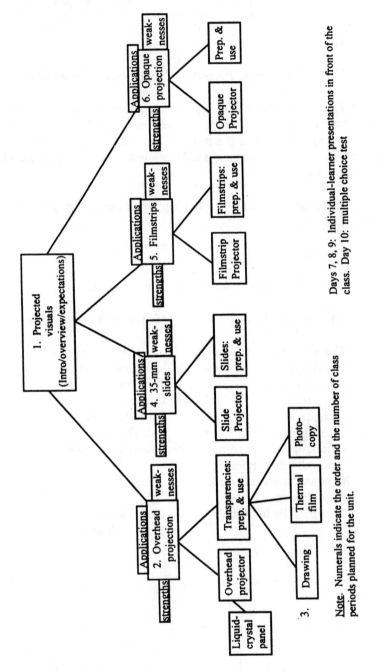

Note. Numerals indicate the order and the number of class periods planned for the unit.

Days 7, 8, 9: Individual-learner presentations in front of the class. Day 10: multiple choice test

4. Column Chart:

Day	Topic	Objectives (They will learn, or be able to,...)	Procedures	Materials	Evaluation*
1.	Projected visuals: intro./ overview/ expectatio ns of unit	...general definitions scope of unit; what tasks (and their criteria) will be	1. Mot. set (5 questions) 2. state goals of unit 3. Give unit outline (explain tasks, evaluation, expectations) 4. Give quick overview of the lab, its personnel, equipment, and procedures	1. Hand-out of unit outline 2. 5-question "test" (to determine their "incoming" knowledge level—*not* for credit)	1. Use "test" results to ascertain what they know (Diagnostic not "formal")
2.	Overhead projection	...proper use of equipmenV materials ...distinguish advantages and limitations ...applications of o.h.	1. Mot. set 2. State obiec tives (warn of quiz) 3. Describe/ demonstrate use of overhead 4. Explain advantages 5. Use "think/ pair/share" to identify disadvantages 6. Short grp. debriefing 7. Give 10-item quiz	1. In lab 2. All equipment and transparencies ready for demonstration	1. Give 10 item quiz on "Day 2" material
3.	Overhead transparen cies	...create three types of transparencies	1. Return quiz 2. Have them correct answers and resubmit 3. Describe and demonstrate 3 production techniques 4. Summarize during and at end	1. In lab 2. All equipment and materials ready	1. Assign all 3 to be created 2. They prepare for their later presentation

4.	35-mm slides	...proper use of equipment/ materials ...distinguish advantages and imitations ...applications of s1ides	1. Mot. set 2. State objectives 3. Describe projector, how to load it, and how to replace bulb 4. Explain how to load slides 5. Gives handout assignment of strengths and weakneRses of using slides (in pair)	1. Projector 2. Slides in tray (some purpose fully inserted improperly)	1. Informal assignment; let pairs work on it 2. Whole-class brief discussion of responses (as a summary)
5.	Filmstrip	...proper use of equipment/ materials ...distinguish strengths/ weaknesses ...applications of filmstrip	1. Do mot. set 2. State objec tives (advise of assignment) 3. Incorporate questions and answers while describing the use of filmstrips 4. Compare/ contrast overhead and slides	1. Do mot. set 2. State objec tives (warn of assignment) 3. Incorporate questions and answer while describing the use of filmstrips 4. Compare/ contrast it with the overhead and slides	1. Individually fill in the evaluation form (they view sample filmstrip) 2. Compare answers with partner's 3. Instructor debriefs with whole group
6.	Opaque Projection	...proper use of equipment materials ...distinguish strength/ weaknesses ...applications of opaque projection	1. Mot. set 2. State objectives 3. Demonstrate uses 4. Present weaknesses 5. Have them brainstorm strengths in pairs	1. Equipment 2. Various documents and flat objects	1. Have pairs share strengths (teacher summarizes on chalkboard)

7. 8. 9.	Individual presentations before class	...transfer their knowledge to "real world" applications	They follow presentation guidelines/ procedures as described on first day hand-out (related to a presentation in their own field)	assure that all equipment is available and in working order	Instructor-self and peer assessments of each person's presentation (as explained on first-day hand out)

* *Evaluation details for the Unit* (100 points)

1. Prepare and deliver 10-15 minute presentations to the class on a topic from your field incorporating the following project visuals:

(3 x 10 points) a. 3 overhead transparencies (one of each of: hand-drawn, Xeroxed, thermal-film)
(2 x 10 points) b. 2 of these 3: some 35-mm slides, a portion of a filmstrip, or one opaque-projection item
(10 points) 2. Overall quality of presentation (content, speaking effectiveness, voice, eye contact, enthusiasm)
(10 points) 3. 10-item quiz (Day 2)
(20 points) 4. Multiple-choice test (Day 10)
(10 points) 5. Participation in group-work, class discussions

5. Bibliography

Ellington, H., & Race, P. (1993). *Producing teaching materials: A handbook for teachers and trainers* (2 ed.). London: Kogan Page.

Heide, A., & Henderson, D. (1994). *The technological classroom: A blueprint for success.* Toronto: Irwin.

Heinich, R., Molenda, M., & Russell, J. (1993) *Instructional media and the new technologies of instruction* (4th ed.). New York: Macmillan.

Robertson, I. (1991). *Audio-visual equipment: A technician's &*

user's handbook. Oxford, UK: Butterworth-Heinemann.

Satterthwaite, L. (1990). *Instructional media: Materials production & utilization* (2nd ed.). Dubuque, IA: Kendall/Hunt.

Wileman, R. (1993). *Visual Communicating*. Englewood Cliffs, NJ: Educational Technology Publications.

Several prepared overhead transparencies from instructor's files: hand-drawn, Xeroxed, thermal-film processed, and computer-generated masters.

Appendix B

Sample Lesson Plan (See "Day 2" of Unit Plan in Appendix A)

Title: "Using the Overhead Projector"

1. *Motivational Set:* Say: "Observe while I present this demonstration. Jot down what you think is correct and incorrect. We will discuss your responses later." Do 3-minute demo using overhead transparencies. Perform some deliberate errors and some correct procedures.

2. *State objectives:* "Today, you will learn how to properly utilize the overhead projector when giving a presentation. You will learn its advantages and disadvantages as a medium."

"At the conclusion of this session you will write a 10-item quiz, for credit, on this material—as described on the unit-plan hand-out that we examined last day."

3. *Methods*: lecture, demonstration, pair-task, large-group discussion, independent work.

4/5. *Activities (and time-frame)*:

Instructor	Learners
3 min.) 1. Do mot. set	1. Observe/listen
1 min.) 2. State objectives	2. Observe/listen
7 min.) 3. Describe projectors & bulb-change (ask questions)	3. Observe/listen, respond to questions
11 min.) 4. Demonstrate/Explain applications and describe advantages as an instructional medium (referring back to mot. set, and asking questions)	4. Observe/listen, respond to questions
8 min.) 5. "Work with partner to identify the disadvantages."	5. Pair-work
5 min.) 6. Debrief, list disadvantages if necessary) with whole class	6. Pairs give responses
5 min.) 7. Do summary by asking key questions	7. Respond to summary questions
10 min.) 8. Give quiz	8. Write quiz

6/7. *Key Questions/Summary*:
1. How do you change a burnt-out bulb?
2. What things did I do correctly in my demo?
3. What did I do improperly?
4. What other uses are there for the overhead?
5. What are the advantages of this medium? The disadvantages?
6. Why should a presenter be skilled in its use?
7. How do you think these overhead transparencies are made?

8. *Evaluation*: Students write 10-item quiz for credit (as explained in unit-plan)

9. *Materials*: projector, screen, several overhead-transparencies of varying quality, spare bulb, extension cord, quiz-papers.

Appendix C

FINAL EXAM

INSTRUCTIONS: Read each question carefully. Answer all questions. Time Limit - 1 hour.

BIOLOGY: Create life. Estimate the differences in subsequent human culture if this form of life had developed 500 million years earlier, with special attention to its probable effect on the English Parliamentary system. Prove your thesis.

COMMUNICATION: 2,500 riot-crazed anarchists are storming the classroom. Calm them. You may use any ancient language except Latin or Greek.

ECONOMICS: Develop a realistic plan for refinancing the national debt. Be brief.

ENGINEERING: The disassembled parts of a high-powered rifle have been placed in a box on the table at the front of the room. You will also find an instruction manual, printed in Swahili. In 10 minutes a hungry Bengal tiger will be admitted to the room. Take whatever action you feel appropriate. Be prepared to justify your decision.

EPISTEMOLOGY: Take a position for or against truth. Prove the validity of your position.

GENERAL KNOWLEDGE: Describe in detail. Be objective and specific.

HISTORY: Describe the history of the papacy from its origins to the present day, concentrating especially but not exclusively, on its social, political, economic, religious and philosophical impact on Europe, Asia, America, and Africa. Be brief, concise, and specific.

MANAGEMENT SCIENCE: Define Management. Define Science. How do they relate? Why? Create a generalized algorithm to optimize all managerial decisions. Assuming an 1130 CPU supporting 50 terminals, each terminal to activate your algorithm; design the communications interface and all control programs.

MEDICINE: You have been provided with a razor blade, a piece of gauze and a bottle of Scotch. Remove your appendix. Do not suture until your work has been inspected. You have fifteen minutes.

MUSIC: Write a piano concerto. Orchestrate and perform it with flute and drum. You will find a portable piano in the desk-drawer at the back of the room.

PHYSICS: Explain the nature of matter. Include in your answer an evaluation of the impact of the development of mathematics on science.

POLITICAL SCIENCE: There is a red telephone on the desk at the front of the room. Start World War III. Report at length on its socio-political effects, if any.

PSYCHOLOGY: Based on your knowledge of their works, evaluate the emotional stability, degree of adjustment and repressed frustrations of each of the following: Alexander of Aphrodisiacs, Rameses II, Gregory of Nicea and Hamurabi. Support your evaluation with quotations from each man's work, making appropriate references. It is not necessary to translate.

SOCIOLOGY: Estimate the sociological problems which might accompany the end of the world. Construct an experiment to test your theory.

EXTRA CREDIT: Define the Universe. Give three examples.